Protecting Mobile Money against Financial Crimes

Protecting Mobile Money against Financial Crimes

Global Policy Challenges and Solutions

Pierre-Laurent Chatain, Andrew Zerzan, Wameek Noor, Najah Dannaoui, and Louis de Koker

Foreword by Bob Christen
The Bill & Melinda Gates Foundation

THE WORLD BANK
Washington, D.C.

ISBN: 978-0-8213-8669-9
eISBN: 978-0-8213-8670-5
DOI: 10.1596/978-0-8213-8669-9

Library of Congress Cataloging-in-Publication Data has been requested.

Cover photo: istock.com
Cover design: Naylor Design, Inc.

Contents

Foreword   *xi*
Preface   *xiii*
Acknowledgments   *xvii*
About the Authors   *xxi*
Abbreviations and Glossary   *xxv*
Overview   *xxix*

Introduction   1
Demand for Insight on the Connection of
    Mobile Money with Anti-Money Laundering
    and Combating the Financing of Terrorism   1
The M-Money Landscape: Potential and Challenges   2
Objectives of This Report   4
Scope of This Report   4
Target Audience   5
Methodology   6
Outline of the Book   6
Notes   7
References   8

Chapter 1   Analysis of the Mobile Money Transaction Flow   9
             Summary   9
             Introduction: Regulating by Provider Type
                 Is Insufficient   11
             Mapping the System: From Mobile Service
                 to Settlement   12
             The Retail Outlet's Role: Customer
                 Interface and User   14
             Who Does What: Multiple Providers   19
             Market Integrity Roles Assumed by Providers   25
             Summary and the Rule of the Account Provider   28
             Notes   29
             References   30

Chapter 2   Assessment of Potential Money-Laundering
             and Combating the Financing of Terrrorism
             Risks and Their Potential Mitigation Techniques   31
             Summary   31
             Integrity Risks in Theory: Placing Them into
                 Four Major Risk Categories   33
             Fieldwork Finding: Perceptions of Integrity
                 Risks May Be Higher Than Merited   37
             Integrity Risks in Reality   40
             Techniques Used to Effectively Mitigate
                 M-Money Risks   49
             M-Money Risks and Mitigation Techniques
                 Specific to the Financing of Terrorism   53
             Balancing Risk Mitigation Techniques with
                 Financial Inclusion Objectives   54
             Notes   58
             References   61

Chapter 3   Overview of Anti-Money Laundering and
             Combating the Financing of Terrorism Regulatory
             Practices and Risk Management Frameworks
             for Mobile Money   63
             Summary   63
             Licensing and Registration of M-Money Providers   65
             Supervision of M-Money Providers   71
             Stocktaking of Current Preventive AML/CFT
                 Obligations   75

The Role of Retail Outlets 92
Notes 99
References 102

Chapter 4   Anti-Money Laundering and Combating the
Financing of Terrorism Policy Guidance for
Countries Regulating Their Mobile
Money Markets **105**
Summary 105
AML/CFT Guidance for Policy Makers 107
AML/CFT Guidance for M-Money Providers 125
Recommendations for the FATF 136
Notes 139
References 142

Appendix A   The Interplay between Financial Inclusion
and Compliance with Anti-Money Laundering
and Combating the Financing of Terrorism
Regulation: Key Issues for Consideration
during Mutual Assessments **143**
Background 144
Financial Inclusion and AML/CFT 145
Policy and the Regulatory Approach 146
Know-Your-Customer Obligations 147
Recordkeeping 149
Retail Outlets 149
Reporting Obligations 151
Statistics 152
Supervision and Enforcement 152
Notes 154
References 155

Appendix B   Mobile Money: Growth Potential, Current
Landscape, and Factors for Success **157**
Potential for Growth 157
The Current M-Money Landscape 158
Profitability of M-Money Providers and the
Factors for Success 162
The Current Global Regulatory Scenario 163
Notes 164
References 165

Appendix C   Customer Due Diligence Obligations and
             Mobile-Money Services: Key Questions
             and Solutions   167
             Know-Your-Customer and the Risk-Based
                 Approach: Principles and Limits   167
             Why M-Money Services Carry Low Risks   169
             Relaxed CDD for M-Money: Three
                 Possible Scenarios   171
             Notes   174
             References   176

Appendix D   Reporting Obligations in the Particular
             Context of Mobile Money   177
             Allocation of Responsibilities   178
             Related Rights, Obligations, and Processes   180
             Contents within an STR   181
             Note   183

Index   185

Boxes
1.1   Defining Closed and Open M-Money Systems   16
1.2   A Hypothetical $10 Deposit and Its Movement into
       a Closed System   20
2.1   ML/TF Threat and Risk Indicators   36
2.2   Cost and Time May Make M-Money Channels
       Unappealing to Criminals   41
2.3   Cases of Consumer Fraud through M-Money:
       The Philippines Experience   46
2.4   The FATF and the Risk-Based Approach to M-Money
       and AML/CFT Compliance   51
2.5   Risk-Based Determination of Transaction Limits
       in the Republic of Korea   52
2.6   South Africa's RICA and Potential Implications
       for Financial Access   56
3.1   Examples of Countries with a Provider-Based
       Licensing Regime   66
3.2   Examples of Countries with a Service-Based Licensing
       Regime (E-Money and Payment Service Licenses)   68

3.3   M-Money in a Technology-Neutral World   70
3.4   Examples of Central Banks with a Separate Department
       for Nonbank Supervision   74
3.5   Examples of MNOs with a Separate Financial Entity   75
3.6   Examples of Relaxed KYC Obligations for
       Lower-Risk Transactions   79
3.7   Examples of National Regulators' Mitigation
       Responses to the Identification Challenge   82
3.8   Examples of Recordkeeping Requirements Observed
       in the Visited Jurisdictions   89
3.9   Examples of Recordkeeping Periods, Usually Exceeding
       the Five Years Recommended by the FATF   90
3.10   Examples of Suspicious Transaction and Threshold
       Reporting Observed during Fieldwork   91
3.11   Examples of Countries Where Providers Assume
       Liability for Retail Outlets   94
3.12   A Country Where Providers Do Not Assume Liability
       for Retail Outlets: Kenya   96
3.13   Examples of APs Managing Retail Outlet Risks   98

Figures
I.1   How Financial Inclusion Leads to a Strong
       AML/CFT Regime   5
1.1   General Anatomy of a Mobile Transaction   12
1.2   Sample Transaction between M-Money Accounts in
       the Philippines and Malaysia, Sending Side   15
1.3   Sample Transaction between M-Money Accounts in
       the Philippines and Malaysia, Receiving Side   15
1.4   Example of a Customer Crediting Account through
       a Retail Outlet in Zambia   18
1.5   Example of a Retail Outlet Crediting Its Own Account
       in Zambia   18
1.6   Providers in an M-Money Transaction   21
1.7   Alternative Provider Type: Celpay in the Democratic
       Republic of Congo and Zambia   24
2.1   Volume of Coins in Circulation and Their Growth Rates,
       2000–08   43
2.2   Document Requirements in Developing Countries,
       Compared with Those in Developed Countries   55

3.1   Example of a Supervision Framework   73
3.2   Gradual KYC Program Adopted by Moneybookers Ltd.,
       an Internet Payment Provider in the United Kingdom   78

Maps

I.1   Jurisdictions Where Domestic or International Person-to-
       Person Transfer via M-Money Is Available, February 2010   3
B.1   Jurisdictions Where Domestic or International Person-to-
       Person Transfer via M-Money Is Available, February 2010   159

Tables

1.1   Steps for a Retail Outlet Cash Withdrawal in Open
       and Closed M-Money Systems   20
2.1   Potential Vulnerabilities for Each Risk Category at
       Each Stage of an M-Money Transaction   37
2.2   Comparative Risks of M-Money and Cash, Before
       and After Controls Are Applied   42
2.3   Number of Suspicious Transaction Reports by
       M-Money Providers in the Philippines, 2007–09   45
3.1   Examples of M-Money Providers' Mitigation Responses
       to the Identification Challenge   84
3.2   Example of the Evolution of Retail Outlets' Regulation
       in Brazil, Various Years   98

Foreword

Two and a half billion people in the world live on less than $2 a day, and 90 percent have no access to savings accounts and other financial services. As a consequence, they tend to resort to risky, expensive, and inefficient ways to conclude financial transactions. Formal financial inclusion has a strong positive impact on development. Research suggests that poor households with access to formal financial services are more likely to invest in education, increase productivity and income, and reduce vulnerability to illness and other unexpected events.

Crown Princess Máxima of the Netherlands, a long-time advocate of financial inclusion for the poor and the United Nations Secretary-General's Special Advocate for Inclusive Finance for Development, recently underlined the potential of bringing people and businesses into the formal financial system to help communities thrive: "Financial inclusion is not an end in itself; it is a means to an end. Financial inclusion helps the development of [the] private sector. It helps create income. It generates jobs and . . . helps people manage cash flow and build assets over time."[1] Financial inclusion also contributes to financial integrity because it helps regulators and supervisors monitor the movement and sources of money and supports law enforcement by diminishing the anonymity of informal transactions.

Given this context, the G-20 has recently encouraged the development of new modes of financial services delivery capable of reaching the poor. Meanwhile, the Financial Action Task Force has made important progress by advancing financial inclusion initiatives. Along the same lines, the Basel Committee on Banking Supervision recently issued the final version of its report, "Microfinance Activities and the Core Principles for Effective Banking Supervision" (http://www.bis.org/publ/bcbs175.pdf), which identifies areas where some degree of flexibility is appropriate in implementing the core principles for microfinance supervision.

The Financial Services for the Poor initiative is working with a wide range of public and private partners to harness technology and innovation to bring quality, affordable savings accounts and other financial services to the doorsteps of poor people in developing economies. The foundation believes that setting aside small sums in a safe place allows people to guard against risks, build assets, and provide opportunities for the next generation.

In this regard, we welcome the timely publication of this book. With more than 80 percent of the world's population now within mobile coverage, burgeoning efforts to enable people to send, receive, and store money using their mobile phones have the potential to greatly improve people's lives and leapfrog more conventional banking models to safer, more affordable alternatives. Often called "mobile money," these services reduce the risks and costs of financial transactions, help increase savings, and bring more people into the formal financial sector. This timely publication investigates the current anti-money laundering/combating the financing of terrorism (AML/CFT) regulatory environment for mobile money and provides guidance on the design of a framework for mobile money that adequately addresses ML/FT risks.

We hope that this work will help countries strike the right balance between the risks associated with the use of mobile money and the objectives of fostering greater financial inclusion and promoting economic development within their countries.

Bob Christen
Director, Financial Services for the Poor
The Bill & Melinda Gates Foundation

Note

1. http://www.uncdf.org/english/about_uncf/docs/SPEECH_HRH_P-MAX-IMA_MDG_SIDE-EVENT_22SEPT2010.pdf.

Preface

Financial inclusion is a key development objective for many developing and emerging countries. It is essential to expand opportunities, particularly for the poorest people. Extending the reach of the financial sector to sections of the society and to geographic areas that were neglected in the past, however, is a challenging objective. There are many barriers to accessing financial services, ranging from limited literacy, to lack of awareness about financial services and products, to high transaction costs and inadequate infrastructure. All around the world, jurisdictions are struggling to promote financial inclusion because it is a necessary condition for sustaining equitable growth.

Financial inclusion is also a core goal of the World Bank Group. We champion it at the international level, particularly in support of the G-20, and we live it with our clients day to day. Lack of access to banking services is currently forcing many people in emerging markets to rely on a cash-based economy that is often insecure. Bringing financial services to unbanked or underserved people is a key element in improving living conditions, and it is crucial for overall economic development.

The rapid development of mobile money is creating unprecedented opportunities for poor people in developing countries to more actively participate in the economy. For millions of underserved individuals around the world, a mobile phone represents more than just a tool for communication; it has become a payment terminal in the pocket. Every day, the number of mobile device—and mobile money—users grows and offers hope to the billions of people without bank accounts.

In a recent survey, the consulting company McKinsey Group forecast that the number of unbanked people with mobile phones will increase from 1.0 billion in 2010 to 1.7 billion by 2012. By that time, as many as 290 million previously unbanked people could be using mobile-money services. In addition, mobile money has the potential to deliver $5.0 billion in direct revenues and $2.5 billion in indirect revenues to mobile operators annually. According to a report prepared for the Groupe Speciale Mobile Association (GSMA) (2007), a 10 percent increase in mobile phone penetration can boost gross domestic product (GDP) growth by 0.6 percent. Moreover, mobile phones are the first consumer technology to be more prevalent in developing countries than in developed ones. According to the GSMA, these findings predict that the growth in mobile money over the next three years will be rapid. In comparison, microfinance institutions currently serve 150 million people.

In this context, governments are increasingly challenged to support the growth of these new services while mitigating the potential risks (including fraud, money laundering, and financing terrorism). Concerns have been raised about potential integrity issues that may stem from the use of mobile money. We believe these concerns deserve our careful attention—first, because we cannot afford to put this vulnerable group of people at risk; and, second, because trust in those services is key to their development. At the same time, it is important not to overestimate these risks, particularly when the alternative is financial exclusion.

Responding to the global financial crisis at the Pittsburgh Summit in September 2009, the G-20 gave additional impetus to this process by committing to support the safe and sound spread of new modes of financial service delivery capable of reaching the poor.[1] The World Bank is highly supportive of this G-20 commitment. We are stepping up our work on responsible finance, including consumer protection regulations, industry codes of conduct for financial service providers, and financial integrity.

Policy makers need to do more and to be more creative, flexible, and agile while keeping in mind that pushing access to financial services should not come at the cost of financial stability and integrity. Bad and overly restrictive regulation is a major obstacle to the expansion of mobile money services to the poor. We need (1) good regulation for nonbank financial services, such as electronic money or payment system regulation; (2) smart and flexible oversight of retailers as agents for mobile money services; and (3) proportionate, risk-based anti-money laundering and combating the financing of terrorism (AML/CFT) rules.

The purposes of this book are to contribute to these debates and to promote well-balanced regulatory approaches. Because international standards are not always clearly understood, too many countries overregulate and, thus, create barriers to business, innovation, and inclusion. Ill-designed and overly rigid AML/CFT regulatory frameworks create conditions that favor informal financial channels, which undermine the very objective of AML/CFT efforts.

It is our view that the approach to AML/CFT needs to reflect this reality. As Paul Vlaanderen, former president of the Financial Action Task Force (FATF) , noted in 2009, AML/CFT must drive financial inclusion; otherwise, it will do little to reduce these crimes in a cash economy.[2] In contrast to financial exclusion and cash, mobile money services bring traceability, recordkeeping, and monitoring.

This analysis recommends a framework that strikes a balance between developing access through innovation and mitigating abuse for money-laundering and terrorist-financing purposes. The authors elaborate on mechanisms through which AML/CFT requirements can be relaxed to the fullest extent possible to facilitate access to financial services for undocumented customers, particularly those in low-income jurisdictions where identification infrastructure is underdeveloped.

FATF supports this idea. We welcome FATF's support and will actively support these efforts. National jurisdictions need further guidance on how much they can relax their AML/CFT regimes while remaining compliant with FATF standards.

Any improvements in these areas will have positive implications for enabling poor people to access appropriate financial services in the safest and most secure regulatory environment. Our expectation is that this work will contribute to the accomplishment of that ultimate goal.

Janamitra Devan
Vice President and Head of Network
World Bank

Notes

1. The G-20 leaders' statement from the September 24–25, 2009, Pittsburgh Summit is available at http://www.pittsburghsummit.gov/mediacenter/129639.htm.
2. http://www.fatf-gafi.org/document/39/0,3746,en_32250379_32236879_43268455_1_1_1_1,00.html.

Reference

GSMA (Groupe Speciale Mobile Association). 2007. "Global Mobile Tax Review 2006–2007." London. http://www.gsmworld.com/documents/tax_review_06_07.pdf.

Acknowledgments

This publication was written by Pierre-Laurent Chatain (task team leader), Andrew Zerzan, Wameek Noor, Najah Dannaoui (all from the World Bank), and Louis de Koker (Deakin University, Australia). The authors are especially grateful to Jean Denis Pesme, manager, Financial Market Integrity Unit, for his guidance and comments in producing this book. The team members would also like to express their gratitude to Latifah Merican Cheong, former program director, who initiated this project during her tenure at the World Bank; and to Kamil Borowik and Raúl Hernández-Coss, who coauthored the 2008 World Bank study, *Integrity in Mobile Phone Financial Services: Measures for Mitigating Risks from Money Laundering and Terrorist Financing*, from which the current study is derived. In addition, the authors thank Deakin University, Australia, for its collaboration.

The internal (World Bank) peer reviewers for this work were Lucie Castets, Massimo Cirasino, Isaku Endo, Nadine Ghannam, Samuel Maimbo, Mariachiara Malaguti, Jean Pesme, Ritva Reinikka, Thomas Rose, Consolate Rusagara, James Seward, and Emiko Todoroki from World Bank and Michael Tarazi from the Consultative Group to Assist the Poor (CGAP).

The external peer reviewers were Claire Alexandre and Ignacio Mas (The Bill & Melinda Gates Foundation), Michael U. Klein, former vice president, Finance and Private Sector Development, World Bank–IFC, Catherine Marty (secretariat of the Financial Action Task Force [FATF]), David Porteous (Bankable Frontier Associates), Lawrence Yanovitch (Alliance for Financial Inclusion), Jan Noll (cochair, Working Group on Typologies of New Payment Methods for FATF), Norbert Bielefeld and Anne-Françoise Lefèvre (World Savings Banks Institute), Meredith Pearson (Vodafone Group Services Limited), Marc Hollanders (special adviser on financial infrastructure, Bank for International Settlements), and Dominic Peachey (U.K. Financial Services Authority).

The labors of our editor, Christine Cotting, are also appreciated. The help of the support staff—Thelma Ayamel, Nicolas De La Riva, Michael Geller, Maria Orellano, and Jocelyn Taylor—has been crucial from start to finish.

The authors would also like to express their gratitude to CGAP—including Chris Bold, Tim Lyman, Sarah Rotman, Yanina Seltzer, Michael Tarazi, and other members of the CGAP team—for their collaboration on several of the country visits and for their informal discussions on fieldwork analysis during the drafting process, which strengthened the manuscript.

The authors also benefited from informal consultation with Thomas Firnhaber (NetSpend), Thaer Sabri (E-Money Association), and Arun Shah (Obopay).

The fieldwork for this study was done in eight markets: France, Kenya, Malaysia, Mexico, the Philippines, the Russian Federation, the United Kingdom, and Zambia. The time given by all the people whom the team met in these locations is acknowledged with appreciation. Although the following list is not exhaustive, the authors would like to highlight some of the people and organizations without whom they could not have produced this book: *France*: Mung Ki Woo (Orange, France Telecom); *Kenya*: Central Bank of Kenya's Bank Supervision Department and National Payments System; Commercial Bank of Africa; the Ministry of Finance; Safaricom Limited; Zain; *Malaysia*: Bank Negara Malaysia; Claire Featherstone, Cynthia Yeo Wee Teng, and Maxis Communications; *Mexico*: Fernando Borja (Banamex); Miguel Calderón (Movista); Christian Carreón Álvarez and Guillermo Zamarripa (Ministry of Finance–Hacienda); Fernando Castrejon (Banorte); Jorge Gonzales, Carlos López-Moctezuma, Carlos Marmolejo, and Carlos Serrano (National Banking and Securities Commision); Pascual O'Dogherty (Banxico); Arturo Rangel (Bancomer); and Luis Urrutia (financial intelligence unit); *The Philippines*: Anti-Money Laundering Council Secretariat and Vicente Aquino (executive director); the Asian Development Bank; Banco de Oro Unibank; Bangko Sentral ng Pillipinas and Nestor A. Espenilla, Jr. (deputy governor), Raymond Estioko, and Pia Bernadette Roman; Globe Telecom; G Xchange and Rizza Maniego-Eala; and Elmer (Jojo) M. Malolos and Maybelle Santos (Smart Communications); *Russia*: Jane Belenkaya (WebMoney); Victor Dostov (E-money); Andrei Emelin (Association of Russian Banks); Oleg Ivanov (Association of Regional Banks of Russia); Boris Kim (National Association of E-Trade Participants); Kirill Kosminskiy (Corporate Governance Department, Ministry for Economic Development); Mikhail Mamuta and Olga Zharkova (Russian Microfinance Center); Alma Obaeva (Settlements Regulation Department, Bank of Russia); Kirill Petrov (I-Free); Evgeniya Zavalishina (Yandex.Money); and Denis Zyryanov (Beeline, VympelCom); *United Kingdom*: Claire Alexandre (Vodafone Group); Jody Ketteringham and Dominic Peachey (Financial Services Authority); Gary Morgan (Mi-Pay UK); Raj Muttukrishnan and Luke Nava (City University London); Marina Solin (GSMA); Lesley-Ann Vaughan (Iceni); and Tony Wicks (Fortent); and *Zambia*: Anti-Money Laundering Investigations Unit; Bank of Zambia Payments Systems Division and Bank Supervision Department; Barclays Bank; Celpay; CellZ and Zamtel; Communications Authority; Mobile Transactions; MTN; Stanbic Bank; Standard Chartered Bank; Zain; and Zambia National Commercial Bank.

About the Authors

Pierre-Laurent Chatain is the lead financial sector specialist at the World Bank's Financial Market Integrity Unit, Washington, DC. Since he joined the World Bank Group in September 2002, he has led several anti-money-laundering assessment missions as part of the Financial Sector Assessment Program in anglophone, francophone, and Spanish-speaking countries. Chatain has also designed and delivered many technical assistance projects and outreach events aimed at strengthening financial market integrity in Africa, Latin America, and the Middle East.

Before joining the World Bank, Chatain worked for the Bank of France for more than 15 years. He held several positions in succession within the legal and inspection departments. He was auditor from 1992 to 1996, then he was promoted to inspector. He also served as mission chief at the French Banking Commission, where he led multidisciplinary, on-site inspection teams in commercial banks in France and overseas. He exercised managerial responsibilities at the Bank of France as deputy director of the On-site Control Department.

Chatain has written extensively in the areas of mediation, conflict resolution, civil bankruptcy, and financial integrity. He coauthored an influential book on the French civil insolvency and bankruptcy regime for individuals. In addition to publishing numerous papers and articles in legal journals in France, he coauthored the books *Integrity in Mobile Phone Financial Services: Measures for Mitigating the Risks of Money Laundering and Terrorist Financing* (2008) and *Preventing Money Laundering and Terrorist Financing, A Practical Guide for Bank Supervisors* (2009), both published by the World Bank.

Chatain holds a master's degree in law from the University of Paris 1 Panthéon-Sorbonne and is a graduate of the French Political Science Institute of Toulouse.

Andrew Zerzan was among the first to publish research on mobile money and anti-money laundering regulation. In 2006, he began working at the World Bank, analyzing the effects of new technologies on the lives of the poor. The following year, he joined a team (led by Pierre-Laurent Chatain) to conduct a cutting-edge study on the different market integrity practices of mobile money providers in developed and emerging markets.

Linked to his role in a United Nations task force on counter-terrorism, he authored the 2009 working paper "New Technologies, New Risks? Innovation and Countering the Financing of Terrorism" that assessed the actual threat of terrorist financing in a variety of advanced payment systems. He has presented at a number of international summit meetings and conferences. Zerzan draws on his private sector experience as a consultant in Japan, where he built a grassroots business that bridged disparities in strategic communications among global companies. He studied financial regulation at the London School of Economics and currently works as an independent expert in the field.

Wameek Noor currently works as a consultant in the Financial and Private Sector Development Network of the World Bank. He has researched, analyzed, and presented globally published research on the best way to expand financial access among the poor without constraining an innovation-friendly environment that fosters private sector growth. He continues to coauthor policy studies on mobile banking, remittances, governance, and anticorruption—key and potentially innovative mechanisms to expand financial sector development by ensuring an effective regulatory and supervisory framework.

Prior to his work with the World Bank, Noor built his knowledge of microfinance and financial access by working with Grameen Bank in Bangladesh, where he was extensively involved with using microfinance to spearhead technology-driven development projects through mobile phones, the Internet, and solar technology. He has also served as a senior analyst at the Corporate Executive Board, a strategy-consulting firm helping client organizations increase their profitability by developing their employee performance, retention, and leadership development programs.

Noor received a master of arts degree in economics and international development from the School of Advanced International Studies at Johns Hopkins University, Washington, DC; and a bachelor of arts in economics and political science from Vassar College, New York.

Najah Dannaoui is a consultant at the World Bank's Financial Market Integrity Unit. Her legal background has equipped her to assess the compliance of countries' legal systems with international standards in the field of anti-money laundering and combating the financing of terrorism (AML/CFT). Her work has also involved promoting financial inclusion through bank and nonbank financial institutions while preserving integrity in the financial markets.

Prior to joining the Bank, Dannaoui worked for four years as a legal consultant at the Embassy of the State of Qatar in Washington, DC She also worked for two years as a litigator in Lebanon, focusing on trade and commercial law.

Dannaoui received her master of law degree in international law from Georgetown University, Washington, DC, in 2004. She also obtained a law degree from the Holy Spirit University in Lebanon in 2000. She was admitted to the New York Bar Association in 2005 and to the Lebanese Bar Association in 2001.

Louis de Koker is a professor of law at the School of Law at Deakin University, Melbourne, Australia. Prior to joining the university, he was the director of the Centre for the Study of Economic Crime and a professor of mercantile law at the University of Johannesburg. He currently leads Deakin University's postgraduate program in financial crime and risk management.

Dr. de Koker's scholarship focuses on money laundering and combating the financing of terrorism laws. Since 2003, he has co-led various research projects to determine the impact of these laws on financial inclusion and to determine regulatory best practice. Projects with Genesis Analytics and FinMark Trust first focused on experiences in South Africa and then broadened to a FIRST-funded study of the AML/CFT impact on financial inclusion in Indonesia, Kenya, Mexico, and Pakistan.

He is a policy advisory consultant on AML/CFT for the Consultative Group to Assist the Poor (CGAP) and a consultant to the World Bank's Financial Market Integrity Unit. In these capacities, de Koker advised various regulators on risk assessment and the drafting of appropriate regulations. In addition to publishing more than two dozen papers and articles on AML/CFT in peer-reviewed journals, he is the author of *South African Money Laundering and Terror Financing Law* (LexisNexis 2007). He is a member of the editorial advisory boards for the *Journal of Money Laundering Control*, the *Journal of Financial Crime*, and *Company Lawyer*.

Dr. de Koker holds various degrees in law, including a doctorate and a master's degree in corporate law from the University of the Free State, South Africa, and a master's degree from the University of Cambridge.

Abbreviations and Glossary

Account	Accounts linked to a mobile money program may be one of three types: (1) A customer may have a bank account directly linked to the formal financial system and accessed via a mobile phone. (2) A customer may have a virtual account in which the transactions can occur only among users in this closed system. Money cannot move to outside accounts. (3) A customer may have a pooled bank account where all money in a closed system is stored.
AML	anti-money laundering
AMLC	Anti-Money Laundering Council (The Philippines)
AML/CFT	anti-money laundering/combating the financing of terrorism
AP	account provider; refers to the party who is ultimately responsible for the delivery and management of the financial services underlying a mobile money program. The AP will typically be responsible for account opening, transaction processing, and recordkeeping—although some of its functions may be outsourced to other parties, such as retail outlets. An AP could be a

	mobile operator, a bank, a different payment services provider, or a partnership or joint venture of such entities.
BSP	Bangko Sentral ng Pillipinas (Central Bank of the Philippines)
CDD	customer due diligence; often used synonymously with KYC (know your customer), but generally refers more broadly to a financial institution's CDD policies, procedures, and processes for obtaining customer information and assessing the value of the information in detecting, monitoring, and reporting suspicious activity.
CFT	combating the financing of terrorism
CGAP	Consultative Group to Assist the Poor
DFID	U.K. Department for International Development
EMI	e-money issuer
e-money	electronic money; refers to the electronic alternative to cash. It is a monetary value stored electronically on receipt of funds and used for making payment transactions. E-money and m-money are the same. *See m-money.*
EMV	Europay, MasterCard, and VISA
EU	European Union
FATF	Financial Action Task Force
FFMS	Federal Financial Monitoring Service (Russia)
FICA	Financial Intelligence Centre Act 38 of 2001 (South Africa)
FIU	financial intelligence unit
GSMA	Groupe Speciale Mobile Association
IMEI	International Mobile Equipment Identity; refers to the unique identifier given to each mobile device.
Java	software created by Sun Microsystems that permits users to conduct various functions, including communicating with a transaction processor.
KYC	know your customer; refers to a set of due diligence measures taken by a financial institution to identify a customer and the motivations behind his or her financial activity. It is a key component of AML/CFT regimes.
ML	money laundering
ML/TF	money laundering/terrorist financing

m-money	mobile money; refers to financial services in which customers send and receive monetary value via a mobile phone. This includes retail payments and remittances from one person to another or between businesses. Salary and benefit distributions into mobile-linked accounts are also encountered in some countries. M-money accounts can be provided by many types of institutions, including banks and non-banks, such as mobile network operators and payment system providers. The category of services includes transaction-enabling services, such as domestic or international person-to-person funds transfers or mobile-based payment services. M-money services are part of the retail payment industry and are covered by the national payment system oversight policy. It is worth noting, however, that m-money is not a term usually adopted by the community of payment regulators.
MMS	multimedia messaging service
MNO	mobile network operator
mobile banking	a broad term for the use of a mobile phone to access financial services and trigger a financial event; it does not assume any specific deployment model or any particular transaction type. For the sake of simplicity, the authors are placing mobile payments, mobile transfers, and m-money in this category. Mobile banking covers both transaction- and nontransaction-enabling services, such as viewing financial and bank account information on a customer's mobile phone.
MORB	Manual of Regulation for Banks
MTZL	Mobile Transactions Zambia Limited
NBFI	nonbank financial institution
NBI	National Bureau of Investigation (The Philippines)
P2P	person to person; refers to the ability of users in a mobile money system to send money to one another.
PII	personally identifiable information
RBA	risk-based approach
retail outlet	generally small local businesses such as gas stations, post offices, airtime sellers, convenience stores, and so forth that are contracted to perform some functions

	face-to-face with customers of an m-money provider. These functions include account opening, cash deposits, and withdrawals.
RICA	Regulation on Interception of Communications and Provision of Communication-Related Information Act, 2002, (South Africa)
SAR	special administrative region
SIM	subscriber identity module; refers to the smart card used in mobile phones. It carries the user's identity for accessing the network and receiving calls and stores personal information, such as phone directory and short-message service messages received.
SMS	short-message service; enables users to send text messages from mobile phones.
STR	suspicious transaction report; refers to a report about possibly criminal activity sent to authorities by financial and relevant nonfinancial institutions.
STK	SIM Toolkit; refers to software placed on the SIM card itself that can be used to hold an m-money application.
telecom	telecommunications company
TF	terrorist financing
UDI	inflation-indexed units
USSD	unstructured supplementary service data; refers to software available on mobile phones that creates a direct link to a central computer system. Unlike SMS, USSD does not store data on the mobile phone itself; when the session is closed, no data are left on the mobile phone.

All amounts are presented in U.S. dollars, unless otherwise indicated.

Overview

Mobile money (m-money)—a term describing the use of a mobile phone to conduct financial transactions—has the capacity and reach to be a global game changer for financial inclusion. Almost 1 billion people without access to formal financial services had a mobile phone in 2009. By fully using the potential of mobile phone services, nearly half of the world's unbanked population can be offered formal financial services.

Addressing concerns about the integrity of m-money is essential to the development of its full potential. These concerns have become particularly acute as the total value of funds transferred through m-money increases. In parallel, m-money programs are now offered in geographic areas that are potentially more vulnerable to money laundering (ML) and terrorist financing (TF).

Financial inclusion and financial integrity are complementary and cross-reinforcing, policy objectives. Regulators, however, are still uncertain about how best to regulate m-money for financial integrity. As more countries draft m-money regulations, operational guidance on the optimal means to develop effective anti-money laundering (AML) and combating the financing of terrorism (CFT) regulatory framework for m-money is proving to be insufficient and incomplete. One driving concern is that regulatory initiatives would be assessed as noncompliant when subjected to an AML/CFT mutual evaluation or assessment—leading to excessive rigidity and conservatism in regulations.[1]

Integrity of m-money goes beyond know-your-customer (KYC) obligations. Customer due diligence (CDD) is a challenging aspect of financial integrity controls—and even more so for m-money. But it is crucial that policy makers also balance other AML/CFT requirements with financial inclusion objectives. The expansion of m-money is highly dependent on the way ML/FT risk assessments are undertaken, the way suspicious transactions are reported, the way recordkeeping requirements are designed, and the way outsourcing and agency relationships are defined and regulated.

Effective policy making on m-money calls for a broad and comprehensive view of ML/TF risks. Too often the focus is solely on m-money products and business models, while the alternative for clients would be cash in many cases. It is important, therefore, that policy makers compare the risk profile of m-money with the risk profile of cash.

M-money is a powerful tool to reduce reliance on cash—a major ML/TF risk. Unlike cash, m-money transactions are generally traceable. M-money also easily lends itself to account monitoring and restrictions on transactions, and restrictions are easier to enforce. For all these reasons, m-money should be highly attractive to countries that wish to attract users of high-risk, cash-based, and informal transactions to a more transparent transactional environment, where consumer protection and integrity can be promoted and ensured.

Efforts should be paid to better disseminate knowledge on the ML/TF risk profile of m-money. In a 2008 report, Chatain and coauthors identified anonymity, elusiveness, rapidity, and poor oversight as the key risk factors relating to m-money. The fieldwork done for this study confirmed those factors' continued relevance. In addition, publicly known cases indicate so far that levels of financial crime abuse of m-money are very low. A few minor cases related to fraud were identified, mainly where victims were required to make payment via m-money. The use of m-money in these cases appears to be largely incidental, and the criminals' recourse to m-money proved to be helpful to law enforcement because the technology facilitated detection and investigation of the criminal schemes. No cases of the abuse of m-money in ML/TF programs were identified.

The ML/TF risk and vulnerability of m-money can be well managed through proportionate regulation and its enforcement. M-money has intrinsic ML/TF risk mitigation features, such as value caps on accounts and transactions. Although criminal abuse can and will occur, this study concluded that the risk of abuse may be kept low when appropriate controls are implemented. Risk profiles may differ from model to model; and appropriate, proportionate regulation is required to ensure the sustainability of m-money.

M-money business models are quickly developing and diversifying. Since 2008, the binary divide between bank-led and mobile network operator (MNO)–led models no longer holds true. The variety and complexity of new and emerging models signal the booming creativity of this industry. One downside of this evolution, however, is the fragmentation of services. It leads to a multiplication of different players, each responsible for some of the key elements of the m-money transaction. MNOs, however, continue to be the backbone of all models because they provide the mobile communications service or channel, whereas money deposited to and withdrawn from the m-money system is stored in an account at a bank or with a third party.

Regulation should ensure that the account provider (AP) is held responsible and accountable for the m-money program as a whole. The AP is the party who is ultimately responsible and ultimately accountable for the delivery and management of the m-money services. The AP typically will be responsible for account opening, transaction processing, and recordkeeping—although some of its functions may be outsourced to other parties such as retail outlets. A regulator, therefore, may hold an AP accountable for failure to take reasonable steps to ensure that retail outlets comply with their AML/CFT obligations. Such reasonable steps would include know-your-agent processes, training and monitoring of retail outlets, and timely intervention when required.

Integrating retail outlets in the regulatory framework is essential to business development and to the management of integrity risks. M-money programs depend on retail outlets to provide the customer interface, including cash-in and cash-out abilities. They are instrumental in any meaningful outreach to nonbanked or underserved customers. Retail outlets may act as agents of the AP or as independent third parties who provide services to the AP. These outlets are generally small businesses with limited infrastructure and capacity. The Financial Action Task Force (FATF) recommendations do not require them to be licensed and regulated. Whether they should be licensed and regulated in a given country context depends on their role in the m-money program and on the country's regulatory strategy. In this regard, policy makers should note that effective regulation and supervision of a potentially large number of small retail outlets will require significant capacity.

In principle, retail outlets should be entrusted with AML/CFT duties, given their unique access to and knowledge of customers. This knowledge of the customer is a cornerstone of effective AML/CFT mitigation measures (CDD, monitoring of business relationships and detection of suspicious activity), and it should designate retail outlets as vital actors in an m-money system. Conversely, in most m-money schemes, retail outlets are also confronted with capacity and resource challenges and typically are barely trained on AML/CFT requirements. As a result, when determining whether an AP should be allowed to entrust certain AML/CFT functions to its retail outlets, the regulator should balance all these considerations and ensure that the outlets actually are equipped to perform any delegated AML/CFT functions.

CDD is the backbone of any regime designed to counter ML/TF activities, and it proves to be challenging in all jurisdictions and for all industries. Some of these CDD challenges are even more acute for m-money systems, particularly in low-capacity countries. Absence of reliable official documentation, business relationships not conducted face to face, the intervention of intermediaries—all these situations are well-known ML/TF risks. Their almost systematic combined recurrence in m-money in emerging markets and developing countries is a challenge for regulators and supervisors, leading too often to regulatory overkill.

In such a context, a risk-based approach is the foundation for the design of appropriate and proportionate regulations and controls. The FATF allows countries to implement a risk-based approach. Although the task force has issued several risk-based guidelines since 2007, these are not well known and are insufficiently used. They also do not address clearly enough the key elements of low-risk scenarios—especially how far countries may go to simplify identification requirements. In that regard, this study explores several options and tools that regulators may wish to consider.

Mapping ML/TF risks is a prerequisite to any effective proportionate approach to CDD. Customer identification and verification requirements can be simplified in specific circumstances, including those in which there is a low ML/TF risk. Everything begins, in theory, with a risk assessment—either at the sector, model, or service provider level. Conducting an ML/TF risk assessment is not a trivial endeavor, and any ML/TF risk assessment first needs to be informed by an understanding of the pertinent risks facing the jurisdictions as a whole. The country profile, the m-money business model, the types of products and services offered, the risk controls that apply to the products and services, and the profiles of likely customers are examples of facts that should be considered in such an assessment.

When ML/TF risks are low, KYC requirements can be simplified in a variety of ways: (1) KYC particulars that are not vital may be reduced, for instance, by dispensing with the need to ask for or verify customers' residential addresses; (2) customers may be allowed to use nonstandard documents and means to verify their personal particulars, for instance, by presenting documents that do not bear a photograph; (3) a tiered approach may be followed, allowing customers to access a basic, low-value product with minimum KYC requirements and requiring them to undergo more extensive KYC checks if they wish to access enhanced products or services; or (4) in low-value transactions with a very low risk profile, institutions may be required to obtain client particulars but not compelled to verify them.

This relaxation of obligations must be counterbalanced by enhanced and ongoing monitoring of business relationships and transactions by the AP as well as by regular reassessment of the risk profile. When designing reduced KYC requirements, regulators should remember that such reduced measures are exceptional and that full anonymity is not acceptable.

Finally, authorities should ensure retail outlets' cooperation in AML/CFT supervision. Effective supervision of AML/CFT m-money compliance requires good cooperation among competent agencies—for instance, the central bank, the financial intelligence unit, and the telecommunications authority. Regulators are advised to ensure an appropriate and clear delineation of duties to avoid any gaps in or duplications of effort.

The right balance of regulation and risk management will give policy makers the required enabling environment for m-money that will provide underserved communities access to modern financial services and that ultimately will promote financial inclusion.

Note

1. The first draft of this report was circulated to peer reviewers and various stakeholders in May 2010. It coincided with the drafting of, and informed the World Bank's input, the 2010 Financial Action Task Force (FATF) report on new payment technologies as well as the FATF's preparatory work for the fourth round of mutual evaluations.

Reference

Chatain, Pierre-Laurent, Raúl Hernández-Coss, Kamil Borowik, and Andrew Zerzan. 2008. "Integrity in Mobile Phone Financial Services: Measures for Mitigating Risks from Money Laundering and Terrorist Financing." Working Paper 146. World Bank, Washington, DC.

Introduction

Demand for Insight on the Connection of Mobile Money with Anti-Money Laundering and Combating the Financing of Terrorism

There has been significant discussion on the potential power of mobile-based technologies to provide unbanked populations with access to financial instruments and channels. Through the specific use of *mobile money (m-money)* services,[1] for example, customers have accessed informational services, such as balance inquiries in their bank accounts, and transactional services, such as sending remittances to other people or paying for goods and services via their mobile phones. M-money has also been used by national governments to pay employee salaries and benefits.

At the same time, however, concerns have been raised about potential integrity issues that may stem from the use of m-money. These concerns have become particularly relevant as increasing amounts of funds are being transferred through m-money and as new m-money schemes develop around the world—including in areas that could be more vulnerable to money laundering (ML) and terrorist financing (TF). Further complicating this concern is that national authorities may not be fully aware of how to regulate and supervise such technological innovations most effectively to minimize potential integrity risks without constraining the policy objectives of promoting greater financial access through these electronic channels. As more countries are attempting to draft m-money–related regulations, demand has increased for operational guidance on how best to develop an effective anti-money laundering/combating the financing of terrorism (AML/CFT) regulatory and supervisory framework for m-money.

This report follows an initial World Bank study titled *Integrity in Mobile Phone Financial Services: Measures for Mitigating Risks from Money Laundering and Terrorist Financing* (Chatain et al. 2008). The study discussed potential ML and TF risks stemming from different m-money services and the way national jurisdictions may apply measures to potentially mitigate such integrity risks. The study was presented to the Financial Action Task Force (FATF) at its 2008 annual plenary in Rio de Janeiro, the first time that integrity concerns related to m-money were comprehensively raised among FATF's constituents. The 2008 report prompted multiple stakeholders, including the FATF, the GSMA (Groupe Speciale Mobile Association), the U.S. Treasury, the U.K. Financial Services Authority, national governments, and others, to demand further research. That demand provided strong motivation to expand research into this area and to publish the findings through this report.

The M-Money Landscape: Potential and Challenges

M-money services hold great potential to expand financial access among poor people.[2] More than 80 percent of the world's population is now within mobile coverage. In 2009, the GSMA's Wireless Intelligence[3] reported that there were more than 4 billion mobile subscriptions globally, with 80 percent of new connections occurring in emerging markets, mostly among lower-income consumers. The growth of global mobile coverage continues exponentially as new mobile network infrastructure and competition in the mobile markets increase worldwide.

At the same time, there are enormous discrepancies between mobile coverage and access to formal financial services. An early-2009 study by the Consultative Group to Assist the Poor, the GSMA, and McKinsey shows that almost 4 billion people worldwide remain without access to formal financial services. Of that amount, 1 billion do not have a bank account, but do possess a mobile phone. By 2012, that number is expected to grow to 1.7 billion, so mobile phones can be leveraged to provide formal financial services to nearly half of the world's unbanked population.

This great potential, however, should be put in context. Although the total revenues generated for the m-money industry are estimated to be nearly \$7.8 billion in 2012, this expected revenue would equal only 4.6 percent of the m-money industry's expected total income. In addition, almost 120 m-money programs are expected by 2012, although it is likely that only a few will succeed and remain sustainable in the long run (CGAP 2009). For the m-money programs that remain viable, their potential impact in postconflict and fragile states such as Liberia[4] may be significant; in such countries where financial sector and landline infrastructure are inadequate, cell phone companies are among the first major enterprises to expand their businesses into these areas.

The number of developed and developing countries in which a domestic or international person-to-person (P2P) m-money transfer was offered as of February 2010 is illustrated in map I.1.[5] The authors have used this map because, in defining an appropriate regulatory framework for m-money, national regulators and supervisors should focus only on the P2P transfer risks associated with m-money. Although m-money goes beyond P2P transfer to include bill payments, these payments do not pose integrity risks and are not reflected in the illustration.

Map I.1   Jurisdictions Where Domestic or International Person-to-Person Transfer via M-Money Is Available, February 2010

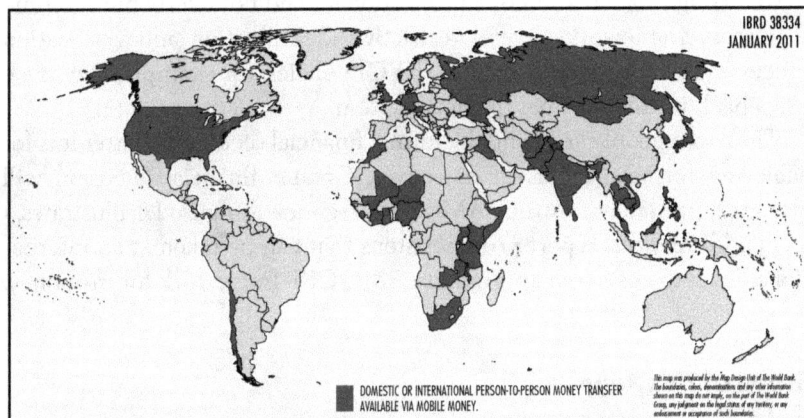

Source: GSMA's Wireless Intelligence unit.
Note: According to the source, this list may not be comprehensive because data are still being collected from additional countries. This map was produced by the Map Design Unit of the World Bank, January 2011. The boundaries, colors, denominations and any other information shown on this map do not imply, on the part of The World Bank Group, any judgment on the legal status of any territory, or any endorsement or acceptance of such boundaries.

Objectives of This Report

Although the general risk analysis and mitigation measures of the 2008 report remain relevant, this report aims to contribute to ongoing policy discussions by providing more targeted guidance on the evolving AML/CFT regulatory and supervisory landscape for m-money.

The project team has developed a guide that gives national authorities practical advice on how to draft AML/CFT regulations and policies that adequately address risk, while permitting both m-money innovation and financial access for unbanked populations. For national regulators, establishing a proportionate and not overly burdensome regulation is important; otherwise, customers will have an incentive to increase their use of informal transfer channels. Informal and formal transfer channels compete with each other. In many countries, informal channels are extremely cost efficient and fast in processing cash transactions, with little or no process for verifying the identification of money senders or recipients. These informal systems are outside the regulatory parameters, and the opacity of these systems is a weak link in AML/CFT regimes focused on financial transactions. The alternative to m-money is arguably pure cash transfers and transactions through these informal channels, not bank-to-bank transfers. The informal alternative would mean that transfers and transactions are not recorded, cannot be traced, and pose higher risks.

Thus, a key objective of this report is to discourage use of informal systems through the creation of a proportionate and not overly burdensome regulatory framework. Overly restrictive identification and verification processes in know-your-customer (KYC) policies, for example, may push users back to the informal financial system.

The more people are using the formal financial sector, the better it is for achieving financial inclusion objectives. Greater financial inclusion will also lead ultimately to strong AML/CFT regimes, as figure I.1 illustrates.

In addition, this report proposes steps that can be taken at an international level to ensure an appropriate AML/CFT framework for m-money.

Scope of This Report

Some governments have moved toward overly restrictive AML/CFT regulations, potentially hindering the m-money market's enormous potential for bringing financial access to the poor. Although it is important that m-money providers have regulatory certainty, it is also important that regulations not be more burdensome than required, be responsive to a

Figure I.1   How Financial Inclusion Leads to a Strong AML/CFT Regime

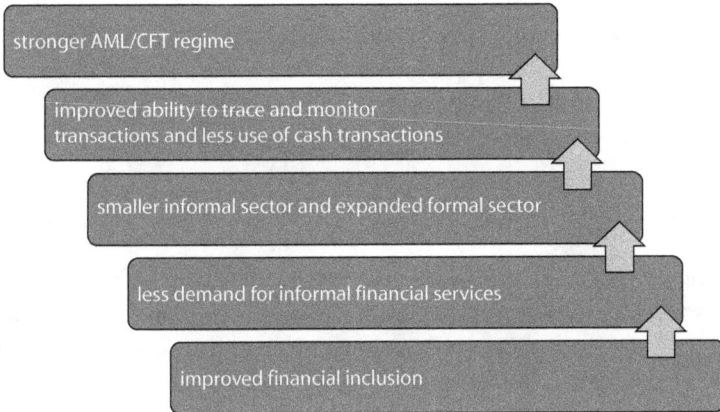

stronger AML/CFT regime

improved ability to trace and monitor transactions and less use of cash transactions

smaller informal sector and expanded formal sector

less demand for informal financial services

improved financial inclusion

Source: Financial Market Integrity Unit, World Bank.

country's local conditions, and be sufficiently flexible to adapt to the different contexts in which they are applied. Excessive regulatory rigidity may stifle greater investment and innovation in m-money programs by unnecessarily raising regulatory compliance costs,[6] increasing barriers to entry, and jeopardizing providers' and regulators' shared goal of reaching lower-income clients in a responsible manner.

The evolution of m-money in Africa and in non-African, low-income countries means that low-income and low-capacity countries are grappling with ways to ensure compliance with international AML/CFT standards.[7] Thus, this report also provides some indications of how the FATF standards[8] can be applied to low-income clients within an m-money context.[9] It does this by presenting various country practices and experiences to enable policy makers to identify the most appropriate solutions for their countries' individual circumstances.

Target Audience

Stakeholders may find helpful guidance on possible methods to best regulate and supervise the continually evolving m-money markets, keeping in mind the objectives of both integrity and financial inclusion. These stakeholders include policy makers from ministries of finance, science, and technology; central banks; telecommunications and financial regulatory bodies; financial intelligence units; and international AML/CFT standard-setting bodies.

To a lesser extent, private sector banks and nonbank financial institutions (microfinance institutions, mobile network operators [MNOs]) and third-party providers (nonbank/non-MNOs) already operating or planning to operate m-money programs may find the report helpful, especially when national authorities are defining the appropriate regulatory and supervisory frameworks to govern the service.

Methodology

This report is based on primary and secondary research and analysis. Fieldwork included extensive interviews with relevant officials in the public sector, including banking and telecommunications regulators, financial intelligence units, central banks, and ministries of finance and telecommunications. From the private sector, MNOs, financial institutions, nongovernmental organizations, microfinance institutions, universities, and donor agencies were also interviewed.

For this report, the study team conducted primary fieldwork in France, India, Kenya, Malaysia, Mexico, the Philippines, the Russian Federation, the United Kingdom, and Zambia.[10] The study team ensured that there was fair representation of input from both developed and developing countries and from both public and private stakeholders.

Outline of the Book

This report is arranged in four chapters and four appendixes, in addition to this introduction:

- Chapter 1 dissects the various business models of m-money programs and outlines the role that each provider can play throughout the mobile payment process. It also identifies the different market integrity responsibilities assumed by each provider as the money flows through the system.
- Chapter 2 provides an assessment of potential risks stemming from m-money services and the mitigation tools that can be applied. It discusses whether there has been an emergence of any new ML/TF risks or mitigation techniques, and reconciles with reality the current perceptions of integrity risks.
- Chapter 3 inventories current regulations and legislation passed in several countries to govern m-money. It assesses how ML/TF concerns

have been addressed from a regulatory standpoint and describes potential interactions or mismatches among the multiple regulations that could govern m-money.

- Chapter 4 makes policy recommendations to the key stakeholders—policy makers and legislators, financial intelligence units and law enforcement agencies, sector regulators and supervisors, and banks and nonfinancial m-money providers. It also proposes new ideas for FATF consideration.
- Appendix A explores what type of guidance assessors may require to integrate financial inclusion questions into the AML/CFT assessment process. It identifies issues that assessors can consider within the broad framework of the current FATF methodology. The discussion is not intended to formally complement the FATF methodology or to be a substitute for any part of it.
- Appendix B provides greater details on the currently evolving m-money landscape, and it discusses general conditions that could determine the success or failure of m-money programs globally.
- Appendix C elaborates on the challenges that m-money providers are currently facing in complying with customer due diligence obligations. It also lifts some misunderstanding or misperceptions of what is expected from service providers, clarifies some concepts that are not always correctly understood by either authorities or the industry, and analyzes the precise obligations under FATF Recommendation 5. Furthermore, this appendix provides some guidance on how best to use the flexibility permitted by the standards and to explore possible alternative options.
- Appendix D outlines the challenges posed by implementing reporting obligations on providers of m-money. In particular, it discusses the different role players; the division of functions; incidental rights and duties; and the information that should be provided in suspicious transaction reports, which are vital to the AML/CFT system.

Notes

1. This new phenomenon should be considered a service rather than a kind of money.
2. For more information on the current m-money landscape—its potential, challenges, and factors that can lead to the success of m-money deployment—see appendix B.
3. Wireless Intelligence, GSMA's marketing information unit, is available at https://www.wirelessintelligence.com/.

4. In Liberia, there is no landline service because it was destroyed in the war and has not been rebuilt. Calls to anyone must be made through a cell phone.

5. For a discussion of cross-border remittances through mobile phones and their associated ML/TF risks, see chapter 3 and appendix A.

6. According to MTN Group representatives operating in the area, m-money providers in Ghana are actually driving to low-income subscribers' houses because they have no other way to verify their addresses, in compliance with KYC requirements.

7. In many regions, for example, the World Bank Financial Market Integrity Unit has seen cases where AML/CFT policy and regulatory frameworks were ill designed, partly because there was no clear understanding of the FATF recommendations and partly because there was an overly conservative policy approach.

8. The World Bank has been working closely with the FATF and FATF-style regional bodies to address the issues of integrity and financial inclusion.

9. In terms of potential flexibility provided by international standards as they relate to AML/CFT, this study places great importance on taking into account a provider's transaction monitoring and pattern systems because they could be key elements in mitigating risks where customer due diligence measures might be more compromised.

10. In complement, the 2008 study conducted fieldwork in Brazil; Hong Kong SAR, China; the Republic of Korea; Macao SAR, China; Malaysia; the Philippines; and South Africa.

References

CGAP (Consultative Group to Assist the Poor). 2009. "Window on the Unbanked: Mobile Money in the Philippines." *CGAP Brief* December.

Chatain, Pierre-Laurent, Raúl Hernández-Coss, Kamil Borowik, and Andrew Zerzan. 2008. "Integrity in Mobile Phone Financial Services: Measures for Mitigating Risks from Money Laundering and Terrorist Financing." Working Paper 146, World Bank, Washington, DC.

CHAPTER 1

Analysis of the Mobile Money Transaction Flow

Summary

This chapter analyzes the mobile money (m-money) transaction structure. It identifies the key steps or elements of a transaction and formulates the "rule of the account provider" as a design principle for an appropriate regulatory framework.

Previous analysis differentiated models on the basis of the type of service provider performing the key functions in a particular m-money business model. This led to a binary approach that differentiated between "bank-led" and "mobile network operator (MNO)–led" models. Governments have increasingly found this approach inadequate to describe and categorize the plethora of models that have emerged. Alternative players are entering the market at an increasing rate. For example, the authors found several third-party m-money providers in the Democratic Republic of Congo, India, Kenya, the Philippines, the United Kingdom, and Zambia—and more are emerging worldwide. These new models cannot fit easily into the binary approach.

The study analyzed the different models and found that their m-money transactions contain the same five elements or functions arranged stepwise:

1. mobile communications service,
2. customer interface,

(continued)

Summary *(continued)*

3. *transaction processing,*

4. *account provision, and*

5. *settlement.*

In the models that were observed, the mobile telecommunications service is delivered by an MNO, and ultimate settlement is carried out by a bank. The responsibility for the other functions, however, is not fixed on any specific provider type. The differences among the various models generally stem from the different ways in which responsibility for the remaining functions is assigned.

The authors believe that it is important to recognize that this great flexibility concerning who can do what in the transaction is vital to understanding how best to regulate. It reinforces the view that regulation must be service based, not provider based.

The chapter is divided into six sections. It first charts the flow of money in an m-money service. Then it outlines the roles that the many providers may play in each step of a mobile payment. That framework is then used to identify the various market integrity responsibilities assumed by the providers as the money flows through the system. The chapter concludes with the rule of the account provider, which identifies the provider of the account as the party best suited to verify the anti-money laundering and combating the financing of terrorism (AML/CFT) practices applied at the other stages of the money flow.

Key Points

- *M-money schemes are complex, with multiple provider types involved.*
- *Business models should not be defined by provider type because all models inherently include various providers.*
- *Five stepwise functions can be identified in an m-money transaction: mobile telecommunication service, customer interface, transaction processing, account provision, and settlement.*
- *Practices that are consistent with AML/CFT procedures are performed in all five functions of the transaction.*
- *Fieldwork indicates that the quality of AML/CFT practices does not vary by provider type.*
- *The provider of the account records is in the best position to oversee the integrity practices conducted during the other stages of the transaction, and ideally should be the party that carries the main responsibility for AML/CFT compliance.*

Introduction: Regulating by Provider Type Is Insufficient

Finding appropriate ways to regulate and supervise m-money requires a close understanding of how m-money actually moves through the system. The role of each participant—whether an MNO, a bank, or another party—is key to determining an optimal AML/CFT regulatory framework.

Each role puts responsibilities on those participants who are best able to accomplish them. For instance, a government may hold a mobile operator responsible for recordkeeping when the records already are being held by a partner bank—a possible redundancy that results in increased costs. In another case, regulations may require a bank staff member to verify a client's identity documents when that verification has already been done by a qualified MNO retail outlet. Again, this duplication of efforts could be an unnecessary burden on the business and ultimately could hinder financial inclusion.

Previous efforts to map the money flows grouped business models into two types: bank-based and MNO-based (later termed bank-led and MNO-led models). But this approach has been insufficient in describing the complex roles that multiple players have in the system. It is also misleading, implying that an m-money provider is exclusively either an MNO or a bank. That implication risks leaving crucial third parties—such as mobile remittance providers or mobile payment system operators—out of the picture. To effectively regulate the system and guard it against abuse, regulators must consider what occurs at each step of the money flow. What function does a provider serve at each stage, regardless of its type?

This analysis defines each stage of the money flow by the function it serves in advancing the transaction toward completion. A transaction could be likened to a relay race: the sender passes a baton to the athlete who specializes in sprints, who then passes it to the athlete who specializes in jumping hurdles, who then passes it to another specialist and then another until the baton is brought to the finish line. Each of the different functions that the athletes perform is critical for the completion of the race. In the same way, each of the different functions performed by the various providers is critical to the completion of the transaction.

What provider performs each function? As will be illustrated in this chapter, most major m-money models are distinct; so far, there is little sign of a general movement toward any particular model as superior or preferred. Therefore, it is important to recognize that most functions of an m-money transaction can be carried out by various types of providers, just as different athletes specialize in different parts of a race. Money transfer orders, transaction processing, account recordkeeping, and so on can be done by a bank, an MNO or remittance retail outlet, and others. Who does what is often the result of market conditions (including the existing licensing requirements), so there is no inherent precondition on who performs each function; rather, it is limited only by regulation.

Mapping the System: From Mobile Service to Settlement

M-money systems observed in fieldwork shared two common characteristics. In the first stage, MNOs always facilitated the mobile service that carried customers' transaction instructions and receipts.[1] And, in the last stage, the money deposited to and withdrawn from the m-money system was always stored in an account of some kind based in a bank.[2] That finding demonstrates how the system always has at least two providers involved in a transaction at any one time. In effect, there is never one single provider.

Figure 1.1 is a diagram of the various stages of a mobile transaction. Note that aside from the beginning and end steps, all middle stages can be performed by many kinds of providers and, therefore, do not inherently necessitate either a bank or an MNO.

Mobile Service

Getting access to a mobile phone that is able to communicate is the first step of an m-money transaction. This access is invariably provided by an MNO. Although it is technically possible for the MNO to monitor activity on the phone, privacy and data protection rights usually make the operator blind to the information communicated. Mobile service can be both prepaid and postpaid, depending on the consumer and on the services offered by the provider. Accounts that are prepaid usually have a ceiling on the amount of credit that can be stored on them at one time. Consumers of postpaid accounts often have to submit to a credit

Figure 1.1   General Anatomy of a Mobile Transaction

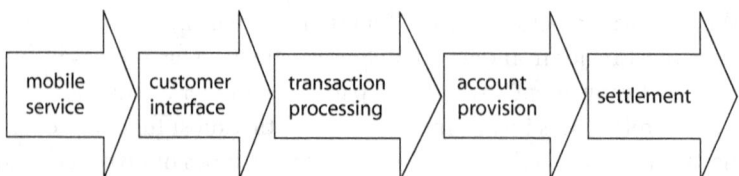

Source: Authors.

check. Prepaid accounts do not pose a risk to MNOs' business and, therefore, are less scrutinized. The MNO faces no danger that the customer will fail to pay his or her bill after he or she has made a purchase because the transaction can be carried out only if the funds are already in the user's account.

Customer Interface

The customer interface is the method through which customers give orders to the m-money system and receive information. It serves the same purpose as a bank teller who answers a call from a customer: the interface connects the customer to the payment system.

Mobile phone manufacturers do not generally put payment system software onto their devices.[3] This means that it is often necessary to put the software on the phone when a customer signs up. Adding the software may be done by downloading it onto the phone via a SIM (subscriber identity module) card (the key that gives the phone access to the mobile network). This is called STK (SIM Toolkit) technology, which is used by Safaricom in Kenya. Alternatively, the consumer may be able to access the network using a special code that prompts the phone to access a menu provided by the transaction processor (this technology is known as unstructured supplementary service data, or USSD).[4]

Retail outlets are also a form of customer interface, and they will be discussed in the next section.

Transaction Processor

The doorway to any m-money program is the transaction processor. Typically, this is a central computer that automatically handles transaction instructions. It receives orders from the user (via the customer interface) and then checks the feasibility of the transaction. For instance, if a consumer requests money be sent to another user in the system, the transaction processor reviews the accounts of each party to verify that funds are available and, possibly, that no limits have been reached (such as transaction amount or quantity limits). Should the request be deemed satisfactory, the processor instructs the account records (discussed subsequently) to be updated with the new balances and sends confirmation messages to the sender and recipient.

Occasionally, this is not conducted automatically through a computer. Providers in parts of Africa have dedicated staff who act as transaction processors, manually updating account records and sending confirmation messages to users.

Account Provision

Account balance information as well as transaction history are usually kept electronically (sometimes with paper backups, depending on regulatory requirements). How long these data are kept and how extensive they are varies from provider to provider and from jurisdiction to jurisdiction. It is frequently, but not always, linked automatically to the transaction processor so that money transfers can occur instantly.

Settlement

The settlement process may be simple—the money that the sender puts into the system is delivered to the recipient, minus fees. Just as settlement between two accounts in the same bank is much simpler than settlement between accounts at different banks, so are m-money transactions. In cases where money is moved within the same financial institution (regardless of the type), settlement is as straightforward as reconciling the account records to the transaction.

When settlement is between accounts at two different institutions, a bank is needed to transfer money from one account to another. For instance, money transferred from an account at a mobile operator in Malaysia (for example, Maxis) to an account at a mobile operator in the Philippines (such as Globe) must go through an intermediary bank. The intermediary credits the bank account of the receiving mobile operator (which then credits the virtual account of its customer) and debits the bank account of the remitting mobile operator (which debits the virtual account of its customer). Figure 1.2 illustrates the flow of money divided into the various functions that must occur to move the money out of the sender's virtual account and to the Philippines where the recipient is located. Notice that the sender's account (that is, his or her virtual account) plays no further role in the transaction after it has been debited and its records are adjusted. The transaction then moves to an actual physical cash settlement in a bank between the two providers (here, Maxis and Globe—both mobile operators).

But the transaction is not done after the receiving provider obtains the transferred funds. The recipient customer's virtual account must still be credited with the money. Figure 1.3 maps this process. Because the funds are coming from outside, the transaction direction is reversed.

The Retail Outlet's Role: Customer Interface and User

Retail outlets are a key component in most m-money systems. These outlets are generally used for opening an account and exchanging cash for credit in the system, or vice versa. Some retail outlets may also keep

Figure 1.2   Sample Transaction between M-Money Accounts in the Philippines and Malaysia, Sending Side

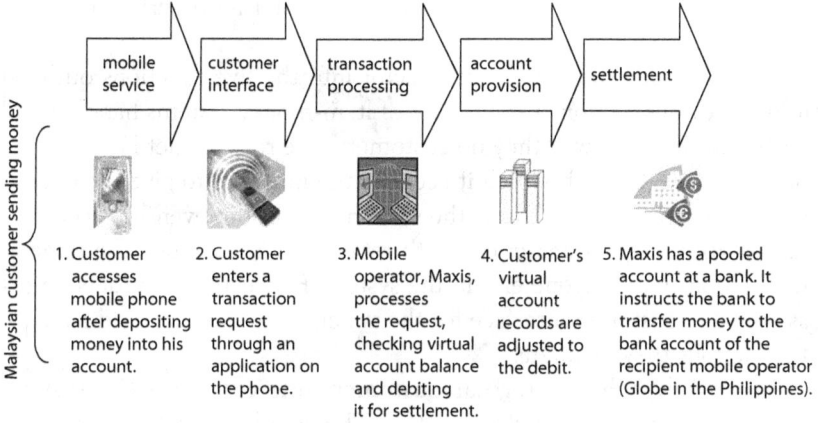

mobile service	customer interface	transaction processing	account provision	settlement
1. Customer accesses mobile phone after depositing money into his account.	2. Customer enters a transaction request through an application on the phone.	3. Mobile operator, Maxis, processes the request, checking virtual account balance and debiting it for settlement.	4. Customer's virtual account records are adjusted to the debit.	5. Maxis has a pooled account at a bank. It instructs the bank to transfer money to the bank account of the recipient mobile operator (Globe in the Philippines).

Malaysian customer sending money

Source: Authors.

Figure 1.3   Sample Transaction between M-Money Accounts in the Philippines and Malaysia, Receiving Side

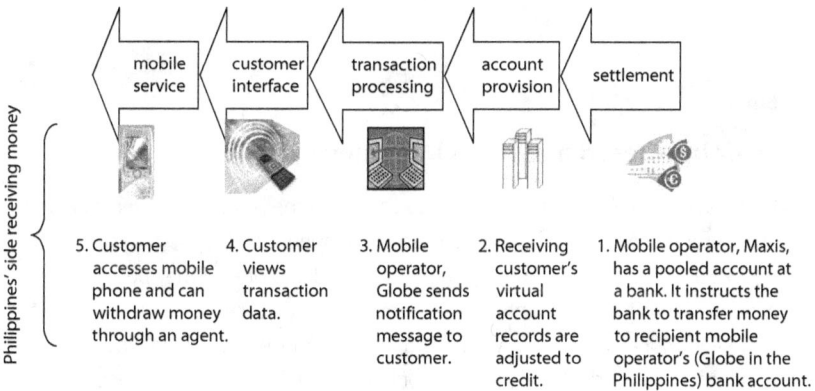

mobile service	customer interface	transaction processing	account provision	settlement
5. Customer accesses mobile phone and can withdraw money through an agent.	4. Customer views transaction data.	3. Mobile operator, Globe sends notification message to customer.	2. Receiving customer's virtual account records are adjusted to credit.	1. Mobile operator, Maxis, has a pooled account at a bank. It instructs the bank to transfer money to recipient mobile operator's (Globe in the Philippines) bank account.

Philippines' side receiving money

Source: Authors.

paper records (such as photocopies of identity documents, applications for account creation, and receipts for cash-in and cash-out) that is not always necessary because the records can be kept electronically with the account provider (AP). From a customer's view, the retail outlet is the central mechanism through which he or she can make deposits[5] and withdrawals[6] when the system is *closed* to outside transactions (that is, when it is a system that does not give users the ability to transact with those who are not registered users). In cases where the system is *open* (that is, when it is interoperable with those who are not registered users), retail outlets may not be as important. See box 1.1 for descriptions of the two system styles.

How does a retail outlet's role factor into the five functions outlined in the previous section? On the face of it, m-money systems handle retail outlets in the same way they do customers. The retail outlet has a mobile phone service through which it accesses the interface to give commands to (and receive receipts from) the system. The outlet even has accounts, just as other users. Transactions with retail outlets are much the same as transactions with anyone else in the system. However, the outlets do act as a type of customer interface for the system and, thus, are paid a fee for transactions they facilitate.

Effectively, when a regular customer puts cash into the system, he or she brings it to a retail outlet. The retail outlet takes the cash and, in return, transfers money from its account to the customer's account. If the account provider (AP) is a bank, the customer receives a deposit into his or her bank account from the bank account held by the retail outlet.

Box 1.1

Defining Closed and Open M-Money Systems

New payment systems such as prepaid cards, Internet money transfer services, and m-money may be categorized as closed or open.

Like a typical bank account, systems are considered open if they permit transactions to and from accounts that are not part of the system. Just as someone may send money from bank A to bank B, an open m-money system would allow a user to move funds directly from his or her m-money account to an account in another financial institution. This means that there are two APs involved—one to send the funds and one to receive them.

Closed m-money systems are set up in a different manner. All transactions occur within the same system, so only one AP is involved. For a customer to move money to someone who does not have an m-money account, the sender must withdraw cash from the system and then use another provider to transfer it to the recipient's account.

Source: Zerzan 2009.

From the AP's point of view, the retail outlet is nearly the same as any other customer. In many programs, a regular user could imitate the function of a retail outlet by taking cash and crediting accounts. However, the different limits put on retail outlet accounts and customer accounts make retail outlet imitation difficult.

Although retail outlet activity in the system is quite similar to that of regular customers (albeit with more transaction frequency and greater account balances), the way in which a retail outlet inputs or withdraws funds from its m-money account can be very different from the way in which customers do so. Retail outlets are almost always required to have accounts in some traditional financial institution (that is, a bank). They cannot exist in the system without such an account, no matter how the program functions. This is because, at some point, retail outlets will want to convert their credit in the system into cash, and vice versa. Customers use retail outlets to do this, but what does the retail outlet do? The amounts retail outlets deal with are much greater than those of regular customers. So how does all the cash that retail outlets receive from customers get deposited into the pooled account?

In closed systems, retail outlets typically will have a bank account in the same settling bank as the AP. If the retail outlet has too much cash on hand at the end of the week or month, it will deposit that cash into this bank account and transfer some or all of it into the pooled account. This transfer will credit the outlet's virtual account. If the retail outlet has too little cash on hand, it makes a cash-out request to the AP. Cashing out moves money from the pooled account to the retail outlet's bank account.

The example of Mobile Transactions Zambia Limited (MTZL)[7] illustrates the process (figure 1.4). Customers of MTZL must have their own mobile phone access, but they need nothing more. When they have opened an account, they may deposit money through a local retail outlet. The retail outlet has its own account on the MTZL system—an account that is essentially the same as the customer's account, but with higher amount and frequency limits. The customer gives his or her cash deposit to the retail outlet, the outlet then transfers credit from its account to the recipient customer's account (minus a fee).

The customer side is complete; but if the retail outlet wishes to recredit its own MTZL account with cash or other funds, it must deposit the cash given by the sender to its (the retail outlet's) MTZL bank account and then transfer it to an MTZL pooled account. The system then credits that amount to the retail outlet's MTZL account (figure 1.5).

Figure 1.4   Example of a Customer Crediting Account through a Retail Outlet in Zambia

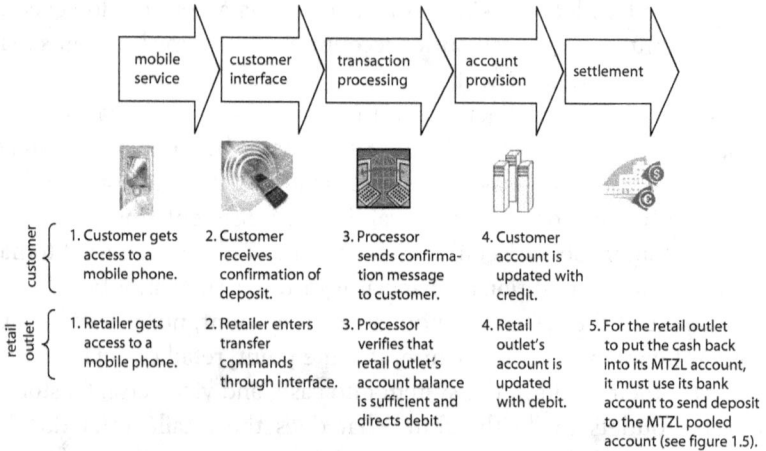

	mobile service	customer interface	transaction processing	account provision	settlement

customer
- 1. Customer gets access to a mobile phone.
- 2. Customer receives confirmation of deposit.
- 3. Processor sends confirmation message to customer.
- 4. Customer account is updated with credit.

retail outlet
- 1. Retailer gets access to a mobile phone.
- 2. Retailer enters transfer commands through interface.
- 3. Processor verifies that retail outlet's account balance is sufficient and directs debit.
- 4. Retail outlet's account is updated with debit.
- 5. For the retail outlet to put the cash back into its MTZL account, it must use its bank account to send deposit to the MTZL pooled account (see figure 1.5).

Source: Authors.

Figure 1.5   Example of a Retail Outlet Crediting Its Own Account in Zambia

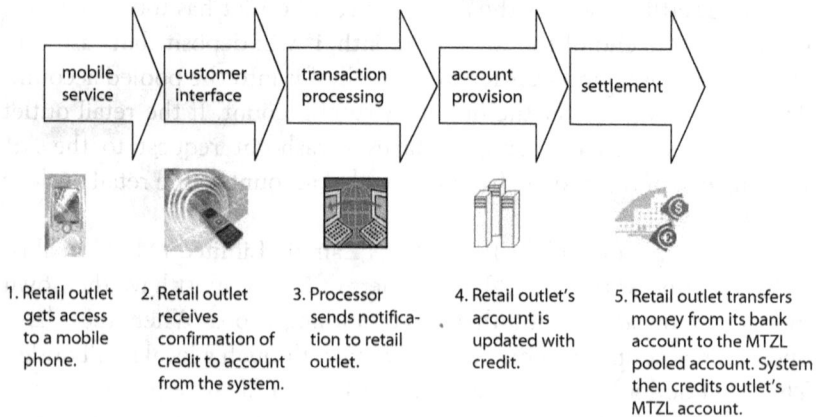

mobile service	customer interface	transaction processing	account provision	settlement

1. Retail outlet gets access to a mobile phone.

2. Retail outlet receives confirmation of credit to account from the system.

3. Processor sends notification to retail outlet.

4. Retail outlet's account is updated with credit.

5. Retail outlet transfers money from its bank account to the MTZL pooled account. System then credits outlet's MTZL account.

Source: Authors.

It is not necessary, however, for the retail outlet to recredit its account because it already has the cash in hand.

Alternatively, there are systems in which all retail outlets and customers have formal bank accounts. Such systems are open m-money systems. M-money is simply an extension of this account and can be used in the same way a debit card is used. For instance, the Kenyan MNO and m-money provider, Orange, does exactly that. Its retail outlets open special bank accounts for customers and act as withdrawal and deposit points—similar to human automated teller machines. Unlike MTZL, Orange retail outlets do not need to keep an intermediary pooled account. If money is in an Orange user's bank account, it is already transferable to other Orange m-money users (and to anybody else in the country).

The lesson here is that although retail outlets may have some unique abilities (such as account-opening rights), the system generally sees their accounts in the same way it sees any other account. Their transactions go through the same process as do customers' transactions. The exception is the way a retail outlet deposits or withdraws cash in a closed system. Whereas customers in either system may deposit or withdraw cash to or from retail outlets, closed system retail outlets have the unique ability to bring new cash into the system, because it is ultimately the retail outlet that will have interaction with the pooled bank account (see box 1.2). Furthermore, only retail outlets receive cash transferred from the pool bank account, as described in table 1.1.

Who Does What: Multiple Providers

Recall the discussion at the beginning of this chapter noting that three of the five steps of an m-money transaction may be facilitated by various types of providers. The exceptions are the mobile service function (the first step to completing a transaction) and the settlement (the last step). Mobile service is always provided by an MNO, and settlement is always performed by a bank. However, the middle three functions—customer interface, transaction processing, and account provision—may be facilitated by various provider types (figure 1.6). The next step in mapping the anatomy of the business is determining who does what. The following analysis examines the various types of providers, demonstrating their increasing involvement in the transaction.

The MNO

MNO participation in the process is technically required only for communications to and from a customer's mobile phone. In instances where the MNO does not have further involvement, the operator may be unaware that m-money services are being provided through its network. Privacy protections and communications security practices generally prevent an MNO from "seeing" the content of communications. In other

Box 1.2

A Hypothetical $10 Deposit and Its Movement into a Closed System

To better visualize the movement of money from a customer to the retail outlet and, ultimately, into the pooled account, we will follow the movement of a customer's hypothetical deposit of $10 to a retail outlet in a closed m-money system. The outlet's assumed fee is $0.50.

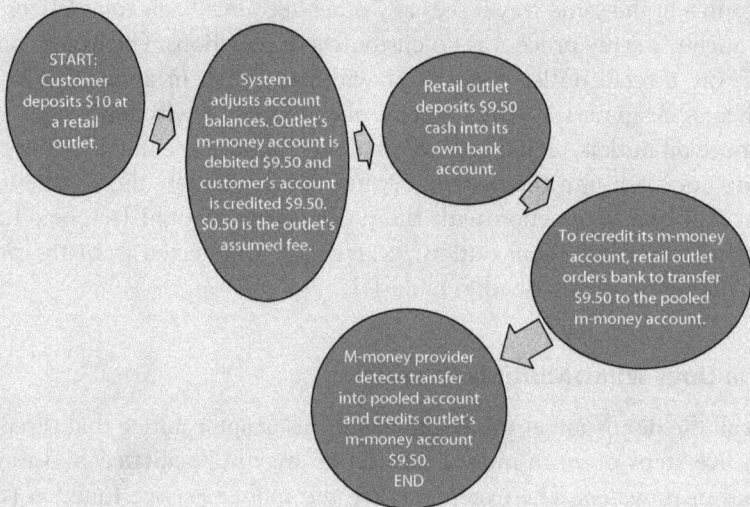

START:
Customer deposits $10 at a retail outlet.

System adjusts account balances. Outlet's m-money account is debited $9.50 and customer's account is credited $9.50. $0.50 is the outlet's assumed fee.

Retail outlet deposits $9.50 cash into its own bank account.

To recredit its m-money account, retail outlet orders bank to transfer $9.50 to the pooled m-money account.

M-money provider detects transfer into pooled account and credits outlet's m-money account $9.50. END

Source: Authors.

Table 1.1   Steps for a Retail Outlet Cash Withdrawal in Open and Closed M-Money Systems

Open system	Closed system
Because funds are already stored in the retail outlet's bank account, the withdrawal process is the same as a regular bank transaction.	(1) Retail outlet makes a cash withdrawal request to the system. (2) System removes funds from virtual account. (3) System debits its own pooled account in a bank and transfers money to retail outlet's account in the same bank. (4) Retail outlet withdraws funds from its bank account.

Source: Authors.

Figure 1.6   Providers in an M-Money Transaction

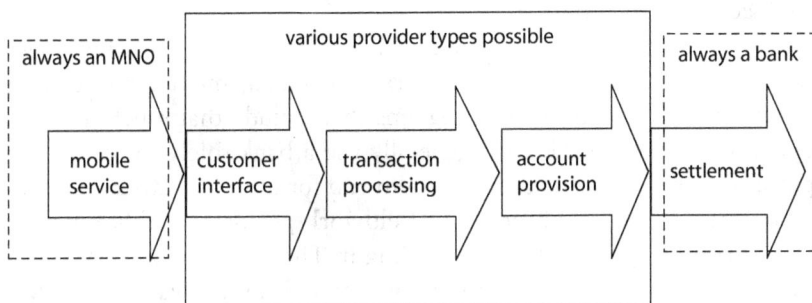

Source: Authors.

words, m-money transactions would simply be charged as a text message or a data download, and what was inside the message or data would be unknown to the MNO.

In many instances, however, MNOs are involved in providing the customer interface. This is certainly the case in the Republic of Korea where SK Telecom provides the mobile service and customer interface for a service called MBank. MBank gives users the ability to access their existing bank accounts through their mobile phones, but banks do not control all the software. The customer interface is provided by the MNO through a dual chip placed in each of its phones. The MNO's role in this is simple: it develops the interface with the four other banks involved (Oh et al. 2005). Although it designed and distributes the platform through which customers transact, the operator, again, cannot "see" individual transactions because of legal restrictions and privacy protections. It is likely, however, that such impediments could be lifted in the case of a law enforcement investigation.

In fact, it is only at the stage of transaction processing that MNO involvement in individual transactions becomes evident. This could be considered the "meat" of the money flow. In fieldwork, it was found that MNOs that performed the transaction-processing function always performed the two preceding functions (mobile service and customer interface). This finding has led some observers to identify the transaction processor as the "leader" of the mobile program. However, the transaction processor is not always a single party. For instance, consider an m-money product marketed in Zambia. The bank that markets the product made an agreement with an MNO. The MNO partially processes transactions on its computers, sending the customers' commands to the bank. The bank then manually approves those commands and adjusts the customers' bank accounts accordingly.

The maximum involvement an MNO can have is covering every function to the point of account record management (the account provision step). In m-money programs that include that much network operator involvement, MNOs generally use a bank solely to handle the physical cash deposited into the system and for ultimate settlement with retail outlets. MNOs observed in fieldwork performing this function also performed all functions preceding it. The most prominent example of this model is the Safaricom model in Kenya. The MNO Safaricom manages the transaction to the point of settlement with retail outlets (which it leaves to the partner banks).

The Bank

Bank involvement can be traced from the other side of the money flow chart. Banks in fieldwork were always the entity providing the ultimate physical cash settlement in an m-money program. At a minimum, they were responsible for holding the funds. If their involvement ends there, it is management of a pooled account under the name of the MNO (or its designate). This is precisely the case of Safaricom in Kenya. Because the MNO manages records, processes the transaction, and provides both the interface and the mobile service, the bank has only to hold the money in a trust account.[8] It does not "see" the day-to-day transactions of customers, but merely the withdrawals from or deposits to the system by retail outlets who have bank accounts at the same bank. In some systems, including that of Safaricom, even the settlement function is carried out by multiple banks where there are several pooled accounts.[9]

If a bank deals with account provision in addition to a settlement function, its participation in the program is greatly enhanced. Account record management means the bank is involved in each transaction in the system. Fieldwork found that when a bank managed this step of the process, the accounts were invariably their own bank accounts as well. That is important because bank accounts are open (except for their regulatory restrictions[10]) and, therefore, directly interoperable with the broader financial system. They can be used to move money to or from nonusers of the m-money system.

In most (but not all) cases in which banks manage account records, banks are also central to the transaction-processing function.[11] Banks that control the mobile transaction processor in an m-money program often had to contract with one MNO or many MNOs to have them provide the technology for the customer interface. Such programs are often the result of the communications authority's reluctance to permit banks to independently set up the interface themselves, without a licensed MNO.[12] When the bank runs the transaction processing, any MNO or third-party involvement in individual transactions is minimal. As mentioned previously, transaction details are usually apparent only to the facilitator(s) of the transaction processing and the AP.

Finally, banks in some countries have gone so far in facilitating m-money as to provide even the customer interface. As mentioned earlier, the customer interface is the function that links the commands or receipts of the customer to the transaction processor. In such cases, the MNO has no more involvement than simply providing the communications platform through which the transaction may occur. It is similar to traditional telephone banking whereby the telecommunications corporation merely provides the line on which the customer speaks to bank staff. Only the bank knows the contents of the call, unless privacy protections are lifted by a court order or other legal means.

Other Providers

As noted in the introductory summary of this chapter, previous analysis and perceptions of m-money programs have often ignored the existence of the plethora of provider types. An m-money service is never provided by one single provider, nor is it limited to just MNOs and banks. Examples are prevalent in the Democratic Republic of Congo (Celpay), India (Obopay), and Zambia (MTZL and Celpay), with other countries considering other providers at the time when fieldwork was being conducted.

Where do these businesses fit on the flow-of-money chart? The mobile communications services are necessarily provided by an MNO, and banks act as the ultimate settlement point in the models that were studied. The remaining three functions (customer interface, transaction processing, and account provision) are delivered by a range of providers, extending from banks and MNOs to nonbank, non-MNO service providers.

Perhaps the most famous third-party provider is Celpay, which classifies itself as a payment service. Celpay is a standalone provider that has made agreements with MNOs and banks so that it can provide its service (and functions in the intermediary three steps).

Figure 1.7 maps the money flow through an account at Celpay. A customer of the Celpay payment service uses his or her existing mobile

Figure 1.7   Alternative Provider Type: Celpay in the Democratic Republic of Congo and Zambia

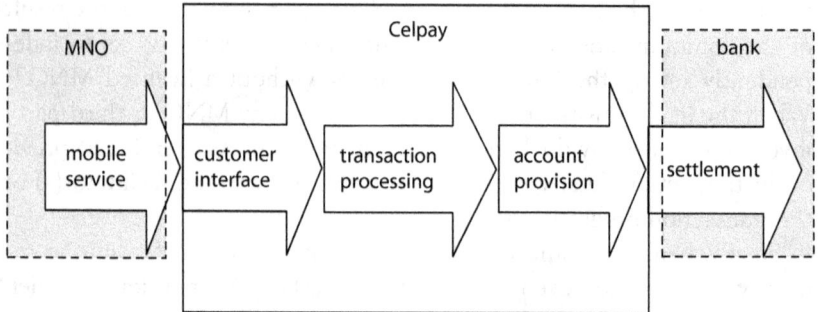

Source: Authors.

service to access a special menu on the phone—a menu designed and downloaded to the phone by Celpay.[13] This menu is the customer interface. Transaction commands are sent and account information is received through this portal. Transaction processing is done at Celpay's offices by its staff. Staff members then manually process the transaction by verifying that available funds are sufficient and limits have not been reached. Account records, also held at the Celpay offices, are updated accordingly; and a confirmation message is sent to both sender and recipient of the funds. Because the system is closed, bank settlement is necessary only when money is withdrawn from or deposited into the system.

Unlike MTZL (an alternative provider type operating in Zambia and discussed earlier), Celpay has no retail outlets. Customers exchange cash and credit at a bank that has an agreement with Celpay. Uniquely, this model gives banks slightly more ability to "see" a customer's activity, but only in terms of his or her deposits and withdrawals. This vantage results from Celpay's lack of a retail outlet network other than bank branches. Because all credit and cash exchanges occur through a bank, all customers must have a bank account at the bank where they deposit and withdraw money. The parallel nature of the two accounts (the customer's Celpay account and the customer's existing bank account) gives users the ability to transact between them. Celpay is blind to what occurs in the bank account (except for deposits and withdrawals from the Celpay system), and the bank is blind to what occurs in the Celpay system (again, except for deposits and withdrawals).

Market Integrity Roles Assumed by Providers

This chapter has outlined a basic framework through which any m-money program can be analyzed. The flow of money is broken into five steps at which a function is carried out to pass the "transaction baton" and advance the transaction toward completion. Furthermore, this chapter has shown that there are many types of business models and providers for m-money.

Now we will look at the relevant AML/CFT procedures carried out by the providers at each step of the transaction.[14] Through this breakdown, we will be equipped to discuss the proper regulatory regime that affects business minimally but leaves no gaps.

Mobile Service Provider

As noted previously, the mobile service is a function always provided by an MNO. Mobile service generally requires an MNO to be supervised and licensed by a jurisdiction's communications authority. This government agency is tasked with regulating the communications industry. Its mandate is broad and rarely covers financial issues, such as AML/CFT. However, it is relevant to ensure the soundness of a company so that it is not controlled by criminals who could use it for illicit ends.

Discussions in the past have questioned whether the communications authority would be equipped to oversee m-money and, in particular, the AML/CFT practices. This concern stems from the case in some countries where the authority is charged with licensing the individual services provided by an MNO.[15] However, the function of providing mobile service is content neutral—that is, the MNO does not necessarily know what is being communicated. It merely carries the message. This function is much the same as a postal worker delivering a water bill—he or she delivers the envelope but is not aware of its contents. Therefore, MNOs whose sole function is the mobile service in a payment program have assumed no AML/CFT responsibilities.

In terms of other possible AML/CFT-consistent practices, some mobile service providers keep basic information (name, address, and telephone number) about their clients. Such information could be used as part of a customer due diligence practice. However, it is mainly for postpaid clients; in many economies, the majority of users are prepaid and little or no information is kept on them. Anecdotal evidence collected in field-work indicates that the number of anonymous prepaid clients may be reduced as governments institute laws requiring MNOs to identify who owns a particular mobile phone number—mandatory SIM registration.

Perhaps unique to telephony, call records and data activity are stored for billing purposes. Geographic data (that is, the location of the person when he or she uses the mobile device or accesses a retail outlet) is also possible to gather through MNO systems, but they are not always recorded. Some observers in law enforcement have called for these data to be captured and linked to that of the transaction, regardless of the MNO's participation in the transaction beyond simply providing the mobile service. Even if the customer's name is unknown by the provider, the phone number is used as a unique identifier for billing.

Customer Interface

The security of the transaction at this point is quite possibly at its greatest risk. Customers usually log on to the software (whatever the type) using a password. Fraud through password sharing and stealing has been detected by various m-money providers. However, to date, no money laundering or financing of terrorism has been detected through shared or stolen passwords.

Fraud is a risk in any payment system. But it is fraud by retail outlets that is one of the foremost concerns of providers—whether MNOs, banks, or other m-money participants. Great efforts have been made to mitigate this risk by all the providers studied in fieldwork, and many of these efforts overlap completely with AML/CFT.[16] In Kenya, for instance, the MNO Zain (now called Airtel Africa) undertakes enhanced due diligence measures on all retail outlets. MNO staff verify the business permits of retail outlets through notaries and perform onsite random visits, including the use of "mystery shoppers."[17] Also in Kenya, retail outlets of Safaricom are required to pass an AML test to ensure their familiarity with integrity issues and procedures.

Furthermore, relevant to AML/CFT is that retail outlets are responsible for verifying a customer's identity (for instance, through identity documents if the customer is unknown to the retail outlet) for cash withdrawals (and for deposits in some programs). This due diligence is meant to prevent fraud by customers and to fall in line with integrity practices.

Transaction Processor

The transaction processor receives a command or instruction from the user. In systems where a non-MNO is the processor, the encrypted command is wired through the MNO's circuits and received by a computer at the provider of this stage of the money flow. This step is not always as simple as it sounds. In some cases noted during fieldwork, the actual transaction processing was manual. The non-MNO provider's staff would have to find the account linked to a particular phone number and enter the data in its separate computer system. For AML/CFT purposes, this manual process means slower internal controls. Some systems have to manually check the names of users for matches on sanctions lists or, at least, wait until the transaction data are entered in the system.

The authors found that when an MNO is the provider of this function, the message is decoded and processed automatically. All MNOs claimed to have the system linked to a screening system that would instantly block flagged names or phone numbers.

Moreover, every provider type performing this function was observed to have placed limits on balance/transaction amounts and frequencies. Attempts to go over these limits were blocked and, in some cases, flagged to the provider.

Account Provider

In all m-money programs studied, account records were a fundamental part of the business. Records included more than just account balances. For instance, there were no cases where money was transferred without a record of the transaction being stored. As with the previous two functions, there are many types of providers managing account records. The period of time for which records were kept varies. They typically are kept for five to seven years because of regulatory obligations; the business need for records is much shorter. By comparison, MNOs keep communications data records for less than two years in most countries. The exception to this is, of course, data on the customer's profile: name, phone number, and other information that varies from plan to plan (for example, date of birth, address, identity documents, and so on).

All of these provider types monitor account activity. But the degree to which they do this varies (although not according to provider type). Account-monitoring procedures vary from sophisticated automated systems that detect patterns to manual ones where the customer base and retail outlet numbers are small.

In terms of reporting suspicious activity, the AP was observed in fieldwork to be the entity that took this responsibility. The practice of filing a suspicious transaction report with the government varied greatly by country, and it did not seem to be linked to the type of provider. The frequency and quality of reporting were more reliant on established practices in the country than on provider type.

Settlement Institution

In all plans, including closed systems, banks involved in the settlement of the transaction stated that they filed suspicious transaction reports with authorities. Closed-system settlement banks that oversaw the pooled accounts filed such documents only for questionable retail outlet activity, however. This is because transactions that occur within the system—that is, from virtual account to virtual account—do not require cash settlement. Because there are no changes in the pooled account that the bank holds, the bank is unable to see such transactions.

After examination of the relevant AML/CFT procedures carried out by providers at each step of the transaction, it is important to emphasize that the regulatory responsibility for each type of provider (MNO, bank, or third-party provider) may vary, depending on the specific type of business model at hand.

Summary and the Rule of the Account Provider

The newness of m-money has inspired many business models and a great variance in the degrees of participation by numerous kinds of providers. Because it is unclear where the market is headed (that is, "which model is best?" if such a question can ever be answered definitively), *a framework for analysis should work in a provider-neutral way*. The three central functions of any m-money scheme (customer interface, transaction processing, and account provision) have been observed to be provided by MNOs, banks, and other kinds of entities.

Procedures relevant to market integrity—including customer due diligence, internal controls, monitoring, reporting, training, and recordkeeping—have all been identified in each of the five steps through which a transaction passes. It seems that in each of these five steps, the provider of the account records is the one that plays the greatest role in AML/CFT obligations.

This finding can lead us to the rule of the account provider: the provider who manages the account records is in the best position to supervise the AML/CFT procedures of the providers at the other stages, and it may be advisable to place the legal burden for regulatory compliance on that provider. This is because the account records function is where the information about customers, retail outlets, and activity all comes together. Whether this function is provided by an MNO, a bank, or another type of entity, the rule holds true. It is important, however, to note that many types of providers may hold the function of an AP. Therefore, regulators must understand that the account provision step may be outsourced to multiple entities, and the regulators should clarify which specific entity would ultimately be legally responsible for any breaches.

Notes

1. This seems natural because only MNOs have the infrastructure available to provide mobile network coverage.
2. Placement in a bank account is not technically necessary because other provider types could choose to store the cash themselves. However, keeping it in a bank reduces the burden on the m-money provider to protect the cash of the m-money system. No m-money provider stores the cash outside of a bank because the cost of guarding cash is too great for nonbanks.
3. Recently, however, Nokia announced plans to start including m-money software in some of its mobile devices sold in developing countries.
4. For further examples, see Mas (2009).
5. Note that to "deposit" is sometimes termed to "cash-in." This report uses the terms interchangeably. To "deposit" is usually the act of putting money into a system that gives interest to a customer (like a bank). To "cash-in" is used in the m-money industry to mean placing money in the system for transfer, usually without accruing interest (like a money transfer service or a remittance provider).
6. Note that to "withdraw" is sometimes called to "cash-out."
7. MTZL is neither an MNO nor a bank. It is a payment provider that facilitates the transaction in the functions of customer interface, transaction processing, and account provision.
8. The trust account in the bank is not in the name of Safaricom; rather, it is in the trust itself, which is a separate legal entity that is affiliated with Safaricom.
9. M-money providers sometimes store the physical cash of the system at multiple banks to mitigate insolvency risks.
10. In South Africa, for instance, m-money accounts are generally not able to transact across borders even though they are bank accounts.
11. Fieldwork done in Zambia found cases where banks were account providers and transaction processing was carried out partially at the MNO.
12. For example, USSD technology often requires licensing from the communications authority in a country. Typically, the authority only grants licenses to MNOs (not to banks and other financial institutions). Non-MNOs then need to pay licensed MNOs to carry their service.
13. Through an agreement with the MNO, Celpay is given the ability to download the software onto a phone's SIM card.

14. The AML/CFT procedures identified are those laid out in Chatain et al. (2008): licensing and registration processes, customer identification, recordkeeping, internal controls and monitoring, guidelines, reporting obligations, supervision and oversight, cross-border transactions, and staff training.

15. Even this practice is diminishing around the world as MNOs are providing an increasing array of services, making it difficult to license individual offerings. Communications authorities are increasingly moving toward a "universal licensing" regime whereby companies are authorized to use a particular channel, frequency, or other method for communications, regardless of the content of the communications.

16. For agency-related fraud abuse that occurred in South Africa regarding low-value products and for guidance on the management of retail outlet risk, see de Koker (2009).

17. Mystery shoppers are staff who visit retail outlet locations and pretend to be regular customers to test the outlet's integrity and competence in carrying out its roles.

References

Chatain, Pierre-Laurent, Raúl Hernández-Coss, Kamil Borowik, and Andrew Zerzan. 2008. *Integrity in Mobile Phone Financial Services: Measures for Mitigating Risks from Money Laundering and Terrorist Financing.* Working Paper 146. Washington, DC: World Bank.

de Koker, Louis. 2009. "The Money Laundering Risk Posed by Low-Risk Financial Products in South Africa: Findings and Guidelines." *Journal of Money Laundering Control* 12 (4): 323–39.

Mas, Ignacio. 2009. "The Economics of Branchless Banking." *Innovations* 4 (2): 57–75.

Oh, Sangio, Hee Jin Lee, Sherah Kurnia, and Robert Johnston. 2005. "Competition and Collaboration in Mobile Banking: A Stakeholder Analysis." Paper presented at the Hong Kong Mobility Roundtable, Hong Kong SAR, China, June 2–3.

Zerzan, Andrew. 2009. "New Technologies, New Risks? Innovation and Countering the Financing of Terrorism." Working Paper 174, World Bank, Washington, DC.

CHAPTER 2

Assessment of Potential Money-Laundering and Combating the Financing of Terrorism Risks and Their Potential Mitigation Techniques

Summary

The growing adoption of m-money (m-money) means that regulators are likely to see new safety problems for consumers and for m-money providers as an increasingly complex financial system gives rise to more sophisticated frauds and increased risks of money laundering (ML) and terrorist financing (TF). A World Bank study in 2008 undertook an evaluation of the ML and TF risk concerns arising from m-money and the potential techniques for mitigating those risks. Given that the m-money market has evolved over the years 2009 and 2010, this chapter determines whether any new integrity risks have emerged and identifies the latest risk-mitigation approaches.

The chapter is divided into six sections. It first categorizes the perceived integrity risks that could stem from m-money, and then shows how there may be elevated risk perceptions among stakeholders of m-money in certain jurisdictions. Following that discussion, the authors argue that a comparative risk-based assessment suggests

(continued)

Summary *(continued)*

integrity risks stemming from m-money services are actually low if providers and authorities take into account risk mitigation measures. Evidence from the field supports that argument. Discussion then turns to the innovative risk mitigation tools currently available to m-money providers and national authorities. The chapter then separates TF from ML and assesses the specific risks and mitigation techniques relevant to TF. It concludes by emphasizing that some countries have applied overly conservative risk mitigation approaches, compromising policy makers' objectives to efficiently and rapidly expand financial access.

Key Points

- *If risks are defined on an absolute level rather than a comparative level, the abuse of m-money could arise from four major risk categories—anonymity, elusiveness, rapidity, and poor oversight.*
- *Poor oversight is an external risk factor potentially creating conditions that increase the likelihood of abuse stemming from the other three major risk categories. The quality of oversight is largely under the capability and discretion of national authorities.*
- *Recent incidents of consumer fraud abuse through m-money channels, anticompetitive business practices by providers, and a lack of formal regulations have heightened integrity perceptions among some m-money stakeholders.*
- *A variety of tools and techniques are available to mitigate integrity risks, and m-money providers generally use most of these tools to avert any reputational risks.*
- *Fieldwork revealed no new ML or TF risks since publication of a 2008 World Bank study. Low amounts of money, traceability, and the monitoring features of m-money programs could make m-money far less risky than other methods of payment, particularly cash.*
- *The risks of financing terrorism and approaches to mitigating those risks are different from those relevant to money laundering, and the approaches have been applied quite differently, depending on the specific circumstances.*
- *A risk analysis of m-money can be accomplished through a more comparative perspective; and if that is done, integrity risks from m-money appear to be comparatively low.*
- *M-money may help move consumers from cash-based transactions to electronic transactions, thus reducing integrity risks on a systemic level through the "electronic" paper trail.*
- *Increasing evidence from fieldwork suggests that certain jurisdictions are implementing overly stringent risk mitigation techniques for ML and TF, potentially increasing regulatory compliance costs among m-money providers and constraining financial inclusion objectives.*

Integrity Risks in Theory: Placing Them into Four Major Risk Categories

Although there is a substantial potential opportunity for m-money to support financial inclusion, significant concerns have been raised regarding the integrity of m-money.[1] Previous analysis, supported by current research and data, suggests that the abuse of m-money could stem from four major risk categories: anonymity, elusiveness, rapidity, and poor oversight. Whereas the first three risk categories may be inherent in the operation of the m-money business model, poor oversight could create conditions that increase the likelihood of abuse emerging from the other three risk factors. Therefore, it should be emphasized again that an enabling environment for m-money must also entail effectively regulating and supervising any potential risk concerns that may arise from these services, including those of ML/TF.[2]

Anonymity

M-money may pose a risk of customer anonymity if proper systems are not in place. Few, if any, m-money transactions can be classified as truly anonymous in the general sense of the word.[3] Many mobile telecommunications and m-money relationships are subjected to identification processes and to verification processes that resemble those applied by normal brick-and-mortar banks to clients who have a similar risk profile. Hence, anonymity in the context of m-money refers specifically to the risk that a criminal may gain access to m-money using a false name or may be allowed to access the services by not disclosing his identity to the MNO or banker.

If identification processes are absent, criminals are able to access m-money with ease. If identification is undertaken, but verification processes deliver weak authentication, it is easier to commit identity fraud successfully. Regarding many of the current m-money programs, there are two main reasons verification processes may not be robust:

1. Responding to the needs of the country, national regulations governing the m-money model allow non–face-to-face verification.
2. The country's verification infrastructure (for example, availability of reliable national identification documentation and electronic databases with identification and profiling data on all residents) is weak.

Both reasons are present in most developing countries, and they may compromise the quality of the verification processes for m-money programs more than for brick-and-mortar banks (de Koker 2009a).

There are many ways these verification processes can be compromised.[4] For example, in some countries, users of prepaid mobile devices are not required to register their phones with the provider, so a user's specific identification data are unknown. As m-money becomes more prevalent, there is concern that criminals could take advantage of this anonymity to send money while masking its source.

Additionally, the use of false identification could present the same problem. The nature of m-money is such that identity may only be verified in a face-to-face manner at the purchase of the phone, and subsequent use will be remote and without the identification normally required for traditional transactions done in person at a bank branch. The possibility that a registered user would hand over his or her phone to criminals to use for illicit activity or that the phone would be stolen for such use could pose dangerous risks.[5] In some countries, such abuse has already been seen among criminal organizations for drug trafficking purposes.[6]

Elusiveness

It is very much in this context that the second risk factor, elusiveness, may exist in the use of m-money to facilitate money movements. Certain cultural practices could provide cover for the true initiator and recipient of a transaction. Mobile phone "pooling," which is used in poorer communities, and the delegation of use in wealthier circles are both examples of exclusiveness. For example, phone pooling is a growing practice in rural villages throughout Africa and Asia. The local community appoints a responsible person to manage a mobile phone that is shared among those in the village. If the phone is registered, it will be under the name of the responsible carrier, not all of those people in the community who may use it.

In wealthier communities that employ phone delegation, a wealthy person authorizes another individual to act on his or her behalf in managing the phone. The phone may be legally registered to the wealthy person, but is never used directly by that person. This practice could be abused for illicit financial activity if the delegated agent misuses the phone to avoid customer profiling. In some countries, financial institutions, law enforcement agencies, and financial intelligence units profile customer activity. This is also true in some markets for m-money. A large transaction may appear consistent with the profile of the wealthy individual to whom the phone is registered, even though that person is unaware that the authorized agent is clandestinely working as an intermediary for criminal activity. The transfer is unlikely to be flagged by authorities because its size is not inconsistent with the customer profile of the wealthy individual registered as its owner.

Furthermore, to increase the difficulty of being detected if engaged in a potentially illicit activity, one may use "smurfing." Smurfing is the use of small transactions to hide the greater sum that ultimately is being transferred. This activity tries to keep money-laundering transactions below the general detection and reporting levels. With the increased detection of smurfing activity, some criminal syndicates have responded by smurfing increasingly smaller sums per transaction. Therefore, U.S. law enforcement agencies have recently coined the phrase "microstructuring" to mean breaking up large sums of proceeds of crime into low-value transactions ranging between $1,500 and $3,000.[7]

Finally, it has been argued that the ubiquity of mobile telephone coverage may pose a heightened integrity concern because the use of cell phones in illegal activities avoids the need to be in the same place all the time; in other words, the nonsedentary nature of using cell phones would likely make illicit activities through mobile-based services more difficult for law enforcement agencies to detect.[8]

Rapidity

The convenience of m-money programs—the ability to use them quickly and practically anywhere at any time—can aid efforts to "layer" a transaction. In ML terminology, layering is the practice of obscuring the origin of funds by complicating their path (for example, transferring them frequently through different accounts within a jurisdiction, and even between jurisdictions[9]). The high speed at which this can be done makes layering much easier than in traditional transfer methods that can require face-to-face interaction with bank personnel at each step. A criminal sitting in one spot with several phones in hand could easily move funds across multiple m-money accounts.

Some of the key risk indicators that have prompted m-money providers and relevant national authorities (such as financial intelligence units [FIUs]) to flag particular m-money transactions as suspicious—based on the perceived risk categories of anonymity, elusiveness, and rapidity—are highlighted in box 2.1.

Poor Oversight

The risk of poor oversight has emerged because current and emerging m-money programs may fall outside anti-money laundering/combating the financing of terrorism (AML/CFT) regulations in some countries. The

Box 2.1

ML/TF Threat and Risk Indicators

- One sender, multiple beneficiaries
- One beneficiary, multiple senders
- High velocity or frequency of transactions
- Incomplete or fictitious information
- Customers whose explanation of the source of the funds is unclear and who decline to provide a satisfactory explanation
- Lack of references or identification
- Structured or recurring, nonreportable transactions
- Multiple third parties conducting separate but related nonreportable transactions
- Transactions structured to lose the paper trail
- Significant increases in the number or currency amount of transactions
- Transactions that are not consistent with the customer's business or income level

Source: The Philippines' Anti-Money Laundering Council.

AML/CFT regulations in place for other financial institutions may not legally apply to the new providers that facilitate m-money (such as telecommunications companies [telecom]) because their primary business is not the provision of financial services. Because the m-money market is generally newer than the AML and CFT legislation in many countries, governments did not consider m-money providers when drafting those laws. Poor oversight may intensify the three inherent risks described earlier because m-money providers will not be detected and sanctioned for unsafe practices in the ways that traditional financial institutions typically are when noncompliant with AML/CFT procedures.

Further complicating the problem is determining the right government authority to oversee m-money. Governments may choose to regulate these businesses through their ministry of communication or technology, but that ministry may not have the mandate or the tools to oversee the industry. In m-money business models where a bank is more extensively involved, there is often a measure of confusion regarding the division of AML/CFT functions between the telecommunications provider and the bank. Countries that have regulated m-money have divided these functions in different ways. Some jurisdictions put the AML/CFT onus on the bank; others shift it to a greater degree to the MNO. Because m-money programs have a variety of different business models (as elaborated in chapter 1), it could be justifiable to regulate and supervise one type of program differently from another. Thus, it is very difficult to determine a consistent approach for all countries to follow in overseeing these electronic channels.

A sample of potential vulnerabilities for each risk category described earlier is provided in table 2.1. The vulnerabilities are presented for the three stages of an m-money transaction—loading the funds, transferring the funds, and withdrawing the funds.

Fieldwork Finding: Perceptions of Integrity Risks May Be Higher Than Merited

A variety of factors might constrain the expansion of m-money programs globally. One of the most significant factors appears to be fears among consumers, service providers, and national authorities about the integrity

Table 2.1   Potential Vulnerabilities for Each Risk Category at Each Stage of an M-Money Transaction

General risk factor	Sample exploitation of vulnerabilities at each stage		
	Loading	Transferring	Withdrawing
Anonymity	Multiple accounts can be opened by criminals to hide the true value of deposits.	Suspicious names cannot be flagged by the system, making it a safe zone for known criminals and terrorists.	Cashing-out of illicit or terrorist-linked funds is possible.
Elusiveness	Criminals can smurf proceeds of criminal activity into multiple accounts.	Criminals can perform multiple transactions to confuse the money trail and the true origin of funds.	Smurfed funds from multiple accounts can be withdrawn at the same time.
Rapidity	Illegal monies can be quickly deposited and transferred to another account.	Transactions occur in real time, making little time to stop them if there is suspicion of terrorist financing or money laundering.	Criminal money can be moved rapidly through the system and withdrawn from another account.
Poor oversight	Without proper oversight, services can pose a systemic risk.		

Source: GSMA risk assessment methodology (Solin and Zerzan 2010).

risks associated with mobile technologies. These fears may not necessarily be based on facts or even reasonable conjecture, but they are understandable, given the novelty of m-money.

World Bank research and fieldwork interviews with authorities in several jurisdictions have indicated that national regulators and supervisors are struggling to understand and assess the actual risks (including those from ML/TF) stemming from such technologies. Most take a conservative position, assuming that these technologies pose a higher risk than they actually do. This view has negatively affected the appetite for and ability of countries to enact legislation permitting m-money and to effectively regulate and supervise m-money services.[10] At the same time, the lack of formal legislation has been one reason that some m-money operators have not ventured into new jurisdictions where there could be great potential for growth in m-money programs.

Even in Kenya, where m-money programs arguably have had significant success without any formal legislation, operators like Safaricom still desire formal legislation that would regulate and supervise them so that more consumers may feel confident in using their services. Although one major reason for Safaricom's success has been consumers' greater trust in MNOs than in commercial banks operating in Kenya (*The Economist* 2009), there are still Kenyan consumers reluctant to use these services because of concerns over the system's integrity. As a result, Safaricom has been working with Kenyan authorities on formal legislation that could have a positive impact on the continued growth of its business, while mitigating perceptions of integrity risks among prospective customers.[11]

Although the general lack of knowledge or the absence of formal legislation in certain jurisdictions has created perceptions of elevated integrity risks among consumers and authorities, banks and MNOs may also have played a role. In some jurisdictions, it appears that banks have blocked MNOs from entering the market for financial services by arguing that MNOs will pose a heightened integrity risk and will threaten market stability because they may not be subject to the same regulation and supervision to which banks are subject. The MNOs, however, view this as a way for banks to prohibit MNOs from engaging in the business for the unbanked because they believe they are more competitive. In other jurisdictions, there have been arguments that MNOs are attempting to force banks out of the m-money business, hindering the potential growth of banks. Banks have attempted to partner with MNOs, but the MNOs have refused. What exacerbates the situation for banks is that unstructured supplementary service data dial numbers (which would allow a financial institution to operate in an MNO's mobile network) are given only to MNOs by the national communications authority of a jurisdiction; therefore, banks must pay MNOs for their use if the bank wants to engage in m-money services.[12] Hence, practices such as these among MNOs and banks have provided both entities an incentive to accuse each other of posing elevated integrity risks, and they may have prevented the emergence of more m-money programs. On another note, the banks' and MNOs' lobbying strength with national authorities in a specific jurisdiction could play a significant role in determining the type of provider allowed to operate m-money services.[13]

There could also be integrity risks arising from the manner in which a particular m-money business model is structured. For example, the m-money operator in one country does not charge a fee to cash-in, but a fee is charged when the consumer transfers the money. Thus, there are reports of small groups of people having pooled their money to cash-in to one specific account, thereby avoiding transfer fees that would have been incurred if each person had done it through his or her separate account. The recipient receives the pooled money and manually disburses it to each respective remittance recipient.

Multiple vulnerabilities may arise from that situation. First, retail outlets may not be in a position to identify the origins of funds pooled into one single account, thereby losing the paper trail. Second, the situation is aggravated by the possibility that a retail outlet is not following procedures and checking the identity and source of funds. And, third, the retail outlets may be involved in the criminal syndicate.[14]

It is difficult to draw any concrete conclusions from the small handful of actual cases of integrity abuse that have surfaced. However, it seems that m-money retail outlets and employees of the MNOs and banking service providers may pose a distinct ML/TF risk. Employees may have or gain access to client details, and they may know the system and controls well enough to circumvent them. Retail outlets, however, can receive substantial volumes of payments and may extract them as a legitimate product of business, perhaps by integrating the funds into legitimate sources of business. Or retail outlets could be fraudulent, defrauding their clients and the banking services provider. Their businesses could also serve as fronts for ML/TF activity. For instance, they may collude with coconspirators who pose as their customers or assist in creating accounts for nonexistent or unwitting clients.[15] Hence, enhanced risk mitigation measures (enhanced due diligence, training, and monitoring[16]) may be needed for retail outlets relative to consumers.

Integrity Risks in Reality

In this section, the authors argue that a comparative and macro-based risk assessment suggests integrity risks emanating from m-money services are low if providers and authorities take into account risk mitigation measures. Evidence from the field supports this argument. Evidence from the field also suggests that a distinction be made between ML/TF and consumer fraud because there have been cases of m-money abuse for consumer fraud, but none of those cases have evidence of ML/TF.

Transition from Cash Transactions to Electronic Transactions

In the previous sections, the AML/CFT risk analysis of m-money focused on the aspects of risks posed individually by each product (absolute risks) and normally relevant within the Financial Action Task Force (FATF) framework. This section considers m-money risk from a broader and more comparative perspective.

M-money is often the first noncash service that clients in developing countries are able to access. Although m-money is not without ML/TF risk, it poses less of a risk than does cash. ML/TF transactions are recorded and traceable, especially if clients are identified. When clients have not been identified, de Koker (2009a) argues that they often are still identifiable. If law enforcement officials wish to identify a particular unidentified client, the m-money framework generally provides them with a rich source of identifying details—for instance, voice recordings, patterns of communication, and patterns of transactions.[17] In addition, the mobile phone acts as a tracking device that can lead investigators to the actual person. Individually and collectively, these facts may render m-money unattractive for abuse, thereby reducing the likelihood that the risk will eventuate.

Also, given that the m-money provider generally has limits on the balance and frequency of m-money transactions, overall costs for ML or TF through m-money relative to other channels may dissuade potential criminals from exploiting the service (see box 2.2).

A risk assessment report undertaken by the GSMA (Solin and Zerzan 2010) compared the risks posed by cash transactions with those posed by m-money. According to this analysis, m-money poses less of an ML/TF risk than do cash transactions, and these risks can be lowered further by proper controls. In sum, because some risk factors

Box 2.2

Cost and Time May Make M-Money Channels Unappealing to Criminals

Depending on the transaction and value caps for m-money, a criminal may launder $10 million in 10 transactions of $1 million each; 100 transactions of $100,000 each; 1,000 transactions of $10,000 each; 10,000 transactions of $1,000 each; or 100,000 transactions of $100 each. Cost- and timewise, it seems unlikely that a criminal would prefer to engage in 100,000 or even 10,000 transactions. A terror financier finds himself or herself in a similar predicament if he or she wishes to abuse capped m-money services to move money.

Nevertheless, regulators should not be comforted only by transaction and value caps imposed by the m-money providers. A comprehensive system of controls and procedures is required to mitigate incentives for criminals to use these services. It is commonly found (for example, with payment cards) that higher security in one segment (such as point-of-sale terminals with EMV [Europay, MasterCard, and VISA] authentication) has displaced criminal activity to other segments (such as card-not-present transactions). The amount of criminal activity in any segment is also a technology-dependent value.

Sources: World Savings Bank Institute; World Bank research.

(anonymity and elusiveness) are lower with m-money than with other payment methods, and other factors (such as rapidity) can be brought to the same level, m-money possesses lower integrity risks than do cash transactions (see table 2.2)—provided that there are effective internal controls and caps on the number of transactions and their values.

As far as the lack of oversight is concerned, each supervisory agency may have varying capacities to understand and mitigate the risks; thus, whereas the risks from m-money are lower after effective internal controls are in place, the extent to which the risk is lowered can vary from country to country. Nevertheless, in all situations, it is arguable that the risks from m-money are lower than those of pure cash that is unrecorded and untraceable.

Evidence regarding how the availability of electronic channels affects the use of cash is emerging. For example, the Bank of Japan, the country's central bank, has already observed a correlation between the increased use of electronic channels (including m-money) and an aggregate reduction

Table 2.2   Comparative Risks of M-Money and Cash, Before and After Controls Are Applied

General risk factor	Cash	M-money Before	M-money Controls	M-money After
Anonymity	HP	SP	Customer profile building to include registration information (name, unique phone number, and so forth)	LR
Elusiveness	HP	SP	Limits on amount, balance, frequency, and number of transactions Real-time monitoring	LR
Rapidity	LR	HP	Real-time monitoring Frequency restrictions on transactions Restrictions on transaction amount and total account turnover in a given period	LR
Poor oversight	HP	LR	Controls that vary by country	LR

Source: GSMA risk assessment methodology (Solin and Zerzan 2010).
Note: HP = highly prevalent risk; LR = low risk; SP = somewhat prevalent risk.

in the level of physical cash. Thus, the overall level of ML/TF risk involved with having physical cash in Japan may also have declined. The advance of electronic money systems in Japan has largely been the result of carrying electronic purses on NFC-enabled[18] mobile phones. A report published by the Bank of Japan (2008) has documented this trend, showing the rate of increase in the amount of large coins (¥500 and ¥100) and an actual decrease in the amount of smaller coins (¥50, ¥10, ¥5, and ¥1) in circulation[19] (see figure 2.1).

M-money therefore can be used strategically to lower national ML/TF risk by facilitating the move away from higher-risk cash transactions to lower-risk m-money transactions.

Risk and Vulnerability Assessment

It is possible to argue that integrity risks arising from m-money are low by determining m-money's vulnerability to abuse and its threat of abuse by prospective criminals (vulnerability + threat = risk).

"Vulnerability" can be defined as a weakness in a specific system or sector arising from weak control measures that are endogenous in nature. Vulnerability also arises from the inherent nature or environment of the particular sector as a result of the products and services offered.

Figure 2.1   Volume of Coins in Circulation and Their Growth Rates, 2000–08
percent

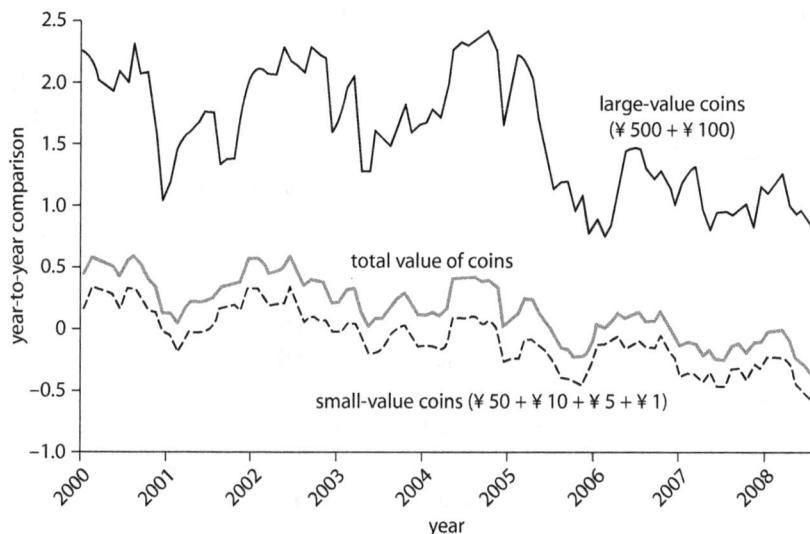

Source: Bank of Japan 2008.

"Threat" can be defined as the likelihood that ML may be attempted. The level of ML threat is influenced by the overall ML environment and attractiveness, which could include exogenous factors at both the national and sector levels (Todoroki forthcoming).

"Risk" can be defined as a residual exposure to threats of ML after taking vulnerability into consideration. Thus, risk is a function of threat and vulnerability. This risk is considered to be potentially inherent in any economic sector; however, the degree of ML/TF risk faced by various sectors may differ.

If this framework is applied to m-money, one can argue that vulnerability is low because there are no novel weaknesses in m-money platforms. Even where national regulatory and supervisory frameworks are absent, m-money providers have internal controls and mechanisms in place. The threat from m-money is also low because the likelihood that ML may be attempted by alternative channels, such as cash, is always likely to be greater than the likelihood that m-money will be used in the attempt. In fact, as box 2.2 demonstrates, the total costs of ML or TF through m-money, relative to other channels, are likely still greater. Hence, because risk is a function of threat and vulnerability, the risk emerging from m-money should also be comparatively low.

Evidence from Fieldwork

M-money poses ML/TF risks, but the study team's fieldwork in a number of jurisdictions where m-money providers have been operating has not found actual evidence of ML/TF abuse through m-money channels. However, the relatively few reports of consumer fraud abuse should provide only limited comfort. This absence of evidence could result from the limited institutional capacity to detect cases of abuse in many developing countries—or perhaps there really is limited risk arising from these services. In this regard, regulators should undertake their own risk assessments of m-money, based on local circumstances and conditions.

Research thus far suggests that the only cases of abuse arising from m-money involve consumer fraud. Cases of consumer fraud have been identified, and suspicious transactions have been reported, but there has been no evidence of ML/TF abuse. In one incident that directly related to the use of a mobile person-to-person transfer, for example, a Safaricom employee was among three suspects arrested in October 2009 over allegations of fraudulent loss of funds through the Safaricom system. The arrests occurred after numerous complaints were received from customers who had lost their e-wallet funds. As a result, Safaricom stated in a press release that it would enhance its current internal AML/CFT controls to mitigate instances of such abuse in the future, particularly because there was no formal AML legislation in Kenya at the time (Momanyi 2009).

Similar incidents of consumer fraud through m-money have been reported in the Philippines. Recent evidence obtained from the Philippines' FIU, the Anti-Money Laundering Council (AMLC), shows an increase in the number of suspicious transaction reports from the two domestic m-money operators since it began recording reports in 2007 (table 2.3). This increase could mean that there is an increase in suspicious activity detected by m-money providers, or it could mean that providers have successful reporting mechanisms in place to ensure that any integrity concerns have been minimized. Furthermore, independent survey work and analysis from the AMLC suggest that the potential ML/TF risks arising from m-money remain relatively low, compared with other ML/TF channels. Two such cases initially flagged through suspicious transaction reports were escalated to law enforcement authorities in the Philippines because they related more closely to petty consumer fraud through the use of these channels. The AMLC found no ML/TF arising from these cases.

It is interesting to note, however, that some of the same processes used to swindle consumers might also be used for TF (and less likely, ML) and

Table 2.3   Number of Suspicious Transaction Reports by M-Money Providers in the Philippines, 2007–09

Name	Year			Cumulative increase (total)
	2007	*2008*	*2009ª*	
M-money provider 1	25	104	152	**281**
M-money provider 2	0	0	2	**2**
Yearly (total)	**25**	**104**	**154**	**283**

Source: The Philippines' Anti-Money Laundering Council.
a. Only data received on or before September 30, 2009 are included.

thus deserve mention. Of the two cases sent to law enforcement agencies, for example, one fraud included swindlers acting as recruiters for overseas positions in a fake recruitment company. The swindlers demanded payment through G-Cash, a mobile phone payment system operated by Global Communications, as a recruitment fee. This fraud was flagged as suspicious by G-Cash because it was tracked as a "many-to-one" suspicious pattern (that is, multiple payments of similar amounts from many different individuals going to the same person).

The other fraud related to the illegal proceeds earned from fraudulently selling iPhones. This case was also flagged as suspicious because most phones have a unique identity number known as an International Mobile Equipment Identity (IMEI).[20] The IMEI made it possible to track the perpetrator because the perpetrator used multiple SIM cards (purportedly of different registered individuals) on the same phone. Through an IMEI, m-money providers can identify a pattern in which the same phone is used to send money to many different individuals (by using different SIM cards on the same phone). That pattern prompts the provider to flag the transactions as highly suspicious. See box 2.3 (which also describes a case documented by the AMLC and not sent to law enforcement agencies in the Philippines).

These cases of consumer fraud have shown that smurfing and layering patterns can be spotted in m-money abuse for the purposes of consumer fraud, and that the internal control mechanisms put in place by MNOs have proved effective in identifying small-value suspicious transactions (even though they are not related to ML or TF). Furthermore, the sophisticated electronic trail, transactional limits, and national regulatory and supervisory oversight of these channels in many jurisdictions may compel criminals to use other means for ML or TF, such as pure smuggling via cash.[21]

Box 2.3

Cases of Consumer Fraud through M-Money: The Philippines Experience

Case 1

Mr. A ordered an iPhone from Mr. B through the eBay Web site. B informed A that the iPhone would be delivered through a courier and instructed A to send the purchase price to B's mobile phone through G-Cash. A cashed-in/sent the amount to B's mobile phone number through G-Cash's business center. However, A never received the iPhone.

The amount sent to B's mobile phone number was transferred to the mobile phone number of Mr. C, who transferred the said amount to the mobile phone number of Mr. D. D then transferred the said amount to the mobile phone number of Mr. E, who went to G-Cash's business center and cashed-out the amount using his mobile phone (see figure B.1).

Figure B.1   Case 1

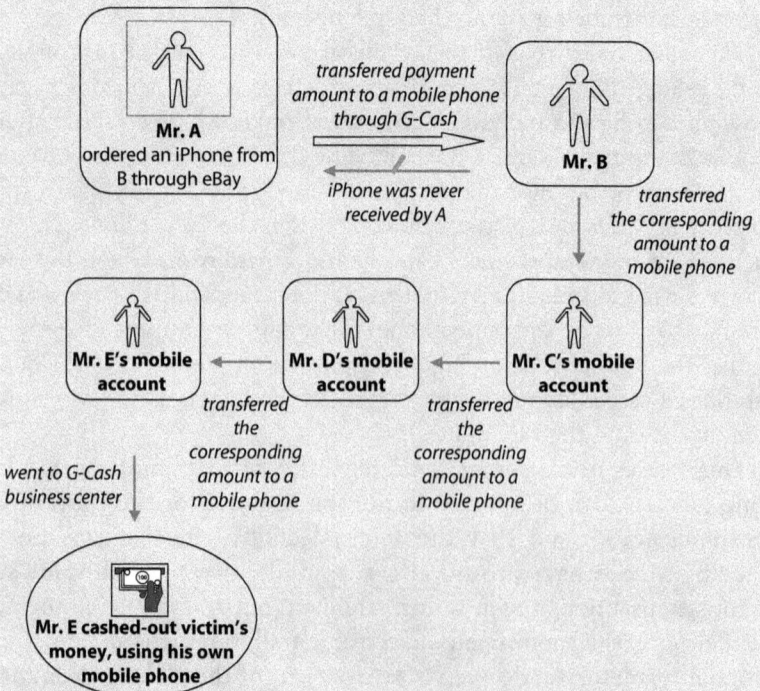

Source: Authors.

Box 2.3 *(continued)*

How the Matter Was Managed by the Authorities
According to IMEI analysis by G-Cash of the mobile phone numbers (SIM card numbers) used by B, C, D, and E, only one mobile phone unit was involved. G-Cash reported the matter to the Philippine FIU. After investigation, the FIU concluded that B, C, D, and E were the same person.

Case 2
In a second fraudulent eBay transaction involving the same perpetrator, Mr. E tried to cash-out from G-Cash an amount cashed-in by an interested iPod buyer who never received the iPod from E.

How the Matter Was Managed by the Authorities
E was not able to cash-out the said amount because the G-Cash company had already blacklisted all the SIM card numbers used by E, given evidence received from case 1.

In coordination with the Philippine FIU, the Anti-Money Laundering Council, law enforcement authorities tried to entrap E, but E eventually realized he was being monitored and never showed up to cash-out the amount.

Case 3
Mr. A, Mr. B, and some additional accomplices recruited several individuals for overseas employment to work as caregivers and nurses in countries such as Italy, the United Kingdom, and the United States. A and B demanded and received from the victims amounts ranging from ₱3,000 to ₱45,000 ($65 to $975) for training fees and processing fees. These fees were collected through G-Cash remittance. The latest victims responded to the *Manila Bulletin* classified ads for the purported available caregiver/nurse positions at Portland Hospital in the United Kingdom, and were informed that overseas travel and processing fees of at least ₱3,000 would have to be paid through G-Cash. Despite the payment of training fees and processing fees by the victims, the promised deployment abroad did not materialize (see figure B.2).

How the Matter Was Managed by the Authorities
When the scam was reported in the *Manila Bulletin* classified ads, the National Bureau of Investigation (NBI) found that the so-called Review and Training Center, represented by A, was not licensed by the Philippine Overseas Employment Administration to recruit workers for overseas employment. In addition, G-Cash's internal transaction monitoring and pattern systems found it suspicious that there were multiple recruitment fees of approximately the same amount from many

(continued)

Box 2.3 *(continued)*

Figure B.2   Case 3

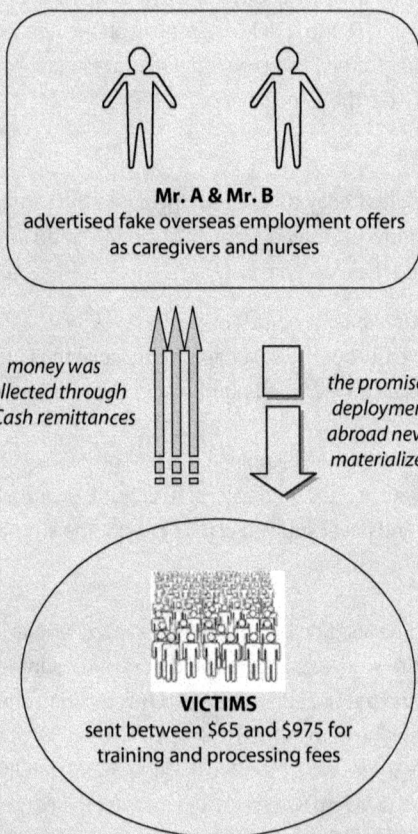

Mr. A & Mr. B
advertised fake overseas employment offers
as caregivers and nurses

*money was
collected through
G-Cash remittances*

*the promised
deployment
abroad never
materialized*

VICTIMS
sent between $65 and $975 for
training and processing fees

Source: Authors.

different individuals going to the same person. G-Cash also discovered that on several occasions Accused A and his cohorts were able to cash-out the funds received from their victims. In an entrapment operation held sometime in April 2009, investigators from the Philippines' FIU and operatives of the NBI were able to arrest A when he attempted to cash-out remittances received from various victims. The arrest warrant for fraud and illegal recruitment was issued by the Regional Trial Court of Manila. The NBI subsequently filed charges of fraud against A and B. Given the small values involved, both men were able to post bail.

Source: The Philippine Anti-Money Laundering Council.

Hence, arguments for placing a more relaxed know-your-customer (KYC)[22] obligation on m-money coupled with strong internal monitoring systems may warrant greater attention and consideration. This is discussed in greater detail in later parts of this report.

Techniques Used to Effectively Mitigate M-Money Risks

As demonstrated earlier, m-money providers generally take steps to mitigate ML/TF risks.[23] Many providers take those steps even though they are not required to do so by law. Interviews with m-money providers suggest that they regard such practices as an important part of good business.[24]

Although m-money is still at an incipient stage in most areas, various jurisdictions have implemented regulatory and supervisory requirements to mitigate any potential risks emerging from this innovation. These requirements include specially set KYC procedures, advanced identification mechanisms, limits on transaction amounts, customer profiling, monitoring and internal controls, centralized registries of account holders, guidelines on AML/CFT, and licensing for m-money providers.

KYC Tailored to M-Money

As discussed earlier, verifying client identity is sometimes challenging for the m-money framework. Some of the possible mitigating factors will be discussed below. However, it is important to recognize that an increasing number of countries now require registration of the SIM card (the unique chip inside each phone). For instance, the telecommunications regulator in Côte d'Ivoire has set a deadline for mobile operators to identify all users of their cellular networks.[25] South Africa implemented a mandatory SIM registration system in 2009, and Nigeria indicated that it soon will follow suit. Mandatory telecommunications registration reduces the risk of anonymity and aids in monitoring accounts for criminal activity.

In response to operators' need to acquire customers using procedures that do not involve face-to-face contact, some jurisdictions have adopted alternative verification measures. The main procedures implemented are (1) legal exceptions to verifying customer's residential address during initiation of the banking relationship (if transactions do not exceed prescribed limits), (2) alternative verification procedures, and (3) restricted functionality. Rather than in-person viewing of verification documentation, customer identity is established by cross-checking customer information against third-party databases—for example, a national tax or social insurance database or other reliable sources such as a telecom's database of active customers. Telecoms enable customers to register for m-money via a mobile phone or the Internet, but these customers are restricted to basic transactions until they have a face-to-face screening.

Innovative Mechanisms for Identification

The security of the mobile telephone device, combined with personal passwords, provides two deterrents that protect against unauthorized third-party m-money use. Fieldwork has revealed use of more advanced measures, such as biometric authentication and electronic signature, to complete financial transactions. To ensure that the costs of such technology are not borne by local retailers (which could impede its adoption in poorer communities), biometric authentification mechanisms are sometimes applied in a centralized way. This means that the advanced biometric technology is based at the company's headquarters rather than spread over multiple retail outlets. MTN Banking, a division of the Standard Bank of South Africa, for instance, has tested a biometric voice identification system for m-money.

Innovative KYC does not always imply a technological solution, however. For instance, South Africa's Wizzit has trained hundreds of local retail outlets that verify customers' identities at their homes and in their communities. This can solve KYC challenges in places where potential clients do not have identification cards or other documentary evidence of their identities.

Transaction Amount Limits

Limited transaction amounts and imposed reporting thresholds are the most popular control measures adopted by regulators and the private sector. The lack of data on m-money means that transaction limits have rarely been set using the strength of a risk-based analysis.[26] Instead, limits for m-money transactions sometimes were set arbitrarily at levels similar to those for other electronic channels, such as automated teller machines or the Internet. The FATF, the international standard-setting body for AML/CFT, nevertheless suggests that a risk-based approach be used (including for new technologies facilitating remittance transfers like m-money) and that the risk-based approach be founded on the local situation and conditions in the country (see box 2.4). Later sections of this report will provide more detail in this regard.

The Republic of Korea is an interesting exception to more arbitrary approaches to limits set by other countries. Korea has set transactional

---

Box 2.4

The FATF and the Risk-Based Approach to M-Money and AML/CFT Compliance

The FATF recommendations provide countries with a number of criteria to take risk into account when determining the extent of the AML/CFT compliance measures that their financial institutions will apply. Thus, implementing AML/CFT compliance measures, countries should assess the money-laundering risk that different financial institutions and particular types of customers, products, or transactions could present in their jurisdictions.

Although the risk assessment for m-money may vary, depending on jurisdiction, several common elements can be identified. Some of the factors to be considered when assessing risks are (1) the effectiveness or existence of the regulatory regime; (2) the volume and destinations of criminal money flows; (3) the number of alternative funds transfer operators, including both formal and informal entities; (4) the extent of law enforcement interdiction and the effectiveness of the suspicious transaction reporting regime; and (5) the size, origins, and locations of migrant communities.

Source: World Bank research and fieldwork.

---

limits using a statistical analysis of the number and magnitude of transactions (see box 2.5).

Customer Profiling

Customer profiles are usually built by the provider, using information gathered at the time of customer acquisition, and they are subjected to ongoing modification. Data collected by providers may include the customer's income level, transaction history, and type of services and channels frequently used. This information may be used by m-money providers to identify any unusual transaction patterns.

Monitoring and Internal Controls

The information systems of m-money operators may also support sophisticated monitoring and internal control systems. They normally have automated controls embedded in information technology systems and supported by some manual controls. This is particularly relevant to AML/CFT risk mitigation because automated controls can quickly scan the name, date of birth, and other relevant identification information and

Box 2.5

Risk-Based Determination of Transaction Limits in the Republic of Korea

Electronic funds transfer law and supervisory regulations have established limits on transactions conducted using m-money in Korea. The limits are based on a statistical analysis of the volume, frequency, and other data gathered by the Financial Supervisory Service. Transaction amounts (in Korean won) are grouped into three categories that fall under increasingly stringent security measures, relative to the transaction amount. Financial institutions may also apply greater security controls, according to the profile of the customer.

Source: World Bank research and fieldwork.

compare the data with various United Nations terrorism lists and others of its kind. The more information received by the m-money provider during the initial customer profiling stage, the better a provider's monitoring and internal control systems can work to monitor customer activities and transactions and to compare those transactions with the initial customer profile.

Issuance of Guidelines

In one country, the government published AML/CFT guidelines for companies entering the m-money market. This publication ensures that providers know their responsibilities and it helps close any regulatory holes.

Supervision, Licensing, and Registration of M-Money Providers

FATF Recommendation 23 stresses the need for jurisdictions to have proper licensing processes for financial institutions. It is amplified by Special Recommendation VI: "Each country should take measures to ensure that . . . legal entities, including agents, that provide a service for the transmission of money or value, including transmission through an informal money or value transfer system or network should be licensed or registered and subject to all the FATF recommendations that apply to banks and non-bank financial institutions." Procedures to ensure that m-money providers, including telecom companies, are acting properly in this regard exist in some of the markets where m-money has taken off. Appropriate licensing and registration of m-money providers will ensure that the business is adequately applying AML/CFT controls. More details and guidance in reference to supervising, licensing, and registration of m-money providers will be offered in later sections.

M-Money Risks and Mitigation Techniques Specific to the Financing of Terrorism

Because the average amount of m-money transferred tends to be comparatively quite low in most jurisdictions and because there typically are limits on the amount and frequency of m-money transactions, there are arguments that the use of m-money channels may be more attractive for TF purposes than for ML purposes.

These arguments generally support on the following aspects:

- TF can involve smaller amounts than does ML. For the 9/11 terrorist attack preparations, for example, the funding provided to the perpetrators appears to have been sent in much smaller transfers than what is normal for other crimes (such as laundering the profits from narcotics trafficking).
- Mobile technology has been used by terrorists in the past to plan attacks or communicate with members of the terror group.[27]
- M-money is a quick, cheap, and anonymous method for moving and storing money.

These concerns about TF have been particularly focused on specific regions that are considered "originators" of "terrorist" activity because m-money programs are in the process of developing in those same regions.[28] In addition, m-money providers, such as those in the Philippines, are currently developing cross-border mobile remittance schemes between the Philippines, Saudi Arabia, and other countries of the Middle East, where many "terrorist" activities are thought to originate.[29]

However, the following factors countering those arguments need to be considered:

- Mobile technology is used for surveillance of terrorism and terror suspects. It has assisted in identifying their locations and has been of help in their arrests and successful prosecutions (for example, see de Koker [2009a]).
- Unlike transactions involving cash, all m-money transactions are recorded. These records may show patterns and may reveal the identities of the parties (de Koker 2009a).

- Caps on m-money transactions force criminals and terrorists to engage in a large number of transactions that increase the likelihood of their being exposed to detection.

As with any other payment channel, it is important to determine if m-money brings any *new* risk to the market. With a greater chance of detection and more burdens for a terrorist financier to move money, it is unlikely he or she would find m-money more attractive than cash or a bank transfer. The 9/11 terrorists, for example, simply used banks. Like most financial services, m-money is not without potential for abuse; but with the correct controls—especially the capping of transactions—the potential integrity risks arising from it can be kept low.

Balancing Risk Mitigation Techniques with Financial Inclusion Objectives

Although integrity risks must be controlled by m-money providers and national regulatory and supervisory authorities, it is also important that regulatory compliance requirements are not unnecessarily conservative. Overly conservative requirements constrain the market, its ability to innovate, and, ultimately, its ability to bring unbanked clients into the network of financial inclusion (de Koker 2004, 2006; Bester et al. 2008; Isern and de Koker 2009).[30] Risk mitigation techniques, therefore, should be *risk based* and *proportionate* so that they can balance with policy makers' objectives, such as those promoting financial access for the poor (Isern and de Koker 2009).[31] In this regard, a working relationship between providers and their regulators is integral so that regulations may support effective business practices (Bester et al. 2008). Providers have a unique ability to understand the needs and requirements of their clients as well as their own business objectives, and regulators are vested with the power to establish and enforce the most effective policies possible, according to the local conditions of the country.

Interviews with some MNOs engaging in m-money services found that a key impediment to their expansion in Africa was the lack of clarity and guidance from some national regulatory agencies concerning the regulatory framework and the business models that they would allow. They noted further that many of the regulatory systems required stringent document-based client identification because the national regulators are concerned about mitigating ML/TF risks (see figure 2.2).

Figure 2.2   Document Requirements in Developing Countries, Compared with Those in Developed Countries

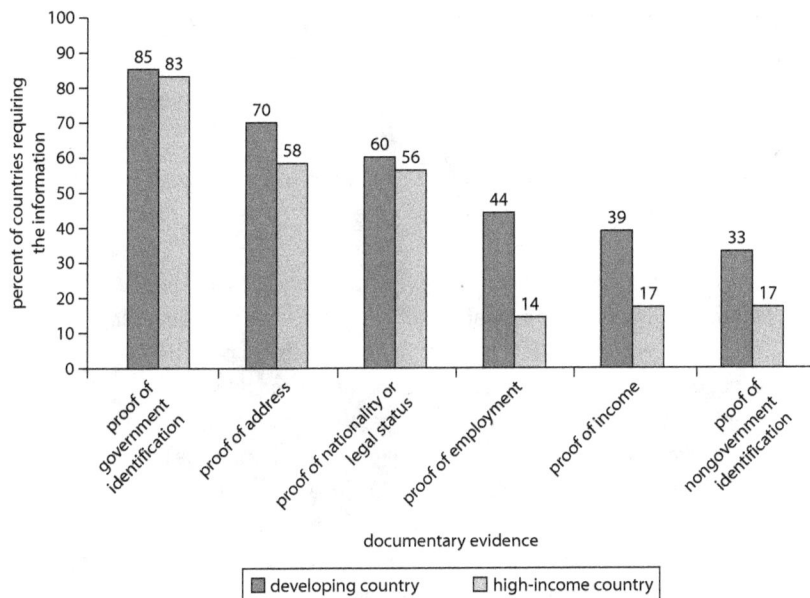

Source: CGAP 2010, http://www.cgap.org/p/site/c/template.rc/1.26.14234/.

However, the cost of excessive documentation requirements may dissuade potential m-money providers. It could also restrict the development of a nonbank-led business model that may have positive effects on financial inclusion in the country.

South Africa is one country that combines flexible, risk-based AML/CFT identification and verification processes (including permitting a non-face-to-face KYC process for mobile money) with a *less* flexible, face-to-face, SIM card–related identification and verification process. Mandatory registration of SIM cards was introduced in 2009 to support the interception of mobile banking communications.[32] The new SIM card identification and verification requirements and the other preexisting AML/CFT requirements are not well aligned. In other words, the new SIM card processes introduced an additional set of customer due diligence requirements to be met prior to opening an m-money account and offset some of the AML/CFT-related financial inclusion flexibility of m-money, as permitted in Guidance Note 6/2008 on mobile banking[33] (see box 2.6).

Box 2.6

South Africa's RICA and Potential Implications for Financial Access

On July 1, 2009, a new amendment to the Regulation of Interception of Communications and Provision of Communication-Related Information Act (RICA), 2002, came into effect. RICA is intended to assist law enforcement agencies in tracing criminals when mobile phones are used to commit major crimes. The new RICA provisions prohibit MNOs from activating a new SIM card unless they have captured the customer's identity and other relevant data. This includes the person's cell phone number, full name and surname, device identity number, and an address (preferably a residential address). The customer's personal information must also be verified by means of a current (green-barcoded) national identity document, a temporary identity certificate, a valid passport, or a travel document. Addresses must be verified with reference to any of a range of documents, allowing also for informal documentation to verify nonformal residential addresses. These processes must be completed face to face.

The RICA and the Financial Intelligence Centre Act (FICA) AML/CFT identification and verification requirements are not well aligned. Clients who were subjected to RICA processes may have to undergo similar (but slightly different) processes for FICA if they wish to open an m-money account. The RICA processes may also not be sufficiently robust to enhance the general m-money integrity.

MNOs such as CellC, MTN, and Vodacom have had to comply with these provisions since July 1, 2009, whenever a new mobile phone number is activated. However, the measures also extend to all existing customers. These customers have 18 months from July 1, 2009, to register both prepaid and contract SIM cards, in accordance with the new provisions. SIM cards of subscribers who fail to comply with RICA within the specified time period will be disconnected from their networks until they are registered.

The new provisions have been controversial. Concerns have been raised in the press regarding their efficacy in fighting crime, the levels of cooperation that could be expected from customers, and the possible abuse of personal data in identity fraud. The integrity of South Africa's national identity documents has also allegedly been undermined by corruption. Citizens have protested that these measures inconvenience honest customers, but do not prevent criminals from accessing the services under assumed names. There have also been cases in which new users were able to obtain SIM cards and access to the networks without complying with the new requirements.

(continued)

Box 2.6 *(continued)*

The government, however, is adamant that the new provisions will assist in combating crime and that the additional regulatory compliance burden among MNOs is justifiable. In this regard, it is interesting to note that some mobile operators in South Africa reported a significant drop in their new customer registrations since the launch of the new amendment of the RICA regulation, thus hindering their ability to tap unbanked populations for financial inclusion. This pattern, however, may be temporary in nature or linked to other reasons, such as the current economic downturn in South Africa.

Source: de Koker 2010.

Given that there have also been cases in which new users were able to obtain SIM cards and access to the networks without complying with the new requirements, these overly stringent requirements may have created the additional risk that, in some cases, airtime dealers are simply registering multiple SIMs in their own names on behalf of their customers to eliminate the new and inconvenient process. It is likely, however, that mobile operators will find ways to address this additional risk, and it ultimately will be the responsibility of mobile operators to express their concerns to the authorities if they deem the new documentation requirements to be too stringent.

One large MNO operating in Africa[34] believes that the stringent documentation and KYC requirements for SIM card registration are not specific to South Africa alone and that other African countries will follow. Thus, they are developing technology to ensure that, at a certain point in the near future, they will not be issuing cell phones and SIM cards without taking additional identity data. These data will be maintained in a file linking a specific phone to a specific person. The data will also include a photograph (taken with a cell phone when the cell or SIM card is purchased), and this photograph will go into the MNO's enhanced electronic database. This MNO is in the process of testing these new procedures in certain countries. It will also set a future deadline by which no new phones will be sold without minimum identification data and a current photo. Another deadline will be set for canceling the mobile coverage of consumers who have not submitted the required information.

The MNO also believes the additional compliance burden involved with taking electronic photos and creating more sophisticated electronic databases will increase provider costs for m-money transactions, and this will ultimately be translated into customer pricing. These additional costs will have direct policy implications concerning the speed through which financial inclusion in Africa may be efficiently and constructively expanded.[35]

Notes

1. Information for this section is extracted from Chatain et al. (2008) and Zerzan (2009).

2. Because of the mandate and expertise of the World Bank division by which this publication is produced, AML/CFT risk concerns and mitigation measures (which also incorporate and mitigate other types of risk) will be the main topics of discussion. A detailed assessment of non-AML/CFT risks is beyond the scope of this report.

3. The mobile telecommunications relationship provides the mobile network operator (MNO) with a number of sources to identify data relating to unidentified clients, and it may even enable locating the client (de Koker 2009a).

4. It must be emphasized that some of the instances discussed here may not be specific to m-money services, but rather are part of more general risks also associated with other new payment methods and even with traditional bank services.

5. In most instances, account operation is protected by a personal identification number held by a specific user.

6. In Brazil, for instance, drug dealers have impoverished people open mobile payment accounts in their own names, thus hiding the dealer's identity. These accounts are called "orange accounts."

7. Isern and de Koker (2009) considered microstructuring and the size of transactions in low-value financial inclusion products. Given the very low values of these transactions, they recognize the theoretical possibility of their abuse for what they call "nanostructuring." They hold, however, that the coordination and effort involved in laundering such small sums make the activity relatively unattractive.

8. These risk concerns also relate to other new payment methods, such as Internet banking. Thus, the risks are not specific to the m-money channel.

9. Cross-border mobile remittance programs are expanding globally.

10. Because there may be multiple types of providers engaged in m-money services, it is perhaps most prudent for national authorities to regulate m-money on the basis of the actual service offered rather than the provider.

11. Findings are from World Bank research and fieldwork interviews with Vodafone officials.

12. The impact of data-enabled phones may change this scenario in the future. Phones that have Internet access would not be dependent on the MNOs, freeing up the banks to do what they please. If there is rapid uptake of data-enabled phones in the next 10 years, the MNO leveraging power may be reduced in branchless banking.

13. World Bank fieldwork has found that, in certain countries, a banking license is required to run an m-money business. It seems that this may be attributed to the historically strong lobbying power of banks over MNOs in many of these jurisdictions, potentially prompting the national authorities to be biased and thus creating legislation that would allow only bank-led models to operate m-money programs.

14. In practice, however, retail outlets often have an incentive to mitigate the first two risks described because they may receive commissions on the number of times a consumer may cash-in. They may be held to strict retail outlet due diligence standards. Also, the internal AML/CFT controls in place among m-money operators generally limit the value and frequency of m-money transactions (which also increases the amount of revenue the m-money provider may receive from the transfer fees).

15. For an example of a retail outlet that opened low-value accounts for acquaintances without their knowledge or permission, see de Koker (2009b, p. 331).

16. These terms will be explained in more detail in later parts of this chapter.

17. However, it should be noted that this information can be provided only if the data are available. World Bank research and fieldwork suggests that MNOs generally do not keep communications data for more than six months.

18. NFC-enabled mobile phones allow for payments and purchases through one's mobile phone as if the phone unit itself were actually another credit or debit card, as long as participating merchants have provisions for this technology.

19. Data were taken from informal remarks made to the study team by Dominic Peachey, Financial Services Authority, U.K.

20. For information on the IMEI, see http://en.wikipedia.org/wiki/International _Mobile_Equipment_Identity.

21. With transaction limits, account monitoring, and the transaction fees in place, it would seem very burdensome and costly to launder money through mobile devices.

22. KYC is the due diligence that financial institutions and other regulated entities must perform to identify their clients and ascertain relevant information pertinent to doing financial business with them.

23. Information for this section comes from the 2009 GSMA risk assessment methodology (Solin and Zerzan 2010), Chatain et al. (2008), and Zerzan (2009).

24. M-money providers have an incentive to undertake proper risk mitigation measures because they want to avert potential reputational risks that could have severe implications for their business growth and sustainability. These risk mitigation measures are not necessarily motivated only by ML or TF concerns, but also by risks of petty consumer fraud.

25. This information comes from a discussion with Sarah Rotman, the Consultative Group to Assist the Poor, about her spring 2009 fieldwork in the region.

26. Another approach is a point-based KYC approach. This system presumes that the more KYC evidence a customer is able to provide (national identification card, driver's license, passport, physical presence, and so forth), the more the customer can be trusted. Services are offered to an extent proportional to the identification provided.

27. Police investigations have concluded that mobile technology was used by terrorists in their attacks in Madrid in 2005 and London in 2006.

28. We place "terrorist" in quotations here because the definition of what is and what constitutes terrorism may vary greatly by ideology, jurisdiction, and other factors.

29. This study does not delve deeper into assessing the comparative ML/TF risks arising from mobile phones for international remittances versus the ML/TF risks arising from the use of brick-and-mortar retail outlets for international remittances. Such analysis is beyond the scope of this study. Credible sources have reported that Saudi national Mohammed Jamal Khalifa has used Overseas Filipinos, such as Abu Sayyaf Group founder Abdulrajak Janjalani, to spread "extremism" and "violence" in the Philippines. The U.S. Department of State considers Abu Sayyaf to be a local Philippine terrorist group (U.S. Department of State 2010).

30. It is important to note that overly restrictive regulations may not necessarily be driven by ML and TF risks, but rather by risks stemming from consumer fraud.

31. Later sections of this report will provide greater details and guidance concerning the risk-based and proportionate approach to regulation and supervision of financial institutions, including country practices.

32. Mandatory registration of SIM cards is now in place in many other African countries, including Tanzania and Uganda.

33. In South Africa, Guidance Note 6/2008 on mobile banking, developed within the framework of Financial Intelligence Centre Act 38 of 2001 Exemption 17,

allows customers to register for mobile banking service by opening their bank accounts remotely, using their mobile phones. This means that there is no need to go to a bank branch initially, provided that a customer is a natural person who is a citizen of or resident in South Africa and who has a valid South African identity number, and provided that transaction and account limits are observed.

34. This mobile services provider operates m-money in Africa and plans to expand its business coverage.

35. All information shared here regarding the MNO came from interviews with the MNO's representatives.

References

Bank of Japan, Payment and Settlement Systems Department. 2008. "Recent Developments in Electronic Money in Japan." Bank of Japan Reports and Research Papers, Tokyo.

Bester, Hennie, Doubell Chamberlain, Louis de Koker, Christine Hougaard, Ryan Short, Anja Smith, and Richard Walker. 2008. *Implementing FATF Standards in Developing Countries and Financial Inclusion: Findings and Guidelines.* Johannesburg, South Africa: Genesis Analytics.

CGAP (Consultative Group to Assist the Poor). 2010. *Financial Access 2010: The State of Financial Inclusion Through the Crisis.* Washington, DC: CGAP. http://www.cgap.org/gm/document-1.9.46570/FA_2010_Financial_Access _2010_Rev.pdf.

Chatain, Pierre-Laurent, Raúl Hernández-Coss, Kamil Borowik, and Andrew Zerzan. 2008. "Integrity in Mobile Phone Financial Services: Measures for Mitigating Risks from Money Laundering and Terrorist Financing." Working Paper 146, World Bank, Washington, DC.

de Koker, Louis. 2004. "Client Identification and Money Laundering Control: Perspectives on the Financial Intelligence Act 38 of 2001." *Journal of South African Law* 4: 715–46.

———. 2006. "Money Laundering Control and Suppression of Financing of Terrorism: Some Thoughts on the Impact of Customer Due Diligence Measures on Financial Exclusion." *Journal of Financial Crime* 13 (1): 26–50.

———. 2009a. "Anonymous Clients, Identified Clients and the Shades In Between— Perspectives on the FATF AML/CFT Standards and Mobile Banking." Paper presented at the 27th Cambridge International Symposium on Economic Crime, Jesus College, Cambridge, U.K., September 4.

———. 2009b. "The Money Laundering Risk Posed by Low-Risk Financial Products in South Africa: Findings and Guidelines." *Journal of Money Laundering Control* 12 (4): 323–39.

————. 2010. "Will RICA's Customer Identification Data Meet Anti-Money Laundering Requirements and Facilitate the Development of Transformational Mobile Banking in South Africa? An Exploratory Note." Center for Financial Regulation and Inclusion, Bellville, South Africa. http://www.cenfri.org/documents/Financial%20inclusion/2010/RICA%20impact%20on%20financial%20inclusion_final.pdf.

The Economist. 2009. "Beyond Voice: New Uses for Mobile Phones Could Launch Another Wave of Development." September 26.

Isern, Jennifer D., and Louis de Koker. 2009. "AML/CFT: Strengthening Financial Inclusion and Integrity." Focus Note 56, Consultative Group to Assist the Poor, Washington, DC.

Momanyi, Bernard. 2009. "Safaricom Staff in MPESA Fraud Probe." *Capital News.* http://www.capitalfm.co.ke/news/Kenyanews/Safaricom-staff-in-MPESA-fraud-probe.html.

Solin, Marina, and Andrew Zerzan. 2010. "Mobile Money: Methodology for Assessing Money Laundering and Terrorist Financing Risks." GSMA Discussion Paper, London.

Todoroki, Emiko. Forthcoming. World Bank Risk and Vulnerability Assessment Project, World Bank, Washington, DC.

U.S. Department of State. 2010. "Background Note: Philippines." http://www.state.gov/r/pa/ei/bgn/2794.htm

Zerzan, Andrew. 2009. "New Technologies, New Risks? Innovation and Countering the Financing of Terrorism." Working Paper 174, World Bank, Washington, DC.

CHAPTER 3

Overview of Anti-Money Laundering and Combating the Financing of Terrorism Regulatory Practices and Risk Management Frameworks for Mobile Money

Summary

This chapter considers aspects of the current anti money laundering (AML) regulatory and supervisory practices and risk management frameworks in relation to mobile money (m-money).

Although there is no one-size-fits-all solution to protect m-money services against fraud and money laundering/terrorist financing (ML/TF), several countries have taken steps to address ML/TF risks by passing laws and regulations. Fieldwork shows, however, that regulations were mainly developed piecemeal and in a fragmented manner. The vast majority of countries have adopted anti-money laundering/combating financing of terrorism (AML/CFT) rules, but uncertainty remains about their application to m-money.[1]

Also considered here are key aspects of the m-money legislation and regulations adopted in several countries. This chapter highlights different regulatory approaches

(continued)

Summary *(continued)*

to ML/TF concerns and describes interactions or mismatches among multiple m-money regulations. The main objectives of this discussion are to facilitate the development of good practice standards, identify possible flaws and loopholes, and formulate some guidance and proposals for international and national policy makers.

The chapter is divided into four sections. The first section discusses the current licensing regimes for m-money providers in various jurisdictions where service is booming or being considered. The second section assesses the current supervision approaches observed in these countries. The third section reviews the scope of the AML/CFT burden imposed on these providers to assess whether it was calculated on the basis of a risk analysis. Specifically, this section will look at customer identification, recordkeeping and suspicious transactions reporting obligations. The final section describes the role of retail outlets in m-money services and identifies trends related to their licensing, responsibilities, and ultimate liability for their activities.

Key Points

- *There are several ways to license and regulate m-money issuers. It is possible to categorize the licenses into two broad categories: (1) provider-based licenses and (2) service-based licenses.*
- *The common practice is to vest the central bank with the power to oversee m-money activities rather than to entrust the job to the communications authority. In rare instances, supervision for AML/CFT compliance has been entrusted to a country's financial intelligence unit (FIU).*
- *Lack of resources, limited experience with AML/CFT issues, and an unstable regulatory regime for m-money may seriously hamper effective supervision.*
- *Most jurisdictions are not fully leveraging the flexibility allowed under the international standards.*
- *No clear and objective assessment of real risks versus perceived risks associated with the various m-money services has been conducted prior to the issuance of regulations.*
- *Know-your-customer (KYC) and customer due diligence (CDD) requirements are problematic, specifically in low-capacity countries that lack effective national identification systems.*
- *Relevant guidelines are generally specified in AML laws and do not take into consideration the special features of such new technologies as short-message service (SMS) and the like.*

(continued)

Summary *(continued)*

• *Mobile network operators (MNOs) are generally required to report suspicious trans-actions and transactions exceeding a certain threshold to the FIU within several days of the transaction date.*

• *Authorities appear to be unsure how to properly license, regulate, and supervise retail outlets that are thought to pose a major (if not the largest) money-laundering threat.*

• *There are no uniform and consistent cross-border standards that determine who may become a retail outlet, the specific activities the outlet may conduct, and its ulti-mate liability.*

Licensing and Registration of M-Money Providers

The stability of the financial system will always be a primary concern for a financial regulator. Ensuring such protection is a juggling act for regulators because they want to balance open regulation and an open environment with control of systemic risks—particularly ML/TF risks (MMT Global Gateway 2009). Doing so requires regulators to have in place appropriate procedures to ensure that providers, mainly MNOs, are acting with proper authorization and are subject to prudent regulatory and supervisory rules. According to Financial Action Task Force (FATF) Recommendation 23, jurisdictions should have proper licensing processes for financial institu-tions—a recommendation that is consistent with the Basel Core Principles (Basel Committee on Banking Supervision 1997). The point is amplified by FATF Special Recommendation VI.

Countries should carefully consider licensing because the type of license granted to mobile operators can influence the degree to which they may participate in the m-money business. The type of license will determine the extent of regulatory burden assumed by MNOs, including AML/CFT obligations.

Fieldwork has shown that there are several ways to license and regu-late MNOs that wish to provide financial services. These different types of licenses may be grouped into two broad categories: (1) provider-based licenses and (2) service-based licenses.

The *provider-based licensing regime* restricts issuance of electronic money (e-money) to existing financial institutions only (that is, to the type of provider). Under this category, MNOs and other nonbank insti-tutions are not allowed to issue e-money on their own; rather, they have to partner with an existing bank. The bank will be the financial service provider and the MNO will be the outsourcing partner. Typically with this type of license, all or the major part of the burden of regulatory compliance (including AML/CFT laws) will be assumed by the partnering bank. The provider-based approach seems to be the prevailing approach among countries such as Brazil, India, Maldives, and South Africa (box 3.1).

This approach is widespread in countries where authorities are risk averse and prefer to entrust traditional financial institutions with the issuance of m-money. They see those institutions as more experienced in dealing with financial instruments and more equipped to monitor and control the flow of m-money, and so they prefer to hold them responsible for AML/CFT compliance.

Box 3.1

Examples of Countries with a Provider-Based Licensing Regime

In **Mexico**, at the moment, all m-money providers must hold a banking license and comply with prudential standards applicable to full-fledged banks. In practice, this means that MNOs have to partner with a bank to get access to the Mexican payment systems. For example, Telcel has partnered with the large banks to provide mobile banking services to account holders (usually in high-end segments). Telefonica, however, is getting ready to launch mobile banking services to lower-income segments of the population by partnering with the banks that focus on this market.[a]

In **South Africa**, all m-money providers must hold a banking license and, as such, meet the central bank's standards. These standards include financial background and strength, governance, customer protection, safety and soundness of the system, background information on shareholders and managers, and business model. In practice, this requirement has resulted in MNOs becoming partners with financial institutions—for example, MTN Group and Standard Bank; Wizzit and Bank of Athens.

Source: Authors' findings from fieldwork in 2009.
a. However, Mexico's National Banking and Securities Commission is preparing regulations for limited-scope banks that would be able to issue e-money and offer a limited range of services, in exchange for lighter prudential requirements and supervision.

The provider-based approach carries some drawbacks to financial inclusion and the ultimate goal of formalizing the financial sector. Without a banking license, MNOs and other nonbanks are not permitted to access the financial sector and issue m-money. This restriction is seen as stringent and not proportionate to the lower risk inherent in m-money services, compared with traditional banking services. Under this bank-based model, the e-money issuers are the banks themselves, so the partnering MNO is not directly regulated per se for the m-money service that is offered. The ultimate liability for m-money lies with the bank.

The *service-based licensing regime*, however, looks at the service rather than the provider. Under this approach, both financial and nonfinancial institutions are allowed to issue m-money, as long as they get the appropriate license or authorization and follow the relevant regulations. This approach is known as a technology-neutral approach because it does not matter what type of provider or technology is used to make a transaction. For example, the m-money issuer may be an MNO, a bank, or a remittance retail outlet. All that matters is the financial service provided (box 3.2).

The service-based licensing approach is seen as an emerging and growing trend among countries that are shifting away from banking licenses. Countries are increasingly aware that bank licenses are stringent and burdensome and that m-money providers should be allowed to issue m-money on their own, without the need to partner with an existing bank.

This approach is gaining popularity because of its perceived positive impact on growth and financial inclusion. The regulatory principle allowing nonbanks to offer payment services is positive for the mobile industry and for consumers. New services and business models become possible—especially for consumers with no or limited access to the current banking system. This is likely to increase competition in the payment services market to extend the range of services offered (GSMA 2008).

Under this approach, the level of prudential regulation is generally lower than that of banking regulation. Nevertheless, the compliance rules still include several requirements as well as full compliance with AML/CFT rules.

Under this service-based regime, all institutions, both financial and nonfinancial, that are planning to become an m-money issuer are generally required to obtain a form of license or authorization prior to engaging in m-money activities (usually in addition to any other license that they may already hold, such as a banking license).

Box 3.2

Examples of Countries with a Service-Based Licensing Regime (E-Money and Payment Service Licenses)

In the **European Union** (EU), regulation for payment of goods and services in the e-sector is contemplated in E-Money Directive 2009/110/EC of the EU. The directive addresses the taking up, pursuit, and prudential supervision of the business of e-money institutions. Article 2 of the directive defines e-money issuers as follows: "Electronic money institution means a legal person that has been granted authorization under Title II to issue electronic money."

Title II in the definition refers to the authorization described under EU Directive 2007/64/EC on payment services in the internal market. It is a special, less-stringent authorization granted to all "payment institutions" before they may provide payment services throughout the community. According to the directive's Article 10, Granting of Authorization: "Member States shall require undertakings . . . who intend to provide payment services, to obtain authorization as a payment institution before commencing the provision of payment services. An authorization shall only be granted to a legal person established in a Member State."[a]

In **Malaysia**, regulation for payment of goods and services in the e-sector is included in Malaysia's Guideline on Electronic Money. Section 5 of this guideline defines e-money issuers as follows: "Any person that is responsible for the payment obligation and assumes the liabilities for the e-money being used."

As for licensing, section 6 refers to the approval described under the Payment Systems Act 2003. In particular, section 6 states: "Issuers of e-money are required to obtain approval from Bank Negara Malaysia pursuant to Section 25(1) of the Payment Systems Act 2003." According to Section 25(1): "No person shall issue a designated payment instrument unless he has (a) submitted to the Bank the documents and information as may be prescribed by the Bank; (b) paid the fee prescribed by the Bank; and (c) obtained a written approval from the Bank to issue a designated payment instrument."

In **Zambia**, regulation for m-money services is authorized under its National Payment Systems Act of 2007. According to Article 3: ". . . this Act shall apply to any person engaged in operating or participating in a payment system or payment system business." According to Article 7: "Any person who intends to operate a payment system shall apply to the Bank of Zambia, in the prescribed form, for designation of the system."

(continued)

Box 3.2 *(continued)*

In the **Philippines**, regulation for payment of goods and services in the e-sector is featured in e-money issuer circular 649 of 2009, published by Bangko Sentral ng Pilipinas (BSP; the central bank), governing the issuance of e-money and the operation of e-money issuers (EMIs) in the Philippines. According to this circular, different types of institutions are allowed to issue e-money after getting a BSP approval. According to section 3 of the circular, Prior BSP Approval:

> *Banks* planning to be an EMI-Bank shall apply in accordance with Section X621 of the Manual of Regulations for Banks (MORB) relating to the guidelines on electronic banking services and with Section X169 of the MORB on outsourcing of banking functions, when applicable.
>
> *Non-Bank Financial Institution*[b] (NBFI) planning to be an EMI-NBFI shall likewise comply with the requirements of Section X621 of the MORB which shall be made applicable to them and with Section 4190Q/S/P/N of the MORNBFI [Manual of Regulations for Non-Bank Financial Institutions] when applicable.
>
> *Non-bank institutions* planning to be an EMI-Others shall register with the BSP as a money transfer agent in accordance with the provisions of Section 4511 of the MORNBFI. To qualify for registration, they have to comply with the requirements detailed in Section 5 of this circular. In case the non-bank institution is already registered with the BSP as a money transfer agent, it is required to meet the additional requirements mentioned under said section to qualify as EMI-Others.

a. EU Directive 2007/64/EC describes the rationale behind introducing a new category of payment service providers as follows: "However, in order to remove legal barriers to market entry, it is necessary to establish a single license for all providers of payment services which are not connected to taking deposits. It is appropriate, therefore, to introduce a new category of payment service providers, 'payment institutions,' by providing for the authorization, subject to a set of strict and comprehensive conditions, of legal persons outside the existing categories to provide payment services throughout the community. Thus, the same conditions would apply community-wide to such services. . . . The conditions for granting and maintaining authorization as payment institutions should include prudential requirements proportionate to the operational and financial risks."
b. According to section 2 of circular 649, these are nonbank financial institutions that are supervised by the BSP.

These licenses are usually referred to as payment system licenses or e-money issuer licenses,[2] and granted to institutions wishing to become payment service providers and to engage in financial activities.

For payment systems licenses, existing laws and regulations that govern payment systems providers (often known as national payment systems laws) will then be applicable. This appears to be the case, for example, in the European Union (EU), Malaysia, and Zambia.

For e-money issuer licenses, other countries have created a specific license for the broad category of e-money issuers, generally encompassing m-money issuers (see box 3.3). This is the case in the Philippines, for example.

Irrespective of whether a payment system license or e-money license is issued, either may be effectively used to regulate m-money services and, thus, the overall distinction between the two does not appear to be so significant. In Zambia, the national payment system law does not actually contain the word "e-money," but it clearly incorporates the concept and is used to regulate different m-money schemes in the country.

Finally, it should be noted that there remain situations in which authorities have not made up their minds about the type of licensing to be used.[3] As far as our current research suggests, there is no real trend

---

Box 3.3

M-Money in a Technology-Neutral World

Fieldwork has shown that authorities are converging toward technology-neutral laws and licenses regarding e-money providers. In other words, the authorities are not issuing specific laws or licenses to control m-money providers because they believe that those providers fall under the broad category of e-money providers. The definitions of "e-money" and "e-money issuers" are drafted to create a broad umbrella that covers all types of e-money issuers and all kinds of e-transactions, including m-money services. For example, EU e-money regulations[a] define these terms as follows:

> Electronic money institution means a legal person that has been granted authorization under Title II of the e-money directive to issue electronic money.
>   Electronic money means electronically, including magnetically, stored monetary value as represented by a claim on the issuer which is issued on receipt of funds for the purpose of making payment, and which is accepted by a natural or legal person other than the electronic money issuer.

Source: E-Money Directive 2009/110/EC, http://eur-lex.europa.eu/LexUriServ/LexUriServ.do?uri =CELEX:32009L0110:EN:NOT.
a. The regulations are presented in E-Money Directive 2009/110/EC of the EU on the taking up, pursuit, and prudential supervision of the business of e-money institutions.

in terms of the licensing or registration of m-money providers (whether under an e-money act, a payment systems act, or some other legislation). The only clear trend is that more countries are learning how to regulate or are regulating the m-money service through the various approaches available.

Supervision of M-Money Providers

Having effective regulation and supervision is pivotal to the success of the AML/CFT system in general and to the stability and integrity of the financial sector in particular. FATF Recommendation 23 and the Basel Core Principles call on jurisdictions to have an effective supervisory regime in place to oversee all types of risks, including ML/TF risks. That recommendation stresses the need for all providers of financial services to be subject to adequate regulation and supervision: "At a minimum, businesses providing a service of money or value transfer . . . should be licensed or registered, and subject to effective systems of monitoring and ensuring compliance with national requirements to combat ML and TF."

Countries often do not have a clear idea whether the communications authority (for example, the Ministry of Telecommunications) or the central bank (or financial supervisory agency that is separate from the central bank) is most appropriate to regulate and supervise m-money issuers. Moreover, fieldwork shows that both entities have serious reservations about taking the lead on this matter—and that complicates the issue further. In many markets, central banks believe they lack the necessary capacity and the expertise to understand (let alone supervise) the technological aspects associated with m-money services. Similarly, communication authorities strongly believe that, besides having limited resources, they have a limited grasp of the financial intricacies and are not equipped to do the supervision.

At the same time, having more than one regulatory and supervisory authority within one jurisdiction adds to the confusion. For example, three agencies in Russia collectively regulate financial institutions, depending on institution type: (1) the central bank, (2) the Ministry of Finance, and (3) the Federal Financial Markets Service.

It is important to note that regardless of who is the primary supervisor for AML/CFT compliance in the m-money industry, examiners will have to be entrusted with the same responsibilities and allowed to carry the same tasks as they do for any type of financial institution. They will be entitled to enter MNOs and other nonbank premises to make on-site inspections. In effect, as contemplated in FATF Recommendation 29, supervisors should have adequate powers to monitor and ensure financial institutions' compliance with requirements to combat ML/TF, including the authority to conduct inspections. As a result, jurisdictions should authorize supervisors to compel production of any information from financial institutions (including MNOs and other nonbanks) that is relevant to monitoring such compliance.

Current Approaches for Supervising MNOs

Fieldwork has shown that several jurisdictions where mobile banking is booming have set up mechanisms to supervise electronic financial services. There is a common tendency to vest the central bank or the primary supervisor for banks[4] and other financial institutions with the power to oversee m-money activities, rather than to trust the telecommunications authority to monitor and enforce AML/CFT compliance.

The authors agree that there are several benefits to designating the central bank—or the competent financial supervisory agency—as the primary regulator and supervisor for m-money activities, and they consider this approach to be the most effective and practical of all. First, supervisory bodies are usually highly skilled and knowledgeable about assessing risks in financial institutions and about the policies and procedures for managing those risks. Second, ML/TF risks typically warrant attention equivalent to that for other types of compliance risks. Third, supervisors are knowledgeable about how financial institutions operate and about the products and services they offer. For m-money, the fact that these financial services are carried out by telecommunications companies (telecoms) or MNOs makes no difference. Hence, even if the account provider (AP) is a telecom or another third-party provider in an m-money business model, it may make sense to regulate it through the central bank.

It is important to note that, in some countries (such as Spain), supervision for AML/CFT compliance is legally entrusted to the FIU, not to the primary financial supervisor. As a result, telecoms and other MNOs fall under the supervisory umbrella of the FIU. This model presents some drawbacks. If the FIU is the primary supervisor, it may well be inexperienced both in financial inspections and in supervisory matters. And the FIU is not likely to be sufficiently equipped to undertake AML/CFT supervision of a new category of reporting entities, such as MNOs. However, if a body other than the FIU is the supervisor, that body may not have access to information supplied through suspicious transaction reports because of legal restrictions imposed on it. Examinations are likely to become more limited in scope and expertise, and multiple regulators and different approaches to compliance supervision for m-money may generate some confusion.

In addition, the FIU may not give AML/CFT compliance the same priority as does a traditional financial supervisor (such as the central bank), and it may not have enough resources to do so. Besides, supervisors have to consider the cost-benefit ratio when imposing high compliance costs on an industry, unless there is credible evidence that the system used involves a high ML risk. Concentrating scarce regulatory or supervisory resources on very low levels of transactions might not be an efficient or effective use of those resources.

Observed Mechanisms for Improving Supervision

To improve supervision, some countries opt to create a separate department within the central bank to supervise and oversee nonbank financial providers (see figure 3.1 and box 3.4).

Along the same lines, and to avoid any potential overlap between financial and telecommunications supervisory authorities, many countries

Figure 3.1   Example of a Supervision Framework

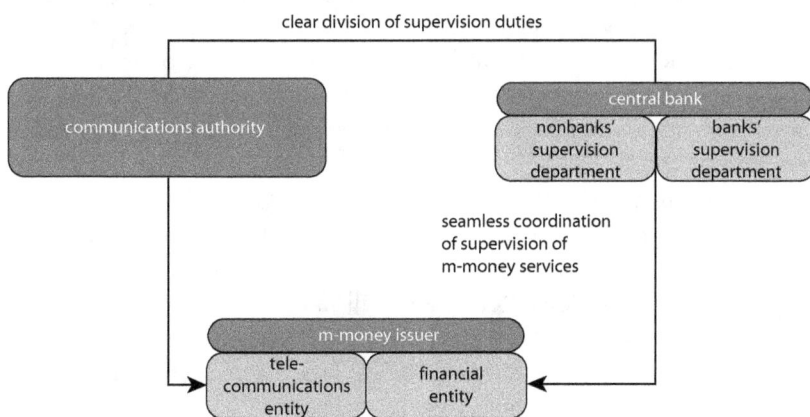

Source: Authors.
Note: Arrows indicate supervision and oversight.

Box 3.4

Examples of Central Banks with a Separate Department for Nonbank Supervision

In **Kenya**, the nonbank providers are monitored, albeit informally, by the recently created National Payment Systems Department within the central bank.

In **Nigeria**, the central bank has set up a mobile payment policy and oversight unit with the mandate to ensure compliance.

In **Zambia**, a separate division within the central bank is in charge of overseeing nonbank payment systems, which are defined as nondeposit-taking institutions.

Source: Authors.

---

now require telecommunications providers to have a separate entity responsible for the financial side of the business (see figure 3.1 and box 3.5).

The authors agree that, when applicable, those mechanisms present several benefits for improving supervision and dividing duties among supervisors.

Supervision Implementation Status

With very few exceptions, supervision of m-money has not really been implemented. The level of acquaintance that supervisors have with these new topics is really uneven; until recently, they were not well versed on the implications of innovative branchless banking and other e-money concepts. Lack of resources, limited experience on AML/CFT issues, and an unstable regulatory regime for m-money may seriously hamper effective supervision.

Even though MNOs should be treated like any other financial provider, it remains unclear whether financial examiners will have access to sensitive information like SMS and other text messages related to m-money transactions. Regulators will have to clarify the perimeter of data that are accessible to financial examiners in the particular context of m-money. Some communications data (like the content of calls) may not be accessible because of privacy laws.

The situation becomes even more complex in the case of cross-border mobile remittances, in which the delineation between home and host

Box 3.5

Examples of MNOs with a Separate Financial Entity

In **Kenya**, the Communications Commission has advised MNOs interested in providing financial services to create a quasi-independent entity for financial services.

In the **Philippines,** the e-money circular requires nonbank entities engaged in activities not related to the business of e-money but interested in providing e-money services to do so through a separate entity that is duly incorporated exclusively for that purpose.

In **Zambia**, the central bank requires MNOs to create a separate financial service team, which serves as a "Chinese wall" between the telecommunications company and the m-money service. This strategy is intended to ensure that there is no conflict of interest between the two product lines (for example, the telecom should not borrow funds from its customers using its m-money arm to build its business). It is also key to avoiding gaps or overlap in supervisory oversight between the communications and financial authorities.

Source: Authors.

supervision is blurred. In effect, these services involve three regulatory spaces: (1) that of the sender, (2) that of the receiver, and (3) that of the international regulations that apply to international remittances.

Stocktaking of Current Preventive AML/CFT Obligations

This section considers the various internal controls that m-money providers should implement to mitigate ML/TF risks. It will discuss successively the issues of customer identification, recordkeeping, and suspicious transaction reporting.

Identifying Customers

Recommendation 5 is probably one of the most important recommendations among the 40+9 FATF standards. It aims to detect possible criminal customers at the conclusion of the relationship between a service provider and a customer. If identification and verification processes are not performed correctly, the integrity of the financial system is at risk because significant amounts of dirty money will continue making the rounds. The damage from money laundering and the financing of terrorism reverberates for years and takes an enduring toll on everything—from the market to the investors and consumers.

However, the recommendation is a particularly challenging obligation, given its potential impact on financial inclusion and integrity. Strict identification and especially verification requirements form barriers that prevent people without the required documentation or data—mainly the low-income and socially marginalized populations—from accessing m-money services (see Isern and de Koker [2009]). Less-stringent provisions, however, may encourage significant integrity abuse.

Indeed, implementing identification and verification requirements has proved quite problematic in low-capacity settings. Many writers have expressed concern that the low-income populations will never be in a position to provide the same type of supporting documents as those sought in developed countries. As a result, the documentation required would prohibit this group from accessing the financial system, especially in remote areas. For example, it is practically impossible in certain countries to require customers to prove a physical address by presenting a utility bill or the like. In South Africa, for example, an estimated one third of households (mostly low income) do not have formal addresses (see CGAP [2009, p. 19]). Also, fieldwork has shown multiple situations in which there are either a poor identification traditions or identity documents that do not carry pictures.

In addition, face-to-face registration is often acquired. This means that the customer has to go to a retail outlet in person and present the required verification documentation. This face-to-face registration can have a negative impact on the speed of enrollment and, by extension, the cost and customer experience.

A recent survey among World Savings Bank Institute (WSBI) members highlighted a number of practical problems regarding identification and verification requirements:

- Obligation to get information on the occupation of the clients and on the use of the funds, which leads to a burdensome procedure for each of the transactions
- Lack of proper identification documents (identity card, passport)
- Lack of official proof of income and residence address
- Lack of understanding by the unbanked population that they need to supply the compliance information (WSBI 2009).

Possible routes for relaxing KYC requirements for low-risk m-money services. The words "identification" and "verification" are generally used in the same sentence of FATF Recommendation 5, one after another. The fact that the FATF standard uses two different words indicates a clear intention to distinguish two different points of the KYC process. *Identification* is the point at which the customer provides information on his or her identity. The customer may give this information verbally or by filling out a form. *Verification* is the process followed to establish the veracity of the identifying particulars that were given or obtained.[5]

There seem to be three acceptable routes for relaxing KYC in the particular context of low-risk m-money services. The first route is that of requiring m-money providers to identify the applicant, but not verify the identity. The authors believe that the identification phase is always useful and a low burden to providers, whereas the verification phase is generally costly and may not always be necessary in cases of low risk. This first route could also mean verifying the identity through alternative means that are not discussed by the Basel Committee.[6]

The second route, following the example of the third EU directive (Directive 2005/60/EC), would apply full KYC exemptions for micro m-money transactions, provided that transactions are subject to close scrutiny to detect abuse. However, the question remains whether this approach would be acceptable from an FATF standpoint.[7]

As a third route, countries may consider applying the so-called progressive KYC/CDD approach whereby payment limits vary, based on the identification check: the better the identification process, the higher the limits. For people without adequate documents, this may imply access to very limited functionalities; and access to broader services (such as higher limits, and transfers, including cross-border) would be allowed only if the customer provides proof of identity and address (see figure 3.2).[8]

It remains clear, however, that appropriate regulation and internal control measures can be determined only in the context of the risk-based approach when a comprehensive risk assessment has been performed. A risk assessment determines whether there are higher or lower risks, and provides grounds for an evidence-based shaping of the regulatory and risk-management regimes to identify those circumstances that will justify reduced KYC measures, as recommended by the FATF. As of today, almost none of the visited countries has adjusted its AML requirements for m-money on the basis of an assessment of risks (see chapter 4).

Figure 3.2   Gradual KYC Program Adopted by Moneybookers Ltd., an Internet Payment Provider in the United Kingdom

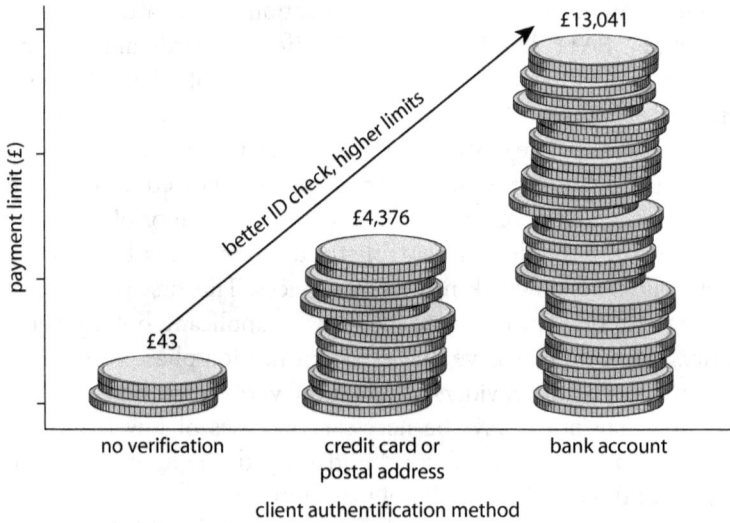

Source: Adapted from Zerzan (2009).
Note: Moneybookers Ltd. increases its 90-day transaction limit, depending on how the user verifies his or her name. If it is confirmed via a credit card, the limit is raised significantly, but not as much as if verified through a bank account.

While customers must be identified to a reasonable standard at the point of entering a business relationship, due diligence should not end at that point. KYC safeguards go beyond simple account opening. They require financial institutions and other nonbank financial providers to formulate a customer acceptance policy and a tiered customer identification program that involves more extensive due diligence for higher-risk accounts and includes proactive account monitoring for suspicious activities.

Observed methods of relaxing the KYC obligation. Fieldwork has shown that MNOs are generally required to identify and verify the identities of prospective customers, for AML/CFT purposes. However, most of these countries have applied their identification and verification requirements across the board, with little regard for risk. Few countries have applied a risk-based approach when determining the AML/CFT requirements.

Among those countries that have applied a risk-based approach, the most common approach has been to relax the verification controls on low-value transactions or products (box 3.6). These approaches have significantly limited the impact of AML on access to financial services.

Box 3.6

Examples of Relaxed KYC Obligations for Lower-Risk Transactions

In the **European Union**, the third EU AML directive[a] allows for simplified CDD for e-money institutions, under certain circumstances.

According to Article 11: ". . . Member States may allow the institutions and persons covered by this Directive not to apply customer due diligence in respect of: . . . (d) electronic money, . . . where, if the device cannot be recharged, the maximum amount stored in the device is no more than EUR 150, or where, if the device can be recharged, a limit of EUR 2,500 is imposed on the total amount transacted in a calendar year, except when an amount of EUR 1,000 or more is redeemed in that same calendar year by the bearer . . . , or in respect of any other product or transaction representing a low risk of money laundering or terrorist financing which meets the technical criteria established in accordance with the Article 40(1)(b)."[b]

In **Germany**, under the Federal Institute for Financial Services Supervision e-money rules, anonymously registered customers may have a total credit of €150 on their mobile phones. Transactions for anonymous customers will be limited to €30 per transaction and €150 per week. According to the rules, this makes simple and anonymous payments with a mobile phone possible without the risk of malfeasance.[c]

In **Mexico**, the new AML/CFT legal framework recognizes three categories of accounts that allow different levels of KYC and CDD requirements.[d] Mobile accounts may fall into either of these categories:

- *"low-transaction accounts" (Mex$8,720 or 2,000 UDI [inflation-indexed units] in monthly deposits):* under this category, clients' files should contain the full name, birth date, and address and be integrated and saved.
- *"low-risk accounts" (Mex$174,400 or 40,000 UDI in monthly deposits and withdrawals):* under this category, clients' files contain complete data related to the client and must be integrated and saved.
- *"unlimited accounts":* under this category, clients' files contain complete data related to the client and copies of the documentation to be integrated and saved.

In the **Philippines**, the Anti-Money Laundering Act of 2001 applies only to transactions in excess of ₱500,000 within one banking day.

(continued)

Box 3.6 *(continued)*

In **South Africa**, Guidance Note 6/2008 on mobile banking, developed within the framework of the Financial Intelligence Centre Act (38/2001) Exemption 17,[e] allows customers to register for mobile banking service by opening their bank accounts remotely, using their mobile phones. This means that there is no need to go to a bank branch initially, provided that a customer is a natural person who is a citizen of or resident in South Africa and who has a valid South African identity number; and provided that transaction and account limits are observed. The client is identified, and reasonable steps are taken to verify the person's identification details (especially comparing the client's personal data to a third-party database with official data). The client, therefore, may start using the mobile banking service by transacting small amounts without going to a bank branch to provide an address. Clients who wish to exceed the strict transaction limits that are imposed under Guidance Note 6/2008 (see below), can submit themselves to the more comprehensive identification and verification requirements of Exemption 17. In this case, the client must normally provide documentary proof of identity in the form of an identification card or number; residential address particulars do not need to be obtained or verified. Clients may migrate from the Exemption 17 products to standard products that are not subject to account and transaction limits by undergoing face-to-face identification and verification processes and providing documentary proof such as their identification cards or numbers and proof of address (de Koker 2009; Solin 2009). This approach, therefore, is proportionate to risk because the identification requirements become more onerous as the transaction sizes—and the related risk—increase.

Financial Intelligence Centre Act (38/2001) Exemption 17
- If an account is opened, maximum balance limit of RF 25,000 ($3,300)
- Transaction restrictions of RF 5,000 ($660) per day and RF 25,000 ($3,300) per month
- No international transactions (except for cash withdrawal in common monetary area)
- One account per person per bank
- Only available to individuals who are citizens or residents of South Africa

Guidance Note 6/2006
- In addition to the Exemption 17 limits, a lower daily transaction limit of RF 1,000 ($130)

(continued)

Box 3.6 *(continued)*

• Non–face-to-face account origination, but the bank must cross-reference the client's national identity number against an acceptable third-party database and must apply enhanced measures to monitor the account for suspicious activity

a. This is EU Directive 2005/60/EC of October 26, 2005, on the prevention of the use of the financial system for the purpose of money laundering and financing of terrorism.
b. This is as specified according to Article 40(1)(b) of the directive.
c. See http://www.newratings.com/en/main/company_headline.m?&id=501499.
d. CGAP country diagnostic for Mexico.
e. The current text of the exemption was the result of market research and an analysis of the needs and reality of the financially excluded population. See Bester et al. (2008) for the development of the exemption.

The flexibility should also extend to the type of documents accepted as proof of identity. As observed in jurisdictions visited, clients were typically required to prove their identities by means of birth certificates, national identity cards, drivers' licenses, or passports. Few countries have gone beyond these standard items to ensure that access to financial services is not impeded by unduly strict or inappropriate verification requirements. Similarly, few banks and financial institutions have implemented innovative mitigation for identification challenges (see box 3.7 and table 3.1).

South Africa is one country that appears to require excessive documentation, claiming it will be more effective in mitigating ML/TF concerns. The country now requires registration of all SIM cards. The government believes this will help meet South Africa's AML/CFT CDD requirements. However, there are counterarguments (and the authors agree) that South Africa's SIM registration requirements are overly stringent and will offset some of the financial inclusion measures introduced through the Financial Intelligence Centre Act (38/2001) (see box 2.6).

Recordkeeping: To Avoid Going beyond the Standards

Recordkeeping systems provide the second plank to an effective AML/CFT system. According to FATF Recommendation 10, financial institutions should maintain all necessary records on transactions (including the amounts and types of currency involved, if any), both

Box 3.7

Examples of National Regulators' Mitigation Responses to the Identification Challenge

In the **Philippines**, the central bank issued Circular 564 of 2007,[a] which broadens the list of valid identification documents acceptable by both financial and nonfinancial institutions. According to this circular,

> the following guidelines governing the acceptance of valid identification cards are issued for all types of financial transactions by banks and non-bank financial institutions, including financial transactions involving overseas Filipino workers (OFWs), in order to promote access of Filipinos to services offered by formal financial institutions, particularly those residing in the remote areas, as well as to encourage and facilitate remittances of OFWs through the banking system.

As for the list of valid identification documents, the circular states the following:

> Clients who engage in a financial transaction with the covered institutions for the first time shall be required to present the original and submit a copy of at least two valid photo-bearing identification documents issued and signed by an official authority. Valid IDs include the following: Passport; Driver's license; Professional Regulations Commission (PRC) ID; National Bureau of Investigation (NBI) clearance; Police clearance; Postal ID; Voter's ID; Barangay certification; Government Service and Insurance System (GSIS) e-Card; Social Security System (SSS) card; Philhealth card; Senior Citizen Card; Overseas Workers Welfare Administration (OWWA) ID; OFW ID; Seaman's Book; Alien Certification of Registration/Immigrant Certificate of Registration; Government office ID (e.g., Armed Forces of the Philippines [AFP], Home Development Mutual Fund [HDMF] IDs); Certification from the National Council for the Welfare of Disabled Persons (NCWDP); Department of Social Welfare and Development (DSWD) Certification; and Other valid IDs issued by the Government and its instrumentalities.

In **Malawi**, when a potential customer does not have the requisite documentation, a close relative (brother or sister) can submit his or her reference (passport details) in support of an application by the person who does not have the necessary documentation. Also, the use of biometrics in the CDD process helped tackle identification challenges and reach more than 200,000 customers in six years.

(continued)

domestic or international, for at least five years to enable them to comply swiftly with information requests from the competent authorities. The rationale is to facilitate reconstruction of individual transactions and to provide evidence for the prosecution of criminal activity, if necessary.

As for the types of targeted information, FATF Recommendation 10 states that financial institutions should keep records on the identification data obtained through the CDD process (for example, copies or records of official identification documents such as passports, identity cards, driver's licenses, or similar documents), account files, and business correspondence for at least five years after the business relationship ends. However, questions have been raised about exactly what should be retained when it comes to customer identity. Some writers hold the view that financial providers should systematically keep hard copies of supporting documents provided by customers for verification purposes because the identification data and transaction records should be available to domestic competent authorities, as required by international standards (FATF 2009, Recommendation 10, para. 3).

In South Africa, for example, the Financial Intelligence Centre Act 38 of 2001 requires financial institutions "to keep record of any document or copy of a document obtained" by the regulated institution to verify a person's identity.[9] In a 2009 press statement (FIC/OBS 2009),

Table 3.1 Examples of M-Money Providers' Mitigation Responses to the Identification Challenge

Country	Provider	Response
Ghana	HFC Bank (Ghana) Ltd.	✓ The bank accepts utility bills, tenancy agreements, and house numbers as evidence of the residence or address of prospective clients.
Lesotho	PostBank	✓ Village chiefs are proposed as points of verification for people in rural areas who wish to open accounts at PostBank. Initially, the chiefs used their resources (stationery and stamps) to authenticate prospective customers. Subsequently, PostBank designed a form that customers complete and take to their village chiefs for date-stamping, in compliance with regulatory requirements.
		✓ Various radio stations have been used by PostBank to communicate the requirements for opening accounts so that people going to the nearest village or town to open a bank account can take with them whatever documentation or certification is needed.
Malaysia	Bank Simpanan National	✓ The bank accepts birth certificates and passports as means of identification for Malaysian citizens; and refugees' cards, student cards, work permits, and letters from colleges and universities for noncitizens.
		✓ Employee address or any other address is accepted to justify a residential address. As for rural areas that do not have any information of residency or address, the bank requires a postal address that is either a communal post box or a neighbor's address.
		✓ Large-scale initiatives are taken to inform the population about the requirements for opening accounts: communication (circulation of pamphlets, or information notice at branch) or campaigns (visits to villages, rural schools).

Philippines	Postal Savings Bank	✓ Barangay certification, a certificate issued by the village master, is accepted as a proof of identification and residence. ✓ The bank accepts also as identity documents passports, driver's licenses, student identification cards, and employment identification. These documents are accepted if issued by official authorities of the Philippines government, its subdivisions, and instrumentalities; government-owned and controlled bodies; and private entities registered and supervised by the BSP, the Securities and Exchange Commission, and the Insurance Commission.
South Africa	Postbank	✓ Postbank accepts any valid documents reflecting the customer's address to identify clients regulated outside the scope of the entry-level Mzansi accounts. These documents include utility bills, bank statements from another bank, recent leases or rental agreements, invoices for municipal rates and taxes, retail account statements, telephone or cellular telephone accounts, valid television licenses, home loan statements from another financial institution, long- or short-term insurance policy documents, motor vehicle registration documents, municipal council letters, corporate or governing body letters or statements, official employer letters for employees residing on company or institution premises, official university or university of technology registration letters, tribal authority letters, and affidavits or declarations.
Uganda	Post Bank	✓ PostBank accepts voter cards that have a photograph, utility bills, references from known customers, and local council letters as alternatives to official proofs of identification. ✓ The bank has also categorized clients into groups, such as sole proprietors, partnerships, individuals, limited liability companies, government departments, associations, clubs, and trustees; and CDD requirements have been customized for each group.

Source: WSBI 2009.

the Financial Intelligence Centre and the Ombudsman for Banking Services stated, "As much as the [Financial Intelligence Centre] Act does not clearly state that a copy of the Identity Document must be made by an accountable institution, the most prudent and practical manner to comply with this obligation would indeed be to make and keep a copy of the identity of the client, in the form of an Identity Document." Therefore, it is not a legal obligation to make a copy of such documents, but the authorities regard it as a prudent and practical way to meet the recordkeeping requirements.

The recordkeeping requirement under the FATF standards does not mandate the retention of a photocopy of the identification documents presented for verification purposes, but it does necessitate storing the information on the documents for five years. A number of other countries (such as Australia, Canada, and the United States) have considered imposing photocopying obligations on their regulated institutions, but they decided against it for a number of reasons—for instance, photocopies could be used to commit identity fraud, may breach privacy laws, and may reveal information about the client that could form the basis of discriminatory practices such as refusal of credit facilities.

Recommendation 10 refers to copies or records of official identification documents, which means that forms of retention other than copies are admissible. M-money providers and their retail outlets in low-capacity countries cannot reasonably be expected to have a copy machine always at their disposal. A mere written annotation or record of the CDD details seen in the materials submitted would suffice, as long as the data are available for at least five years.

Depending on the size and sophistication of a mobile provider's record storage, the following record retention techniques are also acceptable and can constitute a valid alternative to hard copies:

- Scanning the verification material and holding it electronically
- Keeping electronic copies of the results of any electronic verification checks
- Recording reference details (particularly useful in the context of mobile banking where m-money retail outlets are often simple corner shops), including
  - any reference numbers on documents or letters,
  - any relevant dates, such as dates of issue, expiration, or writing,
  - details of the issuer or writer,
  - all identity details recorded on the document.

It is noteworthy that FATF Recommendation 10 goes beyond the identification retention obligation. It also includes other aspects, especially the obligation to keep data on the financial transactions performed by the customer. This requirement is not as simple as it appears, and it raises several questions in practice. Basically, the main issues revolve around (1) what data should be kept and (2) who holds the primary responsibility to retain the information in the particular context of m-money.

As for the type of data, the recommendation states that financial institutions (including m-money providers, whether banks or nonbanks) should retain all necessary records on domestic and international transactions, including the nature and date of the transaction, any amounts and types of currency involved, and the type and identifying number of any account involved in the transaction (see FATF 2009).

Neither Recommendation 10 nor its interpretative note specifies any threshold below which retention of data would not be necessary. This obligation seems to be applied without regard to the amounts of the transactions involved, even in the case of micro or nano payments and transfers.

If something wrong happens with a particular customer, mobile providers should be in a position to assist law enforcement authorities in collecting all evidence for prosecution of any criminal activity. Without a minimum record retention of data, a criminal inquiry would be impossible.

Fieldwork has shown that m-money providers keep customer activity records. Telecoms call these records "customer detail records." They contain data related to a mobile operator's system usage, and they include the identity of the originating and receiving phones for each mobile call, its duration, and other data. In this particular context of m-money, it is not clear whether Recommendation 10 also applies to data that are not exactly "transactional."[10] Is a phone call between the sender and the recipient of m-money operations considered part of the data to be kept under Recommendation 10? What about the SMS that is used by SMS-based mobile banking services to send money from person A to person B?[11] Similarly, should MNOs and banks that provide mobile Internet banking through cell phones[12] retain e-mails that are linked to a particular transaction? Although Recommendation 10 does not provide clear guidance on whether this information should be kept, the authors believe that the rule of the account provider applies. This means that all records that the AP has on a client's financial activity should be kept. The authors suggest that countries determine what data are "financial" and what data are "communications" because the latter would be under the privacy protections discussed below.

Equally important is the issue of possible conflict between data retention under the privacy law and under the AML/CFT law. In most countries, communications data like phone calls and SMS are governed by privacy laws mandating that information be archived for a very limited period of time[13]; AML/CFT laws, however, require providers (including MNOs) to retain data for at least five years. Further clarification is needed on what telephone companies (as financial providers) are compelled to keep when it comes to nonvoice traffic (details of all SMS, MMS, and other similar telecommunications services such as e-mails), and for what period of time the material must be retained. This clarification is of particular importance for mobile banking because supporting materials on the identity of the end user might not be available (see "Adopting Regulation That Balances Financial Inclusion with Financial Integrity" in chapter 4). Policy makers should discuss the framework on data protection, with the aim of balancing the increased exchange of personal data in the particular context of m-money and the fight against the financing of terrorism and organized crime.

Last, regarding the responsibility for keeping records, m-money involves multiple stakeholders, a bank, an MNO, and multiple retail outlets. Recommendation 10 refers to financial institutions, so all parties have to perform their obligations, including delegates such as retail outlets. Retention for at least five years will apply not only to records of identity data, but also to all records of transactions. Because retail outlets have recordkeeping obligations, it is recommended that data to be kept by the retail outlets and data to be sent to the AP for retention be specified clearly.

For more information about the recordkeeping obligations and retention periods in jurisdictions visited, see boxes 3.8 and 3.9.

Monitoring and Reporting Suspicious Transactions

Like all financial institutions, MNOs should have appropriate systems and controls to monitor the transactions of each client in terms of both volume and velocity, and to report to the FIU any transaction or activity that they suspect to be related to money-laundering or terrorist-financing crimes.

According to FATF Recommendation 15, financial institutions must develop programs against money laundering and terrorist financing. These programs should include, among other things, the development

Box 3.8

Examples of Recordkeeping Requirements Observed in the Visited Jurisdictions

In **Kenya**, under the new AML law, a reporting institution must establish and maintain a record that indicates the nature of the evidence obtained (of a person's identity) and that includes either a copy of the evidence or such information as would enable a copy to be obtained.

In **Mexico**, the new AML/CFT legal framework for banks recognizes three categories of accounts that permit different levels of recordkeeping policies for the implementation of mobile banking services:

- Lower obligations: For mobile accounts for natural persons whose monthly deposit transactions are below 2,000 inflation-indexed units (UDIs) (approximately $675), the client file may be integrated with only the client's basic data (name, address, and birth date); it is not necessary to maintain a copy of the documentation.
- Medium obligations: For mobile accounts for natural and legal persons whose monthly accumulated transactions (deposits and withdrawals) do not exceed 40,000 UDIs (approximately $13,500), the file must be integrated with the client's whole list of required data; however, it is not necessary to maintain a copy of the documentation.
- Higher obligations: for mobile accounts for natural and legal persons with unlimited transactions, the file must be integrated with the client's whole list of required data, and the banking institution must maintain a copy of the documentation.

Source: Information on Mexico taken from CGAP, http://www.cgap.org/gm/document-1.9.42401/Updated _Notes_On_Regulating_Branchless_Banking_Mexico.pdf.

of internal policies, procedures, and controls (including appropriate compliance management arrangements) and an audit function to test the system. Recommendation 13 stipulates that if a financial institution suspects or has reasonable grounds to suspect that funds are the proceeds of a criminal activity or are related to terrorist financing, it should be required to report the incident promptly to the country's FIU.

Offering large-volume transaction opportunities to customers will require more control. Where suspicious transactions are detected, APs should have the ability to block further use until the user has provided

Box 3.9

Examples of Recordkeeping Periods, Usually Exceeding the Five Years Recommended by the FATF

In **Kenya**, the new law on proceeds of crime and AML requires that records be kept for a period of at least seven years.

In **Malaysia**, the Anti-Money Laundering Act, 2001, requires financial records be maintained for at least six years from the date an account or a transaction is terminated.

In the **Philippines**, the anti-money laundering act (Revised Rules and Regulations Implementing Republic Act No. 9160, as Amended by Republic Act No. 9194) states that all records of financial institutions must be maintained and safely stored for five years from the date of transaction.

In **Zambia**, the Prohibition and Prevention of Money Laundering Bill, 2001, requires that a business transaction record be kept for a period of 10 years after termination of the business.

Source: Information is taken from legislation. For Kenya:
http://www.kenyalaw.org/Downloads/Bills/2008/The_Proceeds_of_Crime_and_Anti_Money_Laundering_Bill_2008.pdf, for Malaysia: http://www.bnm.gov.my/index.php?ch=14&pg=17&ac=739&full=1, for the Philippines: http://www.amlc.gov.ph/archive.html, for Zambia: http://www.deczambia.gov.zm/docs/The%20Money%20Laundering%20Act.pdf.

additional verification and adequately accounted for the patterns that have given rise to the blockage.

Detecting patterns of suspicious activity among thousands of low-value transactions will not be easy, given the current approaches to detecting suspicious transactions. In practice, suspicions are often triggered by "large and complex" transactions, not by micro or nano operations. Conversely, one could say that limits on transactions restrict the usefulness of the product for either ML or TF and make unusual transactions more detectable. Mobile providers will have to put in place internal monitoring systems to increase the likelihood of spotting any deviant account behavior. Fieldwork in many countries has shown that mobile operators are equipped with internal systems and have adopted risk management procedures, as recommended by the FATF standards (including measures such as a limitation of the number, type, and amount of transactions that can be performed). That fieldwork also has shown that many countries have imposed AML/CFT reporting requirements on m-money issuers. They are generally required to report suspicious transactions to the FIU within several days of the transaction date. In addition, some countries require all transactions exceeding a certain amount to be reported, whether suspicious or not (see box 3.10).

It is noteworthy that authorities are grappling with specific guidelines regarding the information that m-money issuers must report. For example, should regulators require that all or a portion of the content

---

Box 3.10

Examples of Suspicious Transaction and Threshold Reporting Observed during Fieldwork

In **Kenya**, the AML law requires covered institutions to report to the FIU in the prescribed form immediately and, in any event, within seven days of the date the suspicious transaction or activity occurs. A reporting institution must file reports of all cash transactions exceeding $10,000 or its equivalent in any other currency.

In **Mexico,** the new AML/CFT legal framework for banks recognizes different categories of accounts, allowing different levels of applicable reporting policies for the implementation of the mobile banking model:

- Lower level of monitoring and reporting: For mobile accounts for natural persons whose monthly deposit transactions are below 2,000 UDIs (approximately $675), the banking institution is exempt from monitoring and submitting suspicious transaction reports, as long as the transaction level does not exceed 2,000 UDIs.
- Higher level of monitoring and reporting: For all other instances, the banking institution is obligated to monitor the operations and the transaction profiles of its clients. If there is a suspicious case, they must present a suspicious transaction report and particularly report whenever a single transaction exceeds the threshold limit of $10,000.

In the **Philippines,** the AML law requires covered institutions to report to the FIU all covered transactions and suspicious transactions within five working days of the occurrence, unless the supervising authority prescribes a longer period (not exceeding 10 working days). Threshold reporting is for all transactions above ₱500,000.

Source: For the Philippines, information is taken from the Anti-Money Laundering Act of 2001, http://www.amlc.gov.ph/archive.html.

of SMS messages exchanged between the issuer and the receiver, and the call logs between them, be reported when a suspicious transaction report is filed? Would such a requirement violate customer privacy rights and possibly result in a flurry of lawsuits? Would MNOs be reluctant to file reports for fear of losing business? Refer to appendix D for further guidance on these issues.

The Role of Retail Outlets

In many countries, APs do not provide their banking and payment services primarily through branches, but through small retail outlets such as groceries, bakeries, convenience stores, pharmacies, and gas stations. Such retail shops form a crucial part of many mobile banking business models because these shops provide broader and cheaper coverage than does a branch-based model. Although the precise role of such a retailer may differ from model to model, it generally involves providing cash-in and cash-out services and may extend to other customer interface functions, such as account opening and customer care.

Fieldwork has shown that authorities and providers alike are grappling with questions regarding the regulation, supervision, and licensing of these retail outlets for AML/CFT purposes. Questions arise regarding the most appropriate way to ensure integrity and compliance with the law. In particular, the issues of liability and responsibility for AML/CFT are not clearly understood.

The following section addresses successively the issue of status, registration, oversight, and AML duties and responsibilities of such retail outlets.

Licensing of Retail Outlets

In practice, some confusion has been observed as to whether retail shops providing such services should be considered intermediaries, third-party service providers, or retail outlets of the main m-money provider.[14] Some developing countries adopt a fairly strict approach in this regard and treat all such retail outlets as third party service providers, especially in relation to CDD functions.[15]

Determining the correct legal role and status of such retail shops is of paramount importance because it determines their status from a regulatory/supervisory standpoint and defines the scope and nature of their AML/CFT obligations. Therefore, it is important that the legal relationship among the retail shop, the AP (whether a bank or a telecom), and the customer be analyzed to determine the status of the retail shop. It is possible that such a shop can act as an independent third-party service provider, or that the shop may act as such a provider in respect to certain services and as a retail outlet in respect to other services. However, in the models reviewed during the fieldwork, this was not the case.

In the models that were witnessed, the retailers generally acted as the agents of the AP, providing the m-money services in the name of and on behalf of the AP. The agency relationship was established contractually between the AP and the retailer. Customers of the AP would interact with the AP via these retail outlets. Therefore, retailers merely act as outsources of the bank or the telecom. The customers view the retailer as a point of access and as a representative of the AP, rather than as the main counterparty with whom they contract. The authors are of the view that retailers such as these do not deliver the m-money services and, as a result, cannot be compared with an independent intermediary or third-party service provider.[16] Nor would these retailers fall within the category of "introducers" (as contemplated in FATF Recommendation 9), who are generally counterparts (such as lawyers or independent brokers) who do not provide the financial service as such, but do introduce the applicant customer to the bank.

The issue of whether such retail outlets should be licensed and regulated for the m-money service they deliver is debatable. It is not necessary to extend licensing or registration requirements to such retail outlets, provided that the AP is held accountable and responsible for the retail outlet's compliance and noncompliance. In practice, countries have adopted different approaches in this regard (see box 3.11). In the Philippines, for example, each remittance retail outlet must be licensed separately, thereby causing burdensome delays and paperwork. Furthermore, all retail outlets have to undergo AML/CFT training sessions that are available only in Manila. As a result, the Central Bank of the Philippines (Bangko Sentral ng Pilipinas [BSP]) is in the final phase of approving a mechanism by which retail outlets can be "network licensed" or "mass licensed." G-Cash, one of the major m-money providers in the country, is hoping to enlist 15,000 new retail outlets in one step.[17]

Supervision and Oversight of Retail Outlets

Because retail outlets are seen as synonymous with the AP, it is appropriate for supervision and oversight to focus on the AP. Monitoring

Box 3.11

Examples of Countries Where Providers Assume Liability for Retail Outlets

In **Brazil**, the principal is fully responsible for the services rendered by its retail outlets. The central bank requires the principal (1) to control the activities of each of its retail outlets by setting transaction limits and implementing mechanisms to block transactions remotely when necessary; and (2) to ensure compliance with all applicable legal and regulatory provisions, such as AML/CFT, customer protection, and data privacy. A retail outlet must post a notice in its establishment that it acts on behalf of the bank.

In **Colombia**, in the contract between the financial institution and the retail outlet, there is a clear reference to the financial institution's liability for its retail outlets' actions.

In **Mexico**, under current regulations for any type of m-money business model, the liability for regulatory compliance with AML/CFT must fall ultimately on the bank (not telecoms or third-party providers). Thus, a bank-based model has been established. M-money services can be used only if one has a formal bank account with the m-money provider. (Legally speaking, the authorities recognize only the bank as the ultimate provider.)

In **Peru**, final liability rests with the AP, not the retail outlets.

In the **Philippines**, the e-money circular explicitly states that it is the responsibility of the institutions to ensure that their retail outlets comply with all AML laws, rules, and regulations. Section 4 (e) states, "it is the responsibility of the electronic money issuers to ensure that their distributors/e-money agents comply with all applicable requirements of the Anti-Money Laundering laws, rules and regulations."

Source: Authors.

and supervising thousands of retail outlets in accordance with FATF Recommendations 23, 24, and 29 would be impractical and almost impossible, especially in poor countries where supervisory resources are already scarce. However, this does not mean that retail outlets are free of any scrutiny. In fact, scrutiny should be performed by the AP, which should be held accountable and responsible for compliance by the retail outlets. APs' policies, procedures, training, and monitoring of retail outlets should be scrutinized by the supervisor. Where appropriate, the supervisor should visit a representative sample of retail outlets to determine if the AP is performing its required functions correctly.

AML Duties of Retail Outlets

The fact that retail outlets act as an extension of an AP means that the processes and documentation (notably for AML/CFT purposes) are those of the AP (as indicated in the footnote to FATF recommendation 9). Although a general AML/CFT law may extend obligations (such as a duty to report suspicious transactions) to retail outlets, those outlets' main roles and duties and the way they are expected to perform those duties will be determined by the AP.

It is crucial that these duties be clearly specified in the agency agreement whereby the retailer is appointed as a retail outlet of the AP.[18] In practice, the contracts between APs and their retail outlets vary considerably across markets that were studied; but common clauses generally include the duty to perform specified AML/CFT checks, recordkeeping, and reporting obligations.

There are, of course, practical and potential legal limits to the duties that the AP may reasonably delegate to the retail outlet. The authors believe that the retail outlet should have a duty to report a customer's suspicious conduct to the AP, but the retail outlet cannot carry the full burden of conducting on-going due diligence on the business relationship and scrutinizing all transactions undertaken throughout the course of that relationship. Many retail outlets will be modest shops that are not equipped to perform extensive monitoring functions, and they may not have access to the customer profile that the AP holds. This would make it impossible to consider whether a customer's transactions are consistent with the institution's knowledge of that customer. Furthermore, a retail outlet will view only those transactions that are conducted via its shop. The AP, on the other hand, will have a comprehensive record of the transactions conducted by the particular customer.

In conclusion, a comprehensive monitoring regime will combine the strengths of the AP and the retail outlet, instead of relying only on one of the parties. From a policy perspective, however, it is strongly suggested that the main monitoring obligation remains that of the AP because the AP is in the best position to oversee customers' activities. The AP should ensure that the retail outlets provide appropriate support to guarantee that it can meet its obligations in this regard.

Ultimate Liability of Retail Outlets

In the legal relationship between the AP and the retail outlet, the AP is the principal. As the principal in the relationship, it is appropriate that responsibility for AML/CFT compliance (including compliance by the retail outlet), ultimately rests with the AP. This is the case in most of the countries that were visited. This approach means that the AP has strong incentives to ensure that retail outlets comply with their obligations. It must be noted that the only exception in this regard seems to be Safaricom in Kenya, which expressly disavows any liability for its retail outlets' activities—and it is worth noting that, to date, it has not been decided whether that regime is in line with the FATF standards (see box 3.12).

Box 3.12

A Country Where Providers Do Not Assume Liability for Retail Outlets: Kenya

Safaricom describes the relationship with its retail outlets as a de facto (rather than strictly legal) principal–agent relationship. According to Safaricom, the company invests heavily in AML training and supervision for outlets and their personnel to equip them to confront AML situations that might arise. Safaricom is able to exert a lot of control over its outlets, just as in any legal principal–agent relationship. The controls are not optional measures, but mandatory enforcement tools with which the outlets must contractually commit to comply at all times. Because the reputation of the operator is at stake, control over outlets' activities is critical. If an outlet that has the benefit of AML training acts negligently, or willfully permits a money-laundering act to be committed at its outlet, then Safaricom requires the outlet to take responsibility. As such, the outlet agrees to indemnify Safaricom for losses incurred as a result of any wrongful or negligent act or failure to act in relation to the Safaricom service. The individual involved at the outlet also may be liable for breach of the law. The company believes that this is not dissimilar to a legal principal–agent relationship.

Source: Authors.

Internal Scrutiny and Risk Management of Retail Outlets

Because the AP ultimately will bear responsibility in the case of noncompliance (whether by itself or by any of its retail outlets), APs take steps to mitigate their compliance risks. Fieldwork has shown, for example, that they have established due diligence processes before engaging a retail outlet. In practice, small retailers often struggle to produce the required supporting documentation to complete an application to become an authorized retail outlet. Operators like Safaricom, for example, require such documents as certificates of incorporation, bank statements for the past six months, copies of the identification papers for key staff, a list of outlets, and so forth (Davidson and Leishman 2010).

Due diligence measures should be consistent with the risks posed by the agency relationship. When the retail outlet is entrusted with account-opening functions, higher due diligence standards are appropriate. Retail outlets know the AP's system better than the customers know it, so the outlets may be able to abuse their positions within the framework to launder funds and perpetrate other offenses. Generally, they are able to ignore suspicious activities that should be reported to the AP. Depending on the design of the particular m-money model, they may be in positions to falsify records. Even honest retail outlets may render the system vulnerable to abuse by failing to perform their functions diligently.

For that reason, APs must scrutinize their retail outlets closely and manage the attendant ML risk by performing appropriate due diligence measures when engaging retail outlets. When an agency relationship is established, appropriate training and support must be provided. In addition, retail outlets must be monitored for compliance with their AML/CFT duties. This may include on-site visits by compliance representatives of the AP.

Nevertheless, regulators should be informed that although AML/CFT risks arising from retail outlets are greater than risks arising from customers, risk management frameworks for retail outlets are already in place for some providers. For example, Safaricom has built a specific program that incentivizes retail outlets to invest their own funds in the e-money float. In addition, all m-money transactions conducted by the retail outlets are electronic and on a real-time basis, ensuring that the transactions have an electronic trail and reducing the associated integrity risks. (For additional information, see box 3.13 and table 3.2.)

Box 3.13

Examples of APs Managing Retail Outlet Risks

In **Kenya**, Safaricom requires retail outlets to pass an AML test to ensure their familiarity with integrity issues and procedures. Zain verifies the business permits of retail outlets through lawyers and notaries, and it performs random on-site visits by "mystery shoppers".[a]

In **Peru**, financial institutions are obligated to train their retail outlets on KYC and other CDD obligations.

In the **Philippines**, Globe Telecom requires all retail outlets to undergo an accreditation process led by a committee comprising representatives from its finance, legal, business operations, and information technology departments.

In the **Russian Federation**, payment agents are required to register with the Federal Financial Monitoring Service (FFMS) for AML purposes and to have their internal control rules approved by FFMS before accepting payments. In addition, all transactions processed by retail outlets go through the operator's information technology system and will be subject to AML/CFT rules.

In **Zambia**, the central bank reviews applications to ensure that retail outlet personnel are adequately trained in front-end procedures (including KYC) and allows the provider to monitor its retail outlets.

Source: World Bank research.
a. Mystery shoppers are Safaricom employees who visit retail outlets for monitoring purposes, pretending to be customers.

Table 3.2   Example of the Evolution of Retail Outlets' Regulation in Brazil, Various Years

Year	Resolution and description
Before 1999	Only banks can have retail outlets and only in places where there are no bank branches. Services allowed: – loan applications – credit and personal data analysis Subagents are not allowed.
1999	Resolution CMN 2640/99 Additional services allowed: – receipt of account-opening applications (original documents should be analyzed by bank staff) – deposits and withdrawals (subject to CBB's authorization) – bill payments

(continued)

**Table 3.2 Example of the Evolution of Retail Outlets' Regulation in Brazil,
Various Years** *(continued)*

Year	Resolution and description
2000	Resolution CMN 2707/00 Limitation on location is lifted. Retail outlets may be located anywhere, regardless of the presence of a bank branch.
2002	Resolution CMN 2953/02 – Retail outlets are permitted to analyze identification documents for account opening. – In addition to banks, consumer credit companies are allowed to hire retail outlets.
2003	Resolution CMN 3110/03 – All financial institutions are allowed to hire retail outlets. – Subagents are allowed.
2003	Resolution CMN 3156/03 – All other CBB-licensed entities are allowed to hire retail outlets.
2008	Resolution CMN 3568/2008 – Retail outlets are permitted to offer international transfers on behalf of a financial institution (limited to $3,000 per transaction),[a] subject to a simple online CBB registration process.
2008	Resolution CMN 3654/2008 – The need for previous authorization by CBB for banks wishing to hire retail outlets was lifted. – A financial institution willing to deliver services through retail outlets is required only to register each outlet in CBB's online system.

Source: CGAP, http://www.cgap.org/gm/document-1.9.42396/Updated_Notes_On_Regulating_Branchless_
Banking_Brazil.pdf.
Note: In 2006 in Brazil, 95,000 retail outlets, equipped with point-of-sale and bar-code readers, processed 1.53
billion transactions, valued at $ 104 billion. Seventy-eight percent of those transactions were bill payments and
deliveries of government benefits. The remainder included deposits, withdrawals, and loan repayments and dis-
bursements. Six million new accounts were opened in 2006. In Brazil, virtually any entity can be engaged as a
retail outlet. The most common types are lottery kiosks, post offices, grocery stores, and other merchants. Banco
Central do Brasil has issued comprehensive regulations governing other aspects of the business (particularly to
protect consumers), but the lack of prohibitions on who may act as a retail outlet seems to have opened up the
field for innovation and allowed rapid growth (GSMA 2008).
a. It should be noted that person-to-person services are not available, so this transaction limit relates to mobile-
based payments for goods.

Notes

1. As stated by CGAP (Rosenberg 2009), "challenges are intensified by the fact
   that many services have been widely available for only a short while. As a
   result, there are no 'off-the-shelf' regulatory frameworks that can successfully
   mitigate risks and address problems in complex and far-reaching branchless
   banking systems. Nor is there a rich trove of historical data to use in shaping
   policies."

2. It appears that many licenses for m-money are issued as a payment systems license, but contain provisions that directly address e-money services.

3. This indecision is true in Cambodia and Russia, for example. In Cambodia, there is currently no specific regulatory and licensing regime for m-money. M-money services operate on the basis of a mutual understanding between the central bank and the operator. The operator must be guaranteed by a reliable banking institution; the central bank requires the operator to provide monthly reports containing all information necessary for supervisory purposes. Any update to the business operations should be requested from the central bank (see Vada [2009]). In Russia, the country has no specific provision regulating online payments, but a working group on regulating online payments and e-money was established in September 2009. Currently, service providers are registered, but have no AML obligations.

4. For example, the Financial Services Authority in the United Kingdom, Japan's Financial Supervisory Agency, and the Republic of Korea's Financial Supervisory Commission all separated from their central banks.

5. Examples of the types of customer information that banks could obtain, and the identification data that they could use to verify that information, are in the Basel Committee on Banking Supervision's (BCBS) paper on "Customer Due Diligence for Banks" (2001) and subsequently reinforced by a general guide to account opening and customer identification (CDD) in February 2003.

6. Of course, the provider will have to perform full KYC/CDD every time situations arise as defined by the FATF: for example, when there is a suspicion of money laundering or terrorist financing; when the m-money provider has doubts about the veracity or adequacy of previously obtained customer identification data.

7. As already observed in this book, full exemption of CDD is not permitted when an activity is subject to AML/CFT obligations; only reduced measures are acceptable.

8. The quid pro quo for this is that all issuers should have in place the systems and controls to monitor what is going through their systems and the ability to block accounts that exhibit suspicious patterns of activity—unusually high volumes or velocities of circulation.

9. It was debated amongst the regulated institutions for a number of years whether this article required the obligation to photocopy identity documents.

10. Depending on the service provider and the business model, transactions may be initiated by an SMS, a multimedia messaging service (MMS), Java application, or mobile Web session.

11. SMS-based banking systems use plain-text messages for carrying out transactions. For example, the customer needs to send the following SMS message: "PAY[one space][merchant code][one space][amount][one space][debit card number]."

12. In Japan, for example, customers of DOCOMO's i-mode mobile Internet service on the 3G FOMA network are able to remit up to ¥20,000 (about $208) per transfer by inputting the payee's mobile phone number. The payee receives an e-mail notification via his or her DOCOMO mobile phone and is given the option of depositing the money in a domestic bank account or having the amount credited to his or her monthly DOCOMO phone bill.

13. In Europe, for example, Directive 2006/24/EC requires member states to ensure that communications providers retain necessary data as specified in the directive for a period of six months to two years. In the United States, most cell carriers seem to retain content data for three to seven days. In the United Kingdom, SMS, enhanced messaging service, and MMS messages are archived for six months. In the Philippines, a 2008 National Telecommunications Commission circular stipulates that records of traffic data on the origin, destination, date, time, and duration of communications must be retained for a period of two to four months. In Malaysia, Bank Simpanan National (which provides SMS mobile banking) seems to keep data on mobile transactions for only three months.

14. For example, BSP is unclear whether account opening (with actual deposit taking) and KYC can be undertaken by retail outlets that belong to a covered financial institution of the BSP and are compliant with FATF standards, even if the primary financial institution is legally responsible for its retail outlets.

15. This approach has prompted telecom companies to use more complicated business models than may be necessary to be "safe." For instance, a well-known European telecom has felt compelled by regulatory fears to approach local banks in Africa to let it provide mobile financial services. Instead of just being "itself," the company has had to include a local bank to back it up. This action was completely unnecessary for the business model to function, but the company included the bank (and therefore increased its costs) because of liability fears related to CDD.

16. Such a party would often have an independent legal relationship with the customer and would facilitate the provision of the services in a tripartite legal arrangement among the customer, the retail outlet, and the m-money provider.

17. Although it ultimately is left to the authorities to choose the approaches taken, it might be good to consider that, at the international level, the same principle be applied as the one required in FATF Special Regulation VI on retail outlets. In other words, at the minimum, the principal needs to keep the list of its retail outlets, and this list could be submitted to the central bank for its records. One caveat: although remittance retail outlets and m-money retail outlets can be very similar in terms of who they are and what they do for their principals, m-money retail outlets usually do one or more functions (including account opening for customers). The authors are not clear about whether

this function has such an impact that it would require different treatment of retail outlets for m-money than is required for remittances.

18. Regulators also may impose obligations on the retail outlets, beyond those set by the AP.

References

Basel Committee on Banking Supervision. 2001. "Customer Due Diligence for Banks." http://www.bis.org/publ/bcbs85.htm.

———. 1997. "The Core Principles for Effective Banking." http://www.bis .org/publ/bcbs30a.pdf.

Bester, Hennie, Doubell Chamberlain, Louis de Koker, Christine Hougaard, Ryan Short, Anja Smith, and Richard Walker. 2008. *Implementing FATF Standards in Developing Countries and Financial Inclusion: Findings and Guidelines.* Johannesburg, South Africa: Genesis Analytics.

CGAP (Consultative Group to Assist the Poor). 2009. *Financial Access 2009: Measuring Access to Financial Services around the World.* Washington, DC. http://www.cgap.org/gm/document-1.9.38735/FA2009.pdf.

Davidson, Neil, and Paul Leishman. 2010. "Building a Network of Mobile Money Agents." GSMA, London. http://www.gsmworld.com/documents/ Building(4).pdf.

de Koker, Louis. 2009. "The Money Laundering Risk Posed by Low-Risk Financial Products in South Africa: Findings and Guidelines." *Journal of Money Laundering Control* 12 (4): 323–39.

FATF (Financial Action Task Force). 2009. *Methodology for Assessing Compliance with the FATF 40 Recommendations and the FATF 9 Special Recommendations.* Paris, FATF-GAFI. http://www.fatf-gafi.org/dataoecd/16/54/40339628.pdf.

FIC/OBS (Financial Intelligence Centre/Ombudsman for Banking Services). 2009. "Joint Statement: Clarification on the Obligations of Accountable Institutions on Verifying Client Identities, and Record Keeping." Press statement. https://www.fic.gov.za/DownloadContent/NEWS/PRESSRELEASE/ JOINT%20STATEMENT%20Verifying%20and%20recording%20keep%20of %20client%20identities%20trkcm.pdf.

GSMA (Groupe Speciale Mobile Association). 2008. "Understanding Financial Regulation and How It Works." London. http://216.239.213.7/mmt/ financial-regulation.asp.

———. 2009. *Mobile Money for the Unbanked: Annual Report 2009.* London. http://www.mobilemoneyexchange.org/Research/mobile-money-for-the- unbanked-annual-report-2009.

Isern, Jennifer D., and Louis de Koker. 2009. "AML/CFT: Strengthening Financial Inclusion and Integrity." Focus Note 56, Consultative Group to Assist the Poor, Washington, DC.

MMT (Mobile Money Transfer) Global Gateway. 2009. "MMT Explained Part 15: Navigating the Regulatory Minefield with Aiaze Mitha." http://www.mobile-money-transfer.com/mmt_global/mmtex15.

Rosenberg, Jim. 2009. "Which Is Worse—Losing Your Wallet or Your Mobile (Or What If They're the Same Thing)?" Technology blog, CGAP, Washington, DC. http://technology.cgap.org/2009/03/13/which-is-worse-losing-your-wallet-or-your-mobile-or-what-if-theyre-the-same-thing/#more-769

Solin, Marina. 2009. "New Regulatory Change in South Africa Affects Mobile Money." GSMA, London. http://mmublog.org/africa-south/new-regulatory-change-in-south-africa-affects-mobile-money/.

Vada, Kim. 2009. "Mobile Money Regulation. Mobile Money for the Unbanked." PowerPoint presentation to the Mobile Money for the Unbanked Leadership Forum, Barcelona, June 22–25.

Working Group on Cross-border Banking. 2003. "General Guide to Account Opening and Customer Identification." Basel Committee on Banking Supervision, Basel. http://www.bis.org/publ/bcbs85annex.htm.

WSBI (World Savings Banks Institute). 2009. "Anti Money Laundering and Combat Financing Terrorism Rules and the Challenge of Financial Inclusion: WSBI Experience and Proposals to FATF." Position paper, WBSI, Brussels. http://www.wsbi.org/uploadedFiles/Position_papers/0565%20updated.pdf.

Zerzan, Andrew. 2009. "New Technologies, New Risks? Innovation and Countering the Financing of Terrorism." Working Paper 174, World Bank, Washington, DC.

CHAPTER 4

Anti-Money Laundering and Combating the Financing of Terrorism Policy Guidance for Countries Regulating Their Mobile Money Markets

Summary

This chapter provides guidance to relevant stakeholders on how best to design an effective regulatory regime for mobile money (m-money) from an anti-money laundering and combating the financing of terrorism (AML/CFT) perspective. Countries must create a proper enabling environment if m-money is to flourish. An enabling AML/CFT legal and regulatory environment will be sound, clear, nondiscriminatory, and proportionate.

Policy makers, m-money providers, and international standard-setting bodies are all addressing aspects of an appropriate regulatory environment. National policy makers, however, have been grappling with ways to ensure appropriate regulation of m-money providers and their retail outlets, and trying to determine whether their approaches are consistent with the Financial Action Task Force (FATF) standards. In other jurisdictions, m-money providers have difficulty complying with the national

(continued)

Summary *(continued)*

regulations governing m-money, especially in cases in which they were not sufficiently consulted before the regulations were designed and enacted. In addition, international standard-setting bodies—such as the FATF—are working to understand the complexities of the different business models and to formulate appropriate responses to more detailed questions regarding the application of the standards to low-value, low-risk m-money transactions.

This chapter discusses how these stakeholders can address the key issues that face them in relation to m-money. It begins by offering targeted guidance first to national policy makers and then to m-money providers, and it concludes by identifying the key areas that the FATF can consider and toward which it can take action. The chapter's overall findings are highlighted below.

Key Points

Policy guidance in AML/CFT for policy makers:

- *Adopt a more comprehensive approach to AML/CFT.*
- *Conduct an assessment of the m-money ecosystem.*
- *Impose AML/CFT obligations on nonbank providers of financial services.*
- *Adopt technology-neutral regulations.*
- *Promote regulations that balance financial inclusion with financial integrity.*
- *Issue clear and well-articulated AML/CFT guidelines for m-money services.*
- *Impose AML/CFT obligations on retail outlets.*
- *Determine a clear delineation of responsibilities between account providers (APs) and retail outlets.*
- *Implement interagency coordination.*
- *Promote a clear and effective supervisory regime for m-money providers.*
- *Grant relevant authorities the power to make binding rules.*
- *Define an enforceable sanctioning regime for m-money.*
- *Provide AML/CFT training to supervisors.*

Guidelines for m-money providers:

- *Develop AML/CFT internal policies.*
- *Support m-money services with appropriate governance and risk management practices.*
- *Develop internal solutions for money-laundering/terrorist-financing (ML/TF) transaction monitoring.*

(continued)

Summary *(continued)*

• *Require retail outlets to report their suspicions to the AP.*
• *Ensure appropriate information-sharing arrangements among parties, where required.*
• *Ensure that appropriate rules are followed regarding information to be reported.*
• *See that clear internal reporting mechanisms are set by each m-money provider.*
• *Provide staff with ongoing AML/CFT training.*

Recommendations for the FATF:

• *Provide further guidance to identify low-risk transactions and customers.*
• *Identify conditions under which m-money can be supported as a tool to mitigate overall ML/TF risk.*
• *Clarify appropriate customer due diligence (CDD) measures within the low-risk context.*
• *Issue a risk-based guidance report on m-money.*

Implementing AML/CFT standards for m-money services can be discussed at two levels: macro and micro. This chapter provides policy guidance at both levels, targeting both policy makers and m-money providers. Furthermore, this chapter proposes some considerations for the FATF so that financial inclusion is given more attention going forward.

AML/CFT Guidance for Policy Makers

Policy makers can take a number of steps to ensure a more effective facilitative and collaborative approach to regulation.

Designing the Broad Regulatory Framework and Approach

There are a number of facilitative approaches and policy principles that can be adopted by national governments.

Adopt a more comprehensive approach to AML/CFT. In some cases, multiple stakeholders in the m-money community have a narrow AML/CFT approach to m-money that focuses exclusively on customer due diligence (CDD) and FATF Recommendation 5. Although CDD is an essential component of AML/CFT, policy makers should pay equal attention to the other elements of effective AML/CFT regulation. AML/CFT obligations cover a wide spectrum of issues, ranging from CDD to reporting obligations, internal controls and mechanisms, training, dissemination, national and international cooperation, and outreach, among others.[1] Compliance with these other facets of AML/CFT standards[2] is as important as compliance with CDD requirements when a country strives to comply fully with the international standards.

Conduct an assessment of the m-money ecosystem. In an ideal situation, countries should survey the m-money ecosystem and its overall level of integrity risks prior to drafting AML/CFT regulation for m-money activities. The survey should aim to identify all role players in the jurisdiction, understand the products that are offered and are likely to be offered, and potential future patterns and trends. A risk assessment should also be performed to determine the nature, types, and levels of ML/TF risk. Countries will need to identify the main vulnerabilities that are specific to m-money and address them accordingly. Mobile network operators (MNOs) will need to contribute to this process by sharing information about their systems and by identifying higher- and lower-risk customers, products, and services. These assessments are not static; they have to be repeated to identify changes that occur over time, as circumstances develop and threats evolve.

Under ideal conditions, the appropriate regulatory and supervisory approach for m-money should also support the financial system's longer-term systemic stability, rather than merely its current flows. This will be of increasing importance when m-money begins to substitute more fully for the other financial channels and services. In this regard, any reluctance by policy makers to contemplate preventive measures because of their potential costs should be balanced by a consideration of the cost of restoring public confidence if there were any wide-scale incidents involving the m-money channel.

Apply AML/CFT obligations to nonbanks offering m-money. As a general principle, all financial institutions should be subject to AML/CFT obligations.[3] National laws generally require that banks, microfinance institutions, postal services, exchange bureaus, money transfer service providers, and all other types of financial institutions have in place an AML/CFT policy, specialized and trained personnel, reporting systems, and internal controls. Countries should also ensure, however, that nonbanks that offer m-money (for example, MNOs) are explicitly subject to

AML/CFT obligations. The type of license that is granted to a nonbank will normally determine its status with regard to AML/CFT. If the m-money provider is issued a banking license to deliver m-money services, it will automatically be classified as a "financial institution" in relation to such services and, as such, will be subject to the AML/CFT law. If it obtains an electronic money (e-money) issuer license, it might not be subject to that law in some countries. In this regard, authorities should ensure an equitable regulatory environment that treats providers of similar products similarly.[4] When nonbank m-money providers are subjected to AML/CFT obligations, it does not necessarily mean that the full range of requirements should be imposed; flexibility in the way those obligations are applied to m-money services should be considered, particularly in the context of low-capacity countries.

Adopt technology-neutral regulations. Policy makers should avoid adopting AML/CFT regulations that specifically target m-money. What is required is an approach that encompasses the challenges raised by m-money, yet is neither m-money–centric nor m-money–specific. A uniform approach for all new payment technologies and m-money providers (banks, MNOs, and third-party providers) is important because m-money is simply an alternative means of performing financial transactions. Generally, therefore, there is no justifiable reason m-money should be subjected to a regulatory scheme that differs from the one that applies to other new payment technologies. Ideally, a regulatory framework that balances regulation with the need for market access and innovation is indispensable, provided that conditions for an equitable regulatory environment are maintained at all times.

Focus on risks that the product and clients represent. When the regulator considers appropriate CDD controls for m-money, it should focus on the risks that the product and the clients represent.[5] Practical constraints and opportunities presented by the national context should also be considered to ensure a pragmatic and responsive m-money risk-control framework. Countries that identify gaps in their identification and verification frameworks are also advised to consider appropriate improvements. Countries should ensure that there are national or commercial identification frameworks that are proportionate, include all citizens, meet international privacy standards, command industry and consumer support, and deliver value to law enforcement. Mindful of the lack of proper identification mechanisms, several developing countries have recently started to establish and promote new electronic identification systems that enable large coverage of the population, even in the most remote areas.

Adopt regulation that balances financial inclusion with financial integrity. International standards for AML/CFT are challenging—and their flexibility has not always been clearly communicated or understood. In addition, countries very often prefer to err on the safe side to avoid the risk of noncompliance. As a result, too many countries overregulate and, thus, create barriers to business and inclusion. Many countries have not allowed simplified CDD where it was justified by the low risk, as permitted by the FATF's risk-based approach.[6] This has happened because policy makers are not sure about the correct interpretation of aspects of the risk-based approach—especially the interpretation of key phrases in the recommendations, such as "proven low risk"[7]— that would trigger the possibility of full or partial exemption from AML/CFT obligations.

There is already significant flexibility in the international standards that countries could use with more confidence, especially when FATF clarifies its views on low-risk controls. A reduction in regulatory obligations of providers of low-value products will minimize their compliance burden and related costs. Lower costs and affordable fees would enable more of the low-income population to access the services and products. Simplified CDD requirements would also decrease the burden on potential clients to verify their identities, enabling them to access services that may not otherwise have been accessible.

Policy makers, therefore, are encouraged to promote the creation of low-risk, low-value basic accounts and payment and remittance services[8] and to facilitate their development by imposing appropriate reduced and simplified CDD requirements. As long as a country can demonstrate and provide evidence that specific and unique circumstances around a specific functional activity generate a low level of ML/TF risk, partial exemption from AML/CFT obligation is possible.[9]

There are a number of arguments that could be advanced in support of a partial AML/CFT exemption for m-money: Mobile payment services handle much smaller payment transactions than traditional banking services. Usually, transactions are capped; services are restricted to certain geographic areas; most services are purely domestic, with no cross-border activity allowed; and operations in foreign currencies are limited or prohibited. Furthermore, jurisdictions usually limit accounts to one per person.

Last, banks and MNOs have designed sophisticated internal control mechanisms to trace unusual transactions, and those mechanisms mitigate the risks. (For a detailed discussion of the risk profile of m-money, see appendix B.)

Countries may wish to consider the following alternative approaches for simplified CDD in relation to low-risk m-money accounts:[10]

- Reduce the depth of CDD required—for example, by dispensing with the verification of the residential address.
- Expand the list of accepted forms of identification, allowing less-formal evidence to be provided.
- Permit the use of forms of identification that may not bear a picture.
- Establish a tiered customer identification program (or progressive CDD approach), whereby a customer who can provide only minimal verification is restricted to basic services and may access higher levels of services after providing more comprehensive verification.
- In the case of very-low-value transactions (services that most often carry a marginal risk), allow the customer's personal particulars to be obtained without requiring verification of those particulars.

In conclusion, instead of applying traditional banking regulations, regulators should focus on the actual risks of a service offered. AML/CFT controls should be based on a clear understanding of the risks. That understanding can be developed through research, an analysis of national and international ML/TF typologies, and crime analysis. The objective must be to develop a reasonable and well-grounded appreciation of attendant risks that can support a flexible risk-based approach to AML/CFT. Proposed controls must also be based on actual market research and a thorough analysis of the needs and real-life circumstances of those people who are financially excluded.

Sequence the implementation of AML/CFT obligations. The analysis of national AML/CFT frameworks in developing economies shows that a gradual or sequenced implementation of the FATF recommendations can reduce adverse effects on financial inclusion. Sequenced implementation allows the system to be grown and expanded over a period of time to eventually ensure full compliance with the international standards. A sequenced process would start by implementing key FATF recommendations[11] for the sectors and transactions presenting the higher risks of ML/TF; and progressively expand to lower categories of risk as the country develops its capacity to properly identify and mitigate the risks involved.

In many countries, the ability to supervise banks on matters relating directly to the core Basel principles is strained, and AML/CFT implementation is a secondary priority. Capacity constraints often include insufficient staffing and underdeveloped information technology systems, and are exacerbated by weak legal and regulatory frameworks and a lack of coordination among various bodies involved in the AML/CFT framework. As a result, limited guidance is provided, supervision is cursory, and few enforcement actions are taken. Many of the jurisdictions report very few instances of ML/TF abuse, but it is not necessarily clear whether the reports reflect the level of risk or the lack of capacity to identify risks and abuse.

Promote a collaborative, step-by-step approach between financial regulators and industry. One of the main lessons to be learned from the experiences described in chapter 3 is that a successful regulatory outcome requires a participatory approach among all stakeholders—especially the regulators, the banking supervisors, the banking and telecommunications industries, and the national authorities responsible for AML/CFT issues. Furthermore, a step-by-step implementation approach has often proved necessary. It enables construction of basic regulatory models that were refined to adapt to the increasingly sophisticated and diverse business models that emerged. This approach assisted in aligning the regulatory framework with changes in the political, economic, and commercial context. A collaborative test-and-learn approach also facilitates an appropriate analysis and assessment of risk and supports changes in risk mitigation measures when required.

Issuing Guidelines for M-Money Providers
Clear regulatory guidelines for m-money providers have proved helpful.

Issue clear and well-articulated AML/CFT guidelines for m-money services. According to FATF Recommendation 25, "competent authorities" should establish guidelines and provide feedback to assist institutions in applying national AML/CFT measures and particularly in detecting and reporting suspicious transactions. Although suspicious transaction guidance and feedback typically would be provided by the Financial Intelligence Unit (FIU), it may be the national regulator and supervisor of m-money that establishes guidelines to help the supervised entity fulfill its broader AML/CFT obligations. It is, after all, the national regulator and supervisor (for m-money, usually the jurisdiction's central bank) that will subsequently monitor compliance with these obligations.

Guidelines typically are regarded as "soft law" because they are not directly enforceable; but when an m-money provider continually disregards guidance, such conduct may be a factor in decisions on possible future action. Guidance is generic, however, and is different from the recommendations or instructions a supervisor may issue following an inspection—recommendations and instructions that typically are both binding and enforceable and are always directed at an individual institution. Guidance concerns an entire group of supervised entities and may relate to every aspect of the AML/CFT preventive system. It does not impose new obligations on entities, but it does seek to illustrate how certain already-imposed obligations can be fulfilled in practice.

Thus, guidelines are useful to bring clarity to AML/CFT legislation and national and international standards, particularly in cases in which laws were adopted recently. Guidelines for m-money providers can provide information on appropriate ways to interpret obligations and implement AML/CFT policies. It often extends to AML/CFT risk assessments, the design of CDD measures, recordkeeping requirements, suspicious transaction reports (STRs), and maintenance of an adequate level and mix of expertise through staff training.

From an international perspective, the issuing of guidelines reaffirms that the jurisdiction is committed both to developing effective legal instruments and to enhancing the AML/CFT practices of m-money providers. The effect is to enhance the country's credibility in relation to compliance with international standards. It also creates a better climate for doing business. This might attract more m-money providers and enhance the domestic competitive m-money landscape. The net effect of this situation is likely to result in greater financial inclusion among unbanked populations.

Implement guidelines through ongoing collaboration and dialogue between the public and private sectors. National authorities and their supervised entities should be proactive in building a constructive, collaborative relationship. This will enable the regulator to ensure guidelines that are practical, effective, and clear to all relevant stakeholders. Constructive engagement during the drafting of the guidelines is beneficial and can continue after publication of the guidelines. The supervisor may actually wish to engage the supervised entities to disseminate the specific guidelines issued and to conduct open question-and-answer sessions with the companies' compliance officers (rather than simply posting new guidelines on the central bank's Web site, for example). Such engagement will also foster discussion on how best to effectively implement and enforce the guidelines internally within the m-money provider. Furthermore, it is important that national authorities seek continual feedback on the guidelines from the m-money providers: Are the guidelines clear and helpful to the providers? Are they proving easy to implement in the organization? What challenges are being faced in their implementation? Has it been too burdensome on regulatory compliance costs? Comprehensive feedback may lead to amendments and clarification and will help improve the quality and scope of future guidelines issued by the supervisor.

Customize guidelines to specific local circumstances and conditions. To help ensure that guidelines for AML/CFT support financial inclusion, the level of financial infrastructure in the jurisdiction (in both the formal and informal sectors) should be taken into account. Before the designing of the guidelines, it will be helpful to assess the number of unbanked citizens currently served by formal or informal financial services and their specific demographic composition, the overall competitive landscape of the domestic m-money industry, and the prospective interest in the jurisdiction among potential m-money providers.

Regulating Retail Outlets

Appropriate support for the use of retail outlet networks is critical to the growth of m-money. In many countries, banks and other mobile banking providers offer banking and payment services through retail outlets that typically include groceries, bakeries, convenience stores, pharmacies, and gas stations. These outlets complement or replace bank branches and traditional agencies. Because of the network of retail outlets, m-money providers can reach a larger number of customers (including those in rural areas) and provide them with affordable and accessible cash-in/cash-out services. The retail outlet is a critical part of the mobile banking business. It is the customer contact point for cash-in/cash-out functions; but, depending on the model, it can also perform other customer interface functions—for example, customer care support and account opening.

During fieldwork, different approaches to covering retail outlets for AML/CFT purposes were encountered. It was particularly noticeable that authorities and providers alike were struggling to determine the correct and most appropriate status of retail outlets under the AML/CFT supervisory regime. Key questions relate to their responsibilities, and the person or agency that is ultimately liable for the outlets' actions. Ambiguities in or misunderstandings around the international standards further fuel debates and challenges. The retail outlet model presents challenges because some key CDD functions are performed by third parties who are not directly part of the regulated financial institution and who usually have limited AML/CFT capacity and expertise. There are also fears that retail outlets may defraud customers or be linked to criminal organizations. Policy makers, therefore, are struggling to craft appropriate and proportionate regulations to mitigate these risks.

The authors believe that national authorities should consider taking the following steps to design an appropriate regulatory AML/CFT framework in relation to m-money retail outlet networks.

Ensure that regulators know and understand the entities involved in providing accounts. When analyzing an m-money program, regulators generally identify the entity that actively provides the service to customers, takes customers' cash, processes and records transactions, and "issues" m-money as the account provider (AP) in the program. Formally, however, the AP will be the entity defined as such in any applicable legislation for payment services/e-money. This entity might be a mobile operator, a bank, a payment services provider, or a partnership or joint venture involving more than one such entity. If several entities are involved, their respective roles and responsibilities—especially the allocation of liability when breaches occur—must be clear to the regulator(s). The potential for regulatory overlap needs to be minimized while ensuring that all relevant matters are covered.

Determine a clear delineation of responsibilities between APs and retail outlets. The AP is the entity ultimately responsible for the delivery and management of the financial services underlying an m-money program. The AP (whether a bank or a telecommunications company [telecom]) typically will be responsible for account opening, transaction processing, and recordkeeping, although some of its functions may be outsourced to other parties (such as retail outlets). (The role of the AP is discussed in more detail in chapter 1.)

It is of paramount importance to clarify the relationship between the retailer and the AP. In most cases, this relationship will amount to an "agency" or "outsourcing" relationship (although this would not amount to "outsourcing" as discussed by the FATF in its interpretative notes to the recommendations). The authors submit that the retailers do not deliver the m-money services. Rather, they provide the services in the name and on behalf of the main provider; in other words, they merely act as an "outsourcee" of the AP. As a result, retailers should be seen only as representatives or functionaries of the AP who ultimately bears the responsibility for AML/CFT, among other things. In this regard, agency or outsourcing relationships should be contractually established and defined in formal contracts between the retail outlets and the AP.

Fieldwork revealed different approaches to implementing AML/CFT regulations in regard to retail outlets. Some jurisdictions are considering regulating and registering retail outlets. The authors advise caution in this regard. Many jurisdictions, including several members of the European Union, have declined to follow that approach. The FATF standards do not require retail outlets to be licensed or registered. As stated, they are neither the APs nor its outsourcee as interpreted by the FATF. They act as agents or functionaries on behalf of the AP. Regulating retail outlets would imply supervising them; and it is practically impossible, especially in developing countries, to oversee thousands of small, corner shop–type retail outlets.

Know your retail outlets. When the AP is held accountable and responsible for retail outlets' compliance and noncompliance, there is no pressing need to license or register thousands of retailers. However, provision should be made to require that CDD be carried out on retail outlets prior to engaging them. Because retailers can be abused by criminals or be involved in criminal activities themselves, it is advisable that retail outlets that deliver a wide array of services be vetted by the AP prior to beginning any business relationships.

The level of trust that m-money providers invest in their retail outlets is often determined by how well they know them. For large retailers, the "know-your-retail-outlet" process could include the submission to the AP of a full business plan for the retail outlet. It will also entail identifying and verifying the identity of the retail outlet (for example, confirming its registration as a company when the retailer is an incorporated company) and verifying the identities of the business owners and the beneficial owners. When appropriate, policy makers may also require the AP to ensure that retail outlets comply with a suite of security and technological requirements, as set forth in relevant regulations applicable to electronic payments. The AP, however, should be allowed to perform such know-your-retail-outlet measures on a risk basis.

Comprehensive measures will not be required, nor will they be feasible in regard to small, informal retailers. Balancing the need to apply meaningful due diligence measures on retail outlets with the need to grow a large distribution network that can serve the poor is an important and challenging issue for the industry and for the regulators.

Ensure that retail outlets undertake AML/CFT obligations. When the AP is held accountable and responsible for compliance and noncompliance by the retail outlets, it does not mean that retail outlets should not bear AML/CFT responsibilities. On the contrary, they should be tasked with appropriate AML/CFT functions because they are in direct contact with customers. All interested parties are advised to clearly specify the AML/CFT duties delegated to the retailers in the business agreements.[12] This may vary by country, but jurisdictions may wish to consider asking retail outlets to perform some AML/CFT checks, including know-your-customer (KYC) checks and recordkeeping. In addition, it is possible to entrust retail outlets with the duties of conducting ongoing monitoring of transactions and reporting of suspicious activities to the relevant authorities. Depending on the context, however, that may not be practicable. Retail outlets do not necessarily have access to all of the relevant client and transaction information that the AP would hold. Therefore, they may not be able to monitor transactions effectively or identify suspicious transactions accurately. They are, however, in contact with clients and may be able to identify some suspicious behavior. In cases such as these, it is appropriate to require them to relay their suspicions to the AP. The AP then can review the client's transaction patterns and determine whether there are grounds to proceed with a formal STR to the FIU. As for customer monitoring, it is also desirable that the main monitoring obligations rest on the AP because it is best positioned and equipped to oversee customer transactions (and it will be liable ultimately).

Establish mechanisms to scrutinize retail outlets. AML/CFT requirements can be imposed on retail outlets even when they are not directly regulated. In the authors' view, the AP should be required to ensure compliance by the retail outlets. The supervisory authority oversees and regulates the principal, who then oversees the retail outlets. The authors suggest that such an approach is fully consistent with FATF standards.

Retail outlets should be subject to appropriate monitoring to ensure that they comply with AML/CFT obligations delegated to them by the AP. As a result, the contract between the AP and a retail outlet should give the AP the right to audit the retail outlet's performance of its obligations. For example, the AP may wish to use "mystery shoppers"—staff of the AP who visit retail outlets and pretend to be regular customers to test the retail outlet's integrity and competence in carrying out its roles. The AP's policies, procedures, training, and monitoring of retail outlets should be scrutinized, in turn, by the supervisor. To that end, supervisors are advised to perform on-site visits in a sample of retail outlets to determine whether the AP is performing the required functions correctly with regard to its network of retail outlets.[13]

Create an AML/CFT telephone hotline. Because retail outlets are playing a central role in the customer interface and are tasked with several AML/CFT duties, APs may wish to create a hotline for AML/CFT purposes that would be accessible only to their retail outlets. In case of difficulties, the outlets would seek assistance and guidance on issues related to customer identification or unusual operations, among other matters.[14]

Draft clear retail outlet regulations or guidelines. The issue of retail outlets is one of the most contentious and difficult aspects of the regulation of m-money. Jurisdictions should make sure that all responsibilities are clearly understood by all stakeholders. The regulators should consider drafting agency regulations or guidelines that delineate

- minimum provisions to be included in agency agreements;
- basic eligibility criteria for retail outlets;
- technical and operational requirements;
- limits for retail outlet transactions, individually and globally;
- internal controls and reporting requirements for retail outlets;
- the requirement that transactions be conducted online and in real time (that is, each retail outlet must have an account with the bank for real-time financial and accounting settlement);
- different transaction thresholds, based on the level of KYC conducted;
- procedures for authenticating identification of both clients and retail outlets; and
- management of retail outlets directly by the bank or through third parties or network managers.

Cooperating and Coordinating
A constructive and collaborative approach to the drafting and implementation of regulation requires sound communication with all relevant stakeholders and coordination between the relevant government agencies.

Coordinate among regulatory agencies. The field of m-money is not only new and fast evolving; it also sits at the overlap of several regulatory domains—those of banking, telecommunications, and payment system supervisors and of AML/CFT agencies. The overlap substantially raises the risk of coordination failure, where legislation or regulatory approaches are inconsistent or contradictory (Porteous 2006). As a result, implementing a mechanism of interagency coordination is of paramount importance to ensure business growth in a safe and sound environment.

Coordinate with all AML/CFT stakeholders. If day-to-day operational contact among all institutions that play a role in the AML/CFT system is essential to the proper functioning of the m-money system, periodic consultation among high-level representatives of those institutions is equally indispensable if their continuing commitment is to be guaranteed. Through discussions and by becoming aware of the capabilities and objectives of the other actors in the AML/CFT system, these high-level representatives can ensure that duplications and gaps are avoided. FATF Recommendation 31 addresses these goals by recommending that "policy makers, the FIU, law enforcement and supervisors . . . coordinate domestically with each other concerning the development and implementation of policies and activities to combat ML/FT." These high-level meetings generally comprise representatives from relevant ministries, including the Ministry of Telecommunications,[15] law enforcement authorities (both investigative and prosecutorial), all financial supervisors, sometimes the tax administration, the FIU, and industry and professional bodies. Apart from resolving potential difficulties in implementation and otherwise paving the way for cooperation at an operational level, these bodies also may have a formal or informal role in preparing and reviewing draft legislation that is relevant to branchless banking. This input and commentary from the most important stakeholders at the highest level may well facilitate a smooth passage of pending draft legislation.

Coordinate with other supervisors. When supervisors have been granted the power to issue lower supervisory regulations to implement formal legislation, they must coordinate their efforts with those of other supervisors to determine how those regulations are drafted and implemented. This is particularly important for m-money where the primary regulator/supervisor (namely, a ministry of telecommunications) is not necessarily the one in charge of supervising m-money, as observed in many visited countries; in practice, indeed, the central bank—or any other financial supervisory agency—is vested with the power to regulate and oversee m-money providers.

Coordinate with the FIU. Given the expertise of FIUs in the area of AML/CFT, and the fact that they are on the front line in discovering new trends and methods in the domestic domain, there is a valid reason for jurisdictions to make the FIU a key partner in the cooperation mechanism mentioned above. By conducting typologies and research exercises, the FIU can help m-money regulators determine areas of low risk that might justify relaxed AML/CFT requirements. The FIU can also provide basic training for those supervisors or other authorities who are new to the area of AML/CFT and who need a standard introduction. Conversely, of course, the FIU itself may carry out some supervisory tasks and may need training in how to conduct on-site inspections in the particular realm of m-money.[16]

Coordinate with the industry. Regulators and policy makers need to create sufficient certainty in legal and regulatory AML/CFT frameworks to enable the mobile banking ecosystem to develop. Active collaboration among financial and telecom regulators, financial institutions, mobile operators, and handset manufacturers will facilitate a high level of certainty. M-money challenges regulators to respond appropriately and with sufficient flexibility to new issues that appear to extend beyond their traditional domains of expertise. Engagement with the industry will help policy makers and regulators understand constraints that are specific to m-money providers with diverging interests.

Supervising and Enforcing
The primary responsibilities of any AML/CFT supervisor consist of monitoring and enforcing compliance with AML/CFT laws and regulations, and ensuring an equitable regulatory environment to promote fair competition in the financial sector. In this regard, emergence of m-money has posed new challenges to supervisors who have to deal with a new category of role players (namely, MNOs), new products (e-wallets and cell phone banking services), and new customers (unbanked or underbanked populations). Jurisdictions may wish to consider the following steps to ensure appropriate supervision and enforcement.

Determine an organizational model that ensures effective m-money oversight. It is the responsibility of each jurisdiction to devise and establish its own organizational framework for AML/CFT supervision. Neither the Basel Committee on Banking Supervision's core principles for effective banking supervision nor the FATF's international standards provide any guidance on which type of model or supervisory arrangement a country should use or which type is more effective than any other. Decisions to adopt a particular model or supervisory arrangement may be influenced by the country's own context—for example, specific features of the domestic financial system, the powers and resources of existing authorities, and its AML/CFT priorities.

During fieldwork, the authors found that several countries where m-money is booming have chosen the central bank as the primary authority to regulate and supervise MNOs. This model produces a number of benefits. First, central banks have knowledge of and regulatory capacity for payment systems, and they play a pivotal role in maintaining public confidence in money. Second, the staff is usually both highly skilled and knowledgeable about assessing risks in banks and about policies and procedures for managing those risks. Third, ML/TF risks are monitored like other types of compliance risks for which bank supervisors are responsible. Fourth, financial supervisors know how banks operate and they understand the products and services being offered; this knowledge is key to understanding the m-money ecosystem and its related risks.

That model is certainly the most relevant one. However, attention should be given to the following issues. Because of prudential concerns, bank supervisors may not give AML/CFT the same priority as governments would give the issue, or they may not have sufficient resources to do so—especially considering how the growth of m-money is increasing the number of supervised entities. Consequently, compliance issues may get neither the quantity nor the quality of attention that is required.

Countries should also make sure that vesting central banks with supervisory power over m-money providers, including AML/CFT matters, does not contradict or undermine the supervisory responsibilities that may have been delegated to the FIU. Supervision of AML/CFT compliance in some countries is trusted to the FIU only, whereas oversight of other types of issues falls under the umbrella of the financial supervisor. Another key element to consider is the role to be assigned to the authorities in charge of overseeing payment services. Although authorities who are responsible for AML/CFT bear responsibility for mobile operators who provide payment services, authorities supervising payment services may also have an AML/CFT responsibility. In the majority of countries, both functions are located with the central bank because it is the authority responsible for financial stability. However, there is a deep debate regarding appropriate ways to regulate and coordinate these different but overlapping responsibilities within the same authority.[17]

Promote a clear and effective supervisory regime for m-money providers. Supervising the AML/CFT compliance of MNOs is a new topic, and jurisdictions are just beginning to look into it. In a growing number of countries, authorities are devoting more and more attention to the efficiency and efficacy of production, distribution, and use of payment instruments (García 2008). With very few exceptions, however, m-money is not yet prudentially supervised. Supervisors have uneven levels of familiarity with m-money and, until recently, many were not well versed on the implications of innovative branchless banking and other e-money concepts. Lack of resources, limited experience with AML/CFT issues, and an unstable regulatory regime for m-money may seriously hamper effective supervision.

Regardless of who is the primary supervisor for AML/CFT compliance in the m-money industry, examiners will have to be trusted with the same responsibilities and should be able to carry out the same tasks as they would for any type of financial institution. In effect, as contemplated in FATF Recommendation 29, supervisors should have adequate powers to monitor and ensure compliance by financial institutions with requirements to combat ML/TF, including the authority to conduct inspections. Supervisors must not be hampered by any kind of bank secrecy laws that could restrict access to relevant information.[18] The legal means by which the supervisor obtains access to required information is not important, as long as the supervisor can access comprehensive information in a timely manner. The supervisor, therefore, should enjoy unrestricted access to information required for the proper execution of its functions.

As a result, jurisdictions should empower m-money supervisors to compel production from all kinds of providers of any information relevant to monitoring AML/CFT compliance. They should be entitled to enter an m-money operator's premises (including telecoms) at reasonable times to conduct on-site inspections. Supervisors should also access clients' so-called personally identifiable information (PII) that includes names, copies of identification card or number and other identity-related documents (such as a utility bill, if available), correspondence with the provider, and the m-money account balance.

As part of the monitoring process, the supervisor should also be able to determine if the provider's process for filing STRs is sufficient to satisfy its reporting obligations. Supervisors should be allowed to access STR files when performing on-site supervision.[19]

That said, things might be more complicated to implement in practice. Even though nonbank m-money providers should be treated like any other financial provider, it remains unclear whether financial examiners will have access to sensitive information like SMS and other text messages related to m-money transactions. In most of the business models, financial transactions flow across networks through SMS sent by m-money customers; in other words, the SMS is an integral part of the operation. Because prudential examiners need to access the widest range of meaningful information to fulfill their mandates as supervisors, a question remains about whether they are allowed to access SMS when sampling transactions. Regulators will have to clarify the perimeters of data that are available to financial examiners in the particular context of m-money. Some communications data—such as the content of calls—will not be accessible because of privacy laws.

Jurisdictions will also have to address the issue of supervision in the case of cross-border mobile remittances, where the delineation between home and host supervision is blurred. In effect, these services involve three regulatory spaces: (1) that of the sender, (2) that of the receiver, and (3) the international regulations that apply to international remittances. Countries are advised to engage in discussions with foreign supervisors.

Oversight of retail outlets that partner with banks and nonbanks also should be considered for AML/CFT purposes. In countries where m-money providers (whether banks or telecoms) are allowed to use retail outlets to deliver services (such as cash-in/cash-out), it should be determined whether the latter may be subject to on-site supervision. In some countries, the outsourcer is subject to supervision by the central bank, and the bank is held responsible for the retail outlet's actions. As a result, supervisors focus on the outsourcer only. This does not preclude the central bank (or any other relevant authority) from occasionally performing some controls in situ to ensure retail outlets comply with their obligations as well.[20] In Mexico, for example, the National Banking and Securities Commission has the prerogative to conduct on-site inspections of retail outlets when deemed necessary.

Jurisdictions should also provide AML/CFT supervisors with the financial, human, and technical resources they need. These resources should correspond with the size, level of risk, and quality of AML/CFT controls in the m-money sector. Unfortunately, scarcity of resources is a widespread problem in almost all jurisdictions, and the emergence of new

financial products like m-money will make this problem even more challenging. The scarcity can be multifaceted, limiting both the numbers of
technically skilled people and the funds to train them. It is vital that
AML/CFT regimes be effective; for that to occur, sufficient funding must
be provided, as required by international standards.[21] In this regard, the
status and type of license that will be granted to a nonbank's retail outlets will have considerable impact on the supervisory perimeter and, as a
result, on the capacity for supervisors to assume oversight responsibilities
for multiple entities.

Grant relevant authorities the power to make binding rules. The
AML/CFT supervisor, as the body that evaluates nonbank's and bank's
compliance, is in the best position to determine compliance requirements
and to issue rules, regulations, and other forms of guidance. As mentioned
earlier, the central bank is the supervisor for m-money in many countries
and, as a result, already has full power to make rules. In countries where
there is a different arrangement, supervisors may require specific authority to do this, and the jurisdiction should take appropriate measures,
including legislative action, to provide it.

Rules and regulations should be issued in a clear, precise manner so the
meaning of such rules can be easily understood by those who must comply with them—in particular, MNOs. Insufficient clarity may jeopardize
effective implementation of AML/CFT principles in the branchless banking industry and create an unequal business environment. In turn, that
will lead to confusion and to an uneven application of the rules, keeping
the supervisory body from attaining its ultimate compliance objective.
Both public and private sectors benefit when supervisors and financial
institutions collaborate to produce clear rules and regulations.

Define an enforceable sanctioning regime for m-money. Supervisors
should have the power to impose adequate administrative sanctions on
banks and nonbanks that fail to comply with AML/CFT requirements.
Understandably, different jurisdictions adopt different sanctioning
regimes that fit their particular legal traditions, constitutional requirements, and systems of government. Although each country is free to
determine its own regulatory, supervisory, and enforcement systems, one
consistent principle is that all countries—developing and developed—
should adopt a minimum set of measures to sanction m-money providers
who fail to comply with their AML/CFT obligations.

Furthermore, this set of measures should meet FATF requirements as
promulgated in Recommendations 17 and 29. Notably, sanctions should be

effective, dissuasive, and proportionate to the seriousness of the situation. To ensure an equitable regulatory environment, as advocated by the MNO industry, sanctions for not complying with AML/CFT rules should be the same, irrespective of the provider. This also means that equality before the law implies equal treatment in similar circumstances, and this equality is to be reflected not only in the regulations, but also in individual cases. All other things being equal, a nonbank's failure to report suspicious activity to the FIU should not be penalized by a $100,000 fine when a bank would receive a mere warning from the banking supervisor for a similar failure. Although a binding rule at a higher level already goes some way toward securing equality, supervisors must ensure that equality is maintained at the most detailed level and that similar infringements committed by entities supervised by different supervisors receive similar penalties.

Attention should also be paid to possible conflicting situations where the supervision of MNOs is trusted to the central bank and the enforcement power is given to the competent ministry (for example, the Ministry of Finance or the Ministry of Telecommunications).

Jurisdictions should take enforcement seriously—not only to protect the integrity of the system, but also to balance possible weaknesses in other parts of their AML/CFT regime. A relaxed identification regime for m-money may receive a low rating in an evaluation report if there is no evidence of a commitment to enforcement of the relevant obligations.

Provide AML/CFT training to m-money supervisors. AML/CFT compliance supervision in m-money services is a new issue for financial institution examiners. Employees at all levels need continual training on the application of new laws and preventive measures, as well as on new interpretations of existing matters. In addition, training programs need to keep abreast of ever-changing ML/TF techniques and tactics. In this regard, there is clearly a need for broad support and capacity building, especially because weak capacity of supervisors is one of the enduring country risks, as highlighted in chapter 2. Multilateral bodies and donors have a meaningful role to play in this regard.

AML/CFT Guidance for M-Money Providers

Although complying with AML/CFT regulations is standard practice for banks, these rules are not traditionally familiar to MNOs or third-party providers. This section focuses on some of the key aspects of AML/CFT to which m-money providers should pay attention.

Internal Policies

M-money providers should have clear, accessible, and well-documented internal policies and procedures that address any integrity risks arising from their customers. Appropriate internal policies and frameworks will enable providers to comply with relevant regulations as imposed by the national regulator and will help them avoid any reputational risks they may incur as a result of consumer fraud or even ML or TF occurring through their systems. All compliance officers of the m-money providers should be trained on these company policies and held accountable to them if there is any breach of compliance obligations. The quality and depth of the internal compliance policies should be shared with national supervisors for relevant feedback and suggestions. Well-crafted policies that set high standards of operation will prompt national authorities to have greater confidence in the providers. In some jurisdictions, all relevant formal legislation that governs m-money providers—such as AML/CFT laws, e-money laws, or payment systems laws—may not have been formally enacted. This situation greatly increases the importance of having well-documented internal policies in place for m-money providers willing to conduct business in these jurisdictions, and these policies must be adequately implemented and enforced by the organization's compliance officers.

Internal policies developed by m-money providers should revolve around the following practices:

Develop and modify policies through proactive dialogue with the national regulator and partner entities. It appears that a good practice for an m-money provider is to develop an internal AML/CFT policy at the same time it is developing its own m-money product. When Safaricom was established in Kenya, for example, the company developed its own internal AML policy and submitted it to the regulators before formal legislation governing m-money was enacted and before its m-money service was deployed commercially. Although all countries should have formal legislation governing m-money before the industry begins to operate, Safaricom was able to secure approval to operate prior to the passage of such legislation because of the regulator's confidence in Safaricom's internal integrity and risk mitigation frameworks. Furthermore, when formal legislation governing m-money began to be enacted in Kenya, Safaricom was in a position to advise the regulators designing the formal legislation because the company already had assessed the market and its conditions via its own internal analysis and had addressed them in its internal policies.

When it developed its internal policies, Safaricom trained its staff members on AML principles so that they were certified to oversee the risk side of the product. This helped fully prepare the staff for deployment of the m-money service, from pilot stage to commercial operation. Thus, the proactive and timely approach in developing its internal policies helped the company create a climate of dialogue and confidence among all relevant stakeholders, including prospective customers, the internal Safaricom staff, and the national regulator.

If a provider is partnering with another entity for the m-money services, it is also important that the internal AML/CFT policies of the two providers are shared and aligned effectively with each other. For example, when there are potential discrepancies between the internal AML/CFT procedures of two e-money issuers, fieldwork has shown that the more conservative of the two options is often chosen. For cross-border mobile transactions, however, the internal AML/CFT procedures of two e-money issuers may not need to align exactly because they are usually supervised and regulated by two institutions in two countries that typically specify different requirements. This practice has also been observed in regard to the internal AML/CFT policies of e-money issuers' retail outlets (such as Western Union in Malaysia) when they have partnered with other entities for the m-money service.

Survey work to modify internal policies on the basis of a jurisdiction's conditions should also be undertaken. Fieldwork has shown that surveys on the part of the provider led to alterations in national regulatory policies, taking into account the interests of the m-money provider.[22]

Develop and modify policies using an assessment of the risk levels for existing and prospective customers. An assessment of the risk level of each existing and prospective customer is essential, especially if the provider is aiming to expand into new regions, either domestically or cross-border. For example, the provider can apply a graduated customer acceptance policy, which requires more extensive CDD procedures for customers who present a higher risk. When a customer is considered to represent a lower risk of ML or TF, the minimum standard of due diligence may be employed (if that is permitted by domestic law). After these customer acceptance policies and procedures are assessed on the basis of customer risk, they should be clear and well-documented for all employees—especially compliance officers. Employees should be encouraged to offer feedback and suggestions.

Design policies to ensure that companies' compliance officers have an appropriate AML/CFT focus. During fieldwork, it became apparent that many of the m-money providers—especially those in developing economies—are focused more on meeting prudential, systemic, and other requirements than on meeting AML/CFT obligations. Compliance officers of providers, therefore, may be focused more on mitigating other, non-AML/CFT–related risk.[23] To ensure an appropriate focus, regulation should require providers to adopt comprehensive AML/CFT policies. It should also require compliance officers to be adequately trained on AML/CFT to ensure that they understand the importance of AML/CFT compliance, especially in relation to the company's legal liability and reputation.

Risk Management Practices and Transaction Monitoring

Regulation should support appropriate risk management practices and transaction monitoring.

Support m-money services with appropriate governance and risk management practices. Throughout a business relationship, m-money providers (both banks and nonbanks) must conduct ongoing due diligence on the business relationship and must scrutinize transactions undertaken by their customers. As prescribed by the FATF, they have to ensure that the transactions being conducted are consistent with the institution's knowledge of the customer and his or her business and risk profiles, including the source of funds when necessary. As a result, it is the duty of m-money providers to establish clear governance and risk management practices. They also must ensure that regulators responsible for AML/CFT are made aware of their AML/CFT controls and grant approval when necessary.

Develop internal solutions for ML/TF transaction monitoring. Rapid adoption of m-money may generate risks. Even though these risks are low (given the tight limits for transactions combined with stronger monitoring), providers should put in place flagging mechanisms that help detect suspicious activities, according to rules preconfigured in the system. Transaction monitoring is an important means of closely scrutinizing potential criminal activities that might arise from this new type of transaction channel. The ability to trace and monitor transactions is central to AML/CFT efforts.

As stated by the financial industry, "compliance with AML/CFT obligations is a core obligation and the responsibility of any entity participating in the financial services chain, not only because of the societal risk engendered but also because non-compliance by any provider in the chain will cast a shadow on the whole financial industry" (WSBI 2009, p. 1). Implementing the right transaction monitoring solution provides several benefits to the provider, demonstrates higher assurance to customers, and may lead to greater adoption of these services.

In this regard, the challenge faced by mobile providers (especially telecoms) is to adapt their existing transaction monitoring platforms to cover specific ML/TF risks. Providers have already installed technical solutions to combat many forms of potential abuse (for example, firewalls; encryption mechanisms, including those for airtime interface; infrastructure attack monitoring, Uniform Resource Locator filters; application security controls), but ML/TF via m-money constitutes a new class of potential risk. To address this new risk and to conform with international standards, m-money providers will have to add new features to detect suspicious activity specifically related to ML/TF.

Fieldwork has shown that transaction flagging enables an MNO's system to reject a transaction request or to impose artificial delays on suspicious transactions. This approach is an automated facility based on the flags placed on the individual parties in the transaction and the flow of funds between them. In addition to a fully automatic approach, transaction flagging can be used to request manual intervention. Rather than stopping a possible illicit transfer of electronic funds, an operator may be alerted automatically to prevent the receiver from accessing the transmitted funds either by withdrawing cash or sending the money on to a third party. The operator can interrupt the transaction either by freezing the account or by placing the funds in question in a "pending" state. The transaction will be suspended until the user has provided further verification and adequately accounted for the patterns that prompted the alert and suspension.

The provider's information technology system will have to generate periodic reports (daily and monthly) highlighting unusual activity related to m-money operations. Each provider must determine specific internal rules that explain the use of these reports and identify staff accountable for generating, processing, and analyzing them. Guidance will also be needed to establish the alert mechanism when something suspicious has occurred.

Detecting patterns of suspicious activities among thousands of low-value transactions will not be easy, given current approaches. In practice, current approaches trigger suspicions in large and complex transactions, not in micro or nano operations. Conversely, one could say that placing limits on transactions restricts the usefulness of the m-money product for either ML or TF and makes unusual transactions more apparent. Whatever may be the case, mobile providers will have to set up an internal monitoring system to increase the likelihood that any deviant behavior will be spotted. As described in chapter 2, fieldwork has shown that mobile operators in many of the visited countries are equipped with internal systems and have adopted risk management procedures recommended by the FATF standards, including limitations on the number, types, and amount of transactions that can be performed.

Clarify the role of the AP in overseeing AML/CFT procedures. As defined in chapter 1, the AP is the entity responsible for account management and tasked with monitoring AML/CFT procedures across the activity chain. Although account maintenance and recordkeeping may be closely aligned, the entity managing the account records in some programs may not be the party that actually does the accounting (when accounting is outsourced to a third-party processor) and may have no authority or ability to monitor other aspects of the value chain. This is why some laws relating to payment systems (for example, multiparty programs such as e-money transactions[24]) refer to the role of "program operator" or the equivalent to whom the responsibility of core regulatory compliance is assigned—roles that may not be the account manager or even the issuer. Perhaps rather than linking AML/CFT monitoring to the AP, each program should include a role charged with the capacity and responsibility to oversee AML/CFT across the chain.

Establish watch-list screening. One important element of a transaction monitoring process is the use of watch lists. There are different categories of lists. First, as required by FATF standards and international conventions, countries should distribute lists published periodically by the United Nations Security Council Committee, established pursuant to Resolution 1267 (also known as the Al-Qaida and Taliban Sanctions Committee). The lists designate natural and legal persons thought to be associated with these terrorist groups, and all countries are obliged to freeze all funds belonging to or controlled by them. To that end, jurisdictions should ensure that new providers such as telecoms and nonfinancial m-money providers regularly receive these lists.[25] To ensure maximum effectiveness, companies should include the names of terrorists in their internal customer database to automatically raise red flags when an applicant whose name matches the list is encountered. In this way, immediate action can be taken.

A second type of watch list is an internal database that m-money providers (especially telecoms) can design specifically to alert the staff to certain customers who deserve enhanced scrutiny or should be prohibited from accessing services. Although the establishment of such lists is consistent with internal monitoring requirements, using them externally may raise legitimate concerns. Some designers of m-money models have explored the possibility of sharing data between providers to enhance the integrity of the system. In most jurisdictions, sharing the name, account number, and mobile number (the PII) is strictly prohibited by privacy laws, even between similar entities (bank to bank and telecom to telecom).

Therefore, if telecom A notices something suspicious about mobile number 123 on its network, it should be able to send out an alert to telecoms B and C without revealing the PII of the account holder. Mobile number 123 could then be put on a shared watch list and assigned risk level 1. If mobile number 123 shows up again as a suspicious transaction origin (on telecom A) or destination (on telecoms A, B, or C), its risk level rises to 2. The higher the risk level, the more scrutiny is applied to any transaction involving that number.

Some AML/CFT experts have advocated creating a single database to be shared between telecoms and banks. Others have envisioned the possibility of creating a centralized system where all m-money users' information would be regulated by a neutral third party or a government regulatory body who would provide access to various entities, according to business needs and specific credentials. These solutions may be additional tools for combating ML/TF, but their implementation may trigger a contentious debate about consumer protection and privacy rights. Countries wishing to follow these routes should ensure the routes are compatible with their privacy laws.

Reporting Obligations

Because STRs play a key role in the AML/CFT system, it is important to ensure that all parties involved in the provision of m-money services cooperate to share information appropriately, that reporting lines and responsibilities are clear, and that the parties have sufficient capacity to monitor transactions and customers to ensure that suspicious behavior is reported as required. Regulated institutions are required to report suspicious transactions to the government, generally by filing STRs with the national FIU.

In the context of m-money, as many as four types of functions may be relevant to the identification of suspicious transactions: agency, account record provision, mobile telecommunications provision, and settling banking services. Depending on national regulations, these four functions may be combined in as few as two role players or spread among four different role players.

As explained earlier, the MNO may also be the AP in some countries. If the AP is not a bank, the m-money program will have to involve a settling bank to hold the pooled account and the bank accounts of the retail outlets. Although m-money programs may not involve many role players, it is helpful here to focus on a more complex model with four different role players for purposes of guidance.

A framework that draws on the strengths of all four role players will provide the best-quality reports. This can be accomplished by taking the actions described in the following paragraphs.

Charge the AP with identifying and reporting suspicious transactions. The AP should be required to maintain appropriate monitoring systems that enable it to compare a customer's transactions with the customer's profile; compare the customer's transactions and transaction patterns with those of similar customers; and check a customer's name against sanctions lists, lists of politically exposed persons, and other relevant information. A manual system may be appropriate for small programs, but those with large numbers of clients will probably require sophisticated information technology systems to ensure appropriate monitoring. The AP should also have the investigative capacity that enables it to follow up on STRs received from its retail outlets. Where the AP determines that a customer is suspicious or engaged in a suspicious transaction, it should be required to file a report with the FIU.

Require retail outlets to report their suspicions to the AP. Retail outlets deal directly with the clients and may be able to identify suspicious behavior. However, they are not necessarily able to file a high-quality report with the FIU because they do not have access to the customer's records and other relevant information that should be included in a report. Therefore, it is advisable to require retail outlets to report their suspicions to the AP. This reporting obligation may be imposed contractually by the agency agreement. The AP must be required to provide initial and ongoing training to retail outlets to help them identify and report such behavior. The AP must also be required to monitor the ability of retail outlets to report suspicious behavior and to take corrective action when performance weaknesses are identified (including terminating the agency agreement).

The retail outlet's main role in respect to suspicious transactions is to draw the AP's attention to a customer's questionable behavior, thereby triggering a review of that customer's transaction patterns and profile. The AP's reporting rules for retail outlets must be clear and practical, and it must be easy for the retail outlet to file the required reports with the AP. The provider should consider all the relevant information and determine whether there are sufficient grounds for submitting an STR to the FIU.

Ensure appropriate information-sharing arrangements between parties, when required. The general AML/CFT framework of a country may render more than one m-money party responsible for filing STRs. When a settling bank is involved, the bank may be able to identify suspicious transaction patterns relating to retail outlets. General AML/CFT laws will require the bank to report any suspicious transactions directly to the FIU. A nonbank AP, however, is the main manager of retail outlets' ML/TF risk and is responsible for filing STRs. In such a case, the regulator may wish to ensure that all such parties are able to share sufficient information to ensure that AML/CFT risk is properly managed, that STRs are comprehensive, and that multiple STRs are not filed unnecessarily. Such information-sharing mechanisms must comply with the local laws and should comply with international standards, especially those relating to the protection of customers' privacy.

Enable the FIU to access additional information when a report is investigated. It is crucial to set explicit rules governing appropriate and prompt access by investigators to data and information held by the retail outlet, the AP, the MNO, and the settling bank. The STR framework also should reflect the general rules regarding suspicious transactions envisaged in the FATF recommendations, including the protection of parties who file or contribute to such a report and the prohibition against disclosure of potential or actual reports.

Clarify the breakdown of reporting duties when m-money services are provided by international companies. When an international company is one of the service providers, especially when it is the AP, general STR filing duties may be divided among group, regional, and local officers. Where such a splitting of functions is relevant, it is important to clarify the obligations of each party and to ensure that they support effective submission of STRs to the local FIU.

Set appropriate rules regarding the information to be reported. M-money channels also hold communications data. These data may be relevant to the investigation of ML/TF, but normally they will be protected by privacy and general communications laws. It is important to strike an appropriate balance that ensures the reporting of key information in the STR, access by investigators to relevant data, and protection of citizens' privacy.

Set up clear internal reporting mechanisms by each m-money provider. Last, m-money providers—particularly MNOs—should bear in mind that reporting suspicions is not a one-shot task. Any additional suspicious activity that is linked to the original report should be reported as well. The fact that an STR was made does not exempt the provider from filling out additional reports when new suspicions arise regarding the same customer or transaction. The reporting institution should put the reported m-money account under close scrutiny. Also, the AML/CFT reporting officer will have to remind the reporting entity's relevant staff members of their obligation not to tip off the client and to report any further forms of suspicious activity.

Staff and Retail Outlet Training and Awareness

Many staff members of business entities in an m-money program play an indispensable role in mitigating ML/TF risk. It is important to outline their responsibilities and to ensure that they are empowered to meet their obligations.

Provide the staff with continuous AML/CFT training. As noted before, the AP should take the lead in ensuring the AML/CFT policies of the m-money system. This includes making certain that relevant employees and partners (including retail outlets) in the system are adequately trained to handle ML/TF issues. It is the AP's duty to monitor this training and check that the lessons learned are being properly implemented. The AP should also provide employees and partners who handle m-money with AML/CFT guidelines and best practices.

Continuous education in the area of AML/CFT will be necessary as the market continues to change and as regulations adjust to the level of risk faced. Such training should focus on procedures to identify possible criminal abuse as well to report it to the designated compliance officer. Online training solutions are a good tool to keep the staff abreast of AML/CFT requirements.

Some providers, including nonbanks, use testing to certify that an employee or partner is fit to implement the AML/CFT procedures. Such testing helps the organization monitor the effectiveness of its training and the strength of its preventive measures against ML/TF.

Ensure that training targets all staff involved in m-money, at all levels of responsibility. Training should serve the following specific goals:

- All employees know the identity and purpose of the compliance officer.
- Employees receive clear guidance on spotting suspicious activity and reporting it to the compliance officer or that officer's deputy.
- All AML/CFT policies, procedures, and risk assessments are available in written form to all employees at all times. These policies help demonstrate that the company takes its AML/CFT obligations seriously.
- Employees know where to go for more help or information about the AML/CFT regulations and policies.
- Senior management involved in m-money activities complete more detailed AML/CFT training through a professional external body.
- The AML/CFT officer completes a specialist AML/CFT qualification.

Providers should always keep in mind that successful money transfer systems require constant management and ongoing education of all people involved in the m-money chain. In one case observed during field-work, an m-money company created a system that enables in-the-field AML/CFT trainers to log into the system to view the current training status of every employee and issue refresher training reminders via SMS or e-mail.

National authorities should develop the mandated AML/CFT training curriculum for m-money providers and their retail outlets in consultation with all relevant stakeholders, including the m-money providers. This will ensure that the required training takes into account the cost and implementation capacity of the provider. Furthermore, national authorities may wish to ensure that their mandated training is user friendly. As an example, the financial supervisory authority in one jurisdiction where m-money operates allows the m-money provider's retail outlets to be accredited in AML/CFT requirements online through a secure Web site.

Recommendations for the FATF

The FATF recommendations are flexible and the risk-based principles create an appropriate general standards framework for the development of low-risk m-money services. Since 2007, the FATF has issued various guidance notes on the risk-based approach and has provided guidance to low-capacity countries. Despite these positive efforts, studies and interviews conducted during the fieldwork still reflect a measure of policy and regulatory uncertainty. Policy makers and regulators who are keen to promote financial inclusion via m-money models are uncertain whether specific elements of m-money regulatory models will meet approval when their countries undergo a mutual evaluation for compliance with the FATF standards. Some regulators are hesitant to approve certain models, and others are approving only very conservative models that will have a limited impact on the market. The uncertainty is impeding regulatory and market development progress.

During the fieldwork undertaken for this project, it became clear that regulatory intervention is also required to prevent the risk of market distortion. A number of new and emerging m-money providers are competing in this new space, and their models differ markedly. As a result, it is urgent that regulators provide an equitable competitive environment to prevent market distortion. This is important in both national and cross-border contexts, because cross-border m-money services (especially remittance services) are expanding. An equitable domestic and international environment will support the development of appropriate m-money services.

The FATF standards are general in their application, and it is appropriate for the FATF to refrain from providing detailed guidance relating to specific models. However, the FATF also must offer sufficient guidance on key principles to ensure that uncertainty about the applications of its recommendations do not impede appropriate regulatory responses. Clearer principles will help assessors follow a more consistent approach when countries undergo mutual evaluations within the FATF framework. (See Appendix A for further details.)

M-Money Guidance
The issue of financial inclusion is high on the 2010–11 FATF agenda. As a result, several initiatives have been taken to explore solutions that would favor better access to financial services by the poor without compromising financial integrity. Working groups involving FATF members

and observers have been established recently, notably to revisit some key recommendations (such as Recommendation 5 on KYC) and to introduce more flexibility. These initiatives should be encouraged and supported. In this regard, further consideration should be given to the practices described in the following paragraphs.

Provide further guidance regarding the identification of low-risk transactions and customers. Although FATF guidance regarding the identification of high-risk transactions and customers is well developed, less guidance was provided to assist regulators in identifying transactions and customers that pose a low risk. The FATF identifies some examples of low-risk transactions and customers, but these are not relevant to the financial inclusion environment. The FATF recognizes that low transaction value may indicate low ML risk, but also cautions that low-value transactions may be particularly relevant to TF risk. Regulators need to design models that address both ML and TF risks and identify low-risk transactions and clients from both perspectives. Clearer principles that can guide regulators and regulated institutions to distinguish between higher- and lower-risk categories are required to facilitate the development of appropriate business and regulatory models.

Identify conditions under which m-money can be supported as a tool to mitigate overall ML/TF risk. M-money generally poses a lower ML/TF risk than do cash-based transactions. In some countries, the m-money business model may pose less risk than cash, but local conditions may not allow for the imposition of sufficient controls to ensure that the particular model poses only an insignificant measure of risk. For instance, the inherent risk of the model may be assessed at a medium level, but that level may still be significantly lower than the risk posed by cash. M-money is particularly useful in helping users move from cash-based, informal transactions to formal financial services. The regulator may wish to harness this ability of the m-money model to strategically lessen overall ML/TF risk in the system. Doing so will advance the objectives and the spirit of the FATF recommendations, but it is not clear whether such an effort would attract a negative rating when the country undergoes a mutual evaluation. Clarity on the FATF's approach regarding the use of m-money and other financial inclusion initiatives to decrease overall ML/TF risk in a country (including any applicable conditions for such use) is required.

Clarify appropriate CDD measures within the low-risk context.
Additional guidance should be issued regarding appropriate CDD measures in a low-risk context, especially in countries with lower levels of capacity. This guidance should include the following:

- Conditions for partial exemption from CDD requirements in low-risk cases should be considered and better explained.
- The FATF uses monetary limits to define and mitigate the risks of single transactions and wire transfers, but it is unclear whether monetary limits on account-based products are viewed as performing a similar risk mitigation function. The authors believe they are doing so, but that should be made clear in the FATF framework.
- Principles relating to appropriate CDD measures in the context of financial inclusion should be considered, especially relating to identification and verification of customers and beneficial owners in low-capacity countries. Customers may be identified in these countries, but their identifying data cannot necessarily be verified with ease or certainty.
- Additional guidance on the use of retail outlets and non–face-to-face mechanisms to interact with customers in a low-risk context in low-capacity countries is also required. Many financial inclusion business models are only viable if they can operate in a branchless environment, often by using small retail outlets. These outlets do not have the capacity to perform functions that can be performed by banks and their employees. The duties of these retail outlets and principles regarding CDD performed on non–face-to-face customers in a low-risk context should be explained.

M-Money, Financial Inclusion, and the FATF

M-money, financial inclusion, and AML/CFT are dynamic topics in their own right. Their intersection in the context of the FATF framework will continue to prompt new questions. More clearly defined principles will help the FATF address those questions. In addition, it is important to consider a framework for the ongoing engagement of these and related issues, especially in the FATF working groups.

Issue a risk-based guidance report on m-money. In June 2007, the FATF adopted a series of risk-based approach guidance notes for specific regulated sectors to assist both public authorities and the private sector in applying a risk-based approach to AML/CFT. The guidance notes support the development of a common understanding of the risk-based approach; outline the high-level principles involved in applying the risk-based approach, and indicate good practice in the design and implementation of an effective risk-based approach. They set out key elements of an effective risk-based approach and identify the types of issues that both public authorities and financial institutions may wish to consider when using a risk-based model (FATF 2007, para. 1.3).

The FATF should issue regulatory and supervisory guidance that goes beyond assessing potential integrity risks in new payment methods that support increased financial inclusion. In this regard, a separate guidance note for m-money models is advisable.

Be sensitive and responsive to inappropriate compliance procedures. The FATF recommendations set minimum standards of action against ML and TF. The mutual evaluation process is designed to identify a failure to meet these standards. It is not designed to note and evaluate steps taken that exceed the minimum standards. A country that designs and implements an inappropriately strict and rigid AML/CFT compliance framework may exceed the FATF standards, but undermine financial inclusion. The FATF president for 2009–10, Paul Vlaanderen, accepted the relationship between financial inclusion and the task force's financial integrity objectives: if AML/CFT controls are implemented in a manner that unnecessarily undermines financial inclusion, the controls also undermine the FATF's broader integrity objectives. Therefore, the FATF must consider ways to monitor the impact of a country's AML/CFT controls on financial inclusion and must provide guidance on appropriate supportive and corrective actions. The authors believe, for example, that the impact of a too-stringent compliance framework should be considered as part of the mutual evaluation methodology. It is important that supervisors and policy makers are guided to be sensitive to such unintended consequences of inappropriate AML/CFT controls (Chatain et al. 2009).

Notes

1. For a discussion of the multiple components of AML/CFT regulation, see Schott (2006).
2. The range of elements were analyzed during the Global Leadership Seminar on Regulating Branchless Banking, held in Windsor, United Kingdom, on March 8, 2010. The seminar was hosted by the Consultative Group to Assist the Poor, the U.K. Department for International Development, and the Alliance for Financial Inclusion.

3. The FATF identifies financial institutions to be covered by AML/CFT requirements on the basis of the activities or operations that are carried out in those institutions.

4. It should be noted, however, that some mobile operators are obtaining banking licenses that enable them to provide a wider range of financial services. The banking license application process is much more complex than for an e-money license. This justifies strict guidelines and strict procedures that ensure that MNO applicants are screened as rigorously as any other applicant for a banking license.

5. Other risks to consider include delivery channel risks and provider-related risks—for example, the nature of the business, its size, and the nature of the client relationship.

6. Some countries have even been challenging the risk-based approach because it does not really address the particularities of low-capacity countries.

7. There are two conditions that must be met to enable the partial or total exemption of certain financial activities from AML/CFT obligations. It can be done (1) in strictly limited and justified circumstances and (2) when there is a proven low risk of money laundering. The FATF is working on elaborating further guidance in that area.

8. Here, we refer to the type of remittance services that are registered and monitored, as prescribed by FATF Special Recommendation VI.

9. This approach, however, requires a detailed assessment of risks.

10. Note that the FATF does not allow simplified measures in cases where there is a suspicion of money laundering or financing of terrorism.

11. See FATF (2008) for an identification of key recommendations for implementation by low-capacity countries.

12. Some countries, however, are considering subjecting retail outlets to AML/CFT through direct legal obligations.

13. If retail outlets are not directly regulated or indirectly regulated, as proposed in this book, there may be no legal basis for the supervisor to perform on-site visits to the retailer network. Countries should carefully consider this aspect.

14. Depending on the way it is structured, such a solution might prove costly, thereby increasing the overall cost of compliance.

15. According to fieldwork and information from CGAP, the Russian State Duma included representatives of all relevant public bodies when it created its branchless banking working group: the Ministry for Information Technologies and Communication, the Ministry of Finance, the Ministry of Economic Development, and relevant units of the Russian central bank.

16. In some jurisdictions, the FIU is the only authority vested with the power to supervise financial institutions for AML/CFT compliance, while the primary supervisors deal with the oversight of other types of prudential risks.

17. The majority view is (1) to put the burden of licensing (or registering) operators on the payment system overseer because the operators provide a payment service, and (2) either to transfer the AML/CFT responsibility to that overseer or to establish a coordination mechanism between the two functions or departments.

18. FATF Recommendation 4 states, "Countries should ensure that financial institution secrecy laws do not inhibit implementation of the FATF Recommendations."

19. Access to this information is contingent on permission under the national law. In some countries, STRs are accessible only to FIU staff, not to bank examiners of the financial supervisory authority.

20. This discussion assumes that the supervisory authority is legally authorized to oversee nonfinancial institutions like retail outlets.

21. In some countries, the AML/CFT supervisor commissions external auditors to conduct on-site work. This may be a reasonable option in jurisdictions where the supervisor does not have the in-house resources to do such work, although it may be difficult to find auditors with specific expertise in AML/CFT evaluations.

22. For example, for one Malaysia-based provider offering cross-border remittance services with the Philippines, it was found that Bank Negara Malaysia increased the maximum balance limit permissible in the e-wallet for m-money transfers after survey work and analysis was conducted by the provider. The original limit imposed by the bank's regulations on the e-wallet was RM 500, but it was increased to RM 1,500 upon request by the provider. The survey work was initially undertaken to assess the strength and relevance of the provider's internal AML policies and to see if there could be any modifications so more customers could be reached. Following the survey work, the provider argued that a large part of its potential customer base was neglected. It noted that financial access among overseas Filipino workers was hindered because the workers wished to increase the amount of remittances sent per transaction at the lowest possible cost, but the original limit incurred additional expense by forcing them to cash-in several times to send the larger amount. Hence, the bank was convinced that the revised larger limit was still safe and it didn't constrain the business interests of the m-money provider.

23. During fieldwork in one jurisdiction, researchers interviewed a compliance officer of an m-money provider who was not certain to which national entity STRs should be reported.

24. Examples of such laws include Indonesia's 2009 e-money regulations and Nigeria's 2009 mobile payment guidelines.

25. Typically, the central agency responsible for circulating these lists is the central bank, the banking supervisor, or the FIU.

References

Chatain, Pierre-Laurent, John McDowell, Cedric Mousset, Paul Allan Schott, and Emile van der Does de Willebois. 2009. *Preventing Money Laundering and Terrorist Financing: A Practical Guide for Bank Supervisors.* Washington, DC: World Bank.

FATF (Financial Action Task Force). 2007. "Guidance on the Risk-Based Approach to Combating Money Laundering and Terrorist Financing." Paris. http://www.fatf-gafi.org/dataoecd/43/46/38960576.pdf.

———. 2008. "Guidance on Capacity Building for Mutual Evaluations and Implementation of the FATF Standards Within Low Capacity Countries." Paris. http://www.oecd.org/dataoecd/61/28/40248726.pdf

García, José Antonio. 2008. "Regulating and Overseeing Mobile Payments: A Payment Systems Perspective." World Bank Group, Bangkok. http://siteresources.worldbank.org/INTAML/Resources/Regulating_and_Overseeing_Mobile_Payments.pdf.

Porteous, David. 2006. "The Enabling Environment for Mobile Banking in Africa." Report commissioned by the U.K. Department for International Development. Bankable Frontier Associates, Boston, MA.

Schott, Paul Allan. 2006. *Reference Guide to Anti-Money Laundering and Combating the Financing of Terrorism.* 2nd ed. and supplement on Special Recommendation IX. Washington, DC: World Bank.

WSBI (World Savings Banks Institute). 2009. "Integrity in Mobile Phone Financial Services: Contribution to the World Bank's Work in the Context of Working Paper No. 146." Unpublished position paper, Brussels.

The Interplay between Financial Inclusion and Compliance with Anti-Money Laundering and Combating the Financing of Terrorism Regulation: Key Issues for Consideration during Mutual Assessments

A mutual evaluation of a country's levels of compliance with the Financial Action Task Force (FATF) recommendations is undertaken in accordance with the FATF's anti-money laundering/combating the financing of terrorism (AML/CFT) methodology.[1] Currently, this methodology does not provide assessors with specific guidance on the assessment of elements that are unique to mobile money (m-money).

The authors believe it is important to better inform AML/CFT assessors as limited understanding of ways to apply the methodology in such a context can lead to excessive rigidity—at the expense of a thriving m-money industry and of financial inclusion. This discussion identifies matters for consideration that are relevant to m-money. It is not intended to formally complement the FATF methodology or to be a substitute for any part of it. But it does identify issues that assessors may consider within the broad framework of the current methodology and a number of matters that may be included when the methodology is revised.

The methodology prescribes an assessment process that is already time and resource intensive. Therefore, this discussion tries to be comprehensive in identifying relevant topics, without adding unduly to the burdens of countries being assessed or the assessors undertaking evaluations.

Background

In general terms, "financial inclusion" refers to access to appropriate financial products and services for everyone needing them, especially low-income populations. Many countries around the world are exploring ways to make appropriate financial services economically affordable and accessible to these populations. In various jurisdictions, however, many potential customers are unable to provide reliable documentary proof of personal data, such as evidence of their residential addresses or their identification cards. As a result, some of the concerned countries have tailored specific know-your-customer (KYC) regulations to facilitate the extension of financial services to people not currently served. These regulations often simplify customer due diligence (CDD) obligations regarding this particular segment of the population—in most cases, according explicitly or implicitly to the risk particular potential customers pose.

FATF assessors frequently debate the extent to which such simplified CDD regulations meet and advance the objectives of the international standards. The debates extend to the assessment of new role players in services that are targeted at the low-income segment of the population. The rapid development of m-money services has brought many nontraditional financial service providers, such as telecommunications companies (telecoms) and retail outlets, into the AML/CFT framework. AML/CFT evaluations, therefore, should consider whether these entities are relevant in a specific country. Because the FATF methodology does not provide explicit guidance on their assessment, assessors require guidance on AML/CFT and financial inclusion and on more detailed technical issues relating to m-money.

In that regard, the World Bank and a few FATF-style regional bodies (particularly, the FATF of South America—GAFISUD—) have started to explore what type of guidance assessors require to integrate financial inclusion questions into the assessment process. The following discussion is a contribution to that effort. It aims, in particular, to identify key questions that should be considered when assessing the conformity of m-money-related AML/CFT laws and controls to international standards.[2] After a general discussion of financial inclusion, matters relevant to FATF recommendations 5, 10, 13, 20, 23, 25, 26, 28, 29, 30, and 32 will be addressed.

Financial Inclusion and AML/CFT

Assessors should consider specific issues regarding financial inclusion when assessing the quality of a country's AML/CFT framework. This is not an easy task because financial inclusion raises quite a wide range of issues. Properly contextualizing and assessing a country's policy and regulations regarding m-money is key.

From an assessment viewpoint, financial inclusion initiatives might be perceived as introducing risks of money laundering (ML) and terrorist financing (TF). By nature, the aim is to provide financial services to those people for whom such services were not previously available, especially people who are unable to provide documentary proof of identification or residence. It also involves cash-intensive businesses that are normally regarded as high-risk entities. Moreover, financial inclusion usually leads to the development of cross-border financial services that frequently are classified as higher-risk services.

It is important, however, to understand that financial inclusion is intended to bring the excluded population that is currently in the informal, undocumented, unmonitored, and unregulated system into the formal, transparent, and protective financial system. This is a central and crucial AML/CFT objective. In this regard, new modes of financial service delivery capable of reaching the poor—such as m-money services—assist society and promote good governance in the following ways:

- They help increase social inclusion and combat poverty, thereby decreasing related terrorist-financing risks and the level of poverty-linked crimes.
- They reduce the use of cash and increase the traceability of transactions.
- They increase the ability to protect consumers against fraud and other financial abuses that generate illegitimate proceeds and undermine public trust in the formal financial system.

In short, the general financial integrity objectives of the AML/CFT framework are elusive when large parts of a society are excluded from formal and regulated financial services. Therefore, financial inclusion and AML/CFT are complementary policy objectives.[3]

In addition, there are other mutual benefits (like the development of sound global financial markets) that serve large parts of the populations in those jurisdictions that are complying with global standards and principles. Together, AML/CFT and financial inclusion may also enhance adherence to other standards, including financial sector supervisory best practices. The complementarity between the two is now well accepted, and the FATF has already started exploring ways to further financial inclusion and financial integrity. Assessors, therefore, should consider the interplay between AML/CFT and financial inclusion when performing an AML/CFT assessment.

Policy and the Regulatory Approach

As part of the overall consideration of a country's national context and its AML/CFT policy and regulations, it is appropriate for assessors to consider whether the authorities have managed to strike a balance between the risks associated with the use of m-money and the country's objective of fostering greater financial inclusion. That requires assessors to consider:

- whether the country supports financial integrity objectives with a financial inclusion policy;
- whether financial inclusion initiatives, if any, pay due regard to and are aligned in their objectives with and implementation of the international standards; and
- whether the country has taken care to ensure that AML/CFT controls are not unnecessarily undermining financial inclusion.

A country that does not take steps to address deficiencies in financial inclusion is actually undermining its broader AML/CFT objectives. That fact should be reflected in the evaluation of the AML/CFT regime's overall adequacy. Financial inclusion initiatives that are too flexible may not be aligned with the FATF recommendations, but AML/CFT controls that are overly burdensome or rigid will form a barrier to new users who wish to move from the informal financial system to formal financial services. In such a case, the AML/CFT regime may have the perverse consequence of encouraging a significant portion of the population to resort to risky, inefficient, nontransparent and informal ways to conduct financial transactions.

Assessors should give credit to appropriate policies that aim to discourage use of informal systems and to encourage a proportionate financial regulatory framework. In this regard, FATF Recommendation

20 is highly relevant to m-money. Authorities promoting m-money that carries lower risks (see chapter 2) should receive credit because they encourage "the development of modern and secure techniques of money management that are less vulnerable to money laundering" (FATF Recommendation 20).

As a result, assessors may wish to consider the following questions:

- How well aligned are the country's policy on financial inclusion, if any, and its AML/CFT regulations?
  - What is the current level of financial inclusion in the country?[4]
  - Does the country's national AML/CFT risk assessment consider the impact of transactions that occur in the informal sector and cash economy?
  - Did the authorities tailor the regulatory framework—and the AML/CFT regime in particular—to encourage entry into the formal financial sector? If so, how did they determine the appropriate level of integrity protection for a particular financial environment?
- How effective are the steps, if any, that the country is taking to formalize financial activity and extend financial inclusion?

Know-Your-Customer Obligations

When it comes to assessing compliance with FATF Recommendation 5 on customer identification and verification, assessors should determine whether the regulators employed a flexible approach to permit undocumented populations to access m-money services and, if so, whether the regime is proportional and justified. The assessors will need to consider a range of issues relating to the extent of any exceptions that were granted and the justification for those exceptions.[5]

In this inquiry, the first step assessors may wish to take is to consider the risk environment. To justify an exemption from CDD measures, a country should establish that a particular activity carries a low risk of ML/TF. In this regard, the targeted markets for financial inclusion tend to have unknown or unassessed risks. In addition, many products, services, and delivery channels will be new; and risk assessments have to be dynamic. Although all assessments of risk will have to be designed to address the particular context, assessors should at least consider the following questions:

- Did the country undertake a risk assessment before relaxing KYC for specific low-risk m-money products?

- Is the risk assessment sufficiently robust to satisfy authorities and assessors that m-money products carry a low risk?
- Were this assessment and its conclusion documented?
- Are the KYC exemptions clearly defined?[6]

Assessors should keep in mind that it may not be possible to comprehensively assess the risks of new m-money products because tangible evidence is not immediately available.[7] Therefore, the risk should be monitored over time as evidence is gathered and its regulation and supervision are standardized.

Furthermore, assessors should consider how AML/CFT requirements—particularly those relating to customer identification—have been reduced or simplified to facilitate the access of undocumented customers. To this end, the following questions are relevant:

- Are there expanded lists of acceptable forms of identification or is the use of alternative forms (that is, ones that do not necessarily bear a picture) permitted?
- What criteria were used to determine the validity and reliability of the range of identification options?
- When a tiered customer identification program is permitted,[8] is this program effectively implemented and monitored by the account provider (AP) to discover any outliers?

In addition, assessors should consider how the supervisor is ensuring appropriate client risk management by the AP. In this regard, assessors may wish to verify if supervisors conduct some checks on the way m-money providers have determined criteria and controls for low-risk and low-value products. In practice, most APs mitigate ML/TF risks by setting caps and limits that restrict functionalities of the service. From an assessment standpoint, it would be relevant to determine whether supervisors address the following questions:

- Are these thresholds and caps based on a documented analysis of risk? Does the analysis consider known typologies in the specific country?
- Does the system permit a customer to exceed a cap?[9] If so, does the level of identification and verification and of monitoring increase?
- Are customers monitored for attempts to circumvent the limits, such as one customer holding multiple accounts?

The FATF assessment methodology in relation to KYC is wide ranging. It is challenging for assessors and assessed countries alike, and further guidance in this regard is required.

Recordkeeping

FATF's Recommendation 10 requires financial institutions to maintain all necessary records on domestic and international transactions for at least five years to enable them to comply swiftly with information requests from the competent authorities. Because the provision of m-money services involves new players, such as telecoms and retail outlets, it is advisable to include these new entities in the scope of the assessment of Recommendation 10.

Assessors should consider whether telecoms are subject to any record retention obligations for m-money services. If the AP (be it a telecom or a bank) is relying on retail outlets, attention should also be given to the recordkeeping obligations that may extend to them. In this regard, issues such as the following should be analyzed:

- recordkeeping obligations that apply to the AP, retail outlets, and other service providers;
- the legal nature of the obligations and how compliance is ensured;
- the ability of competent authorities who follow legal due process in seeking records from nonfinancial entities to access relevant information and evidence in a timely fashion.

Retail Outlets

The reliance on retail outlets in the context of m-money may complicate the application of more flexible or relaxed CDD rules to low-risk customers and products. It is important to determine what the status of retail outlets is; whether they have any AML/CFT obligations; and, if so, how compliance is ensured. Some retail outlets may act as agents of the AP and some may act as independent service providers. Their specific operations may impact their obligations and the allocation of responsibility to ensure compliance.

For assessors, the first matter to consider is the status of retail outlets under the AML/CFT regime. This is a central point because the implications for the country and the scope of issues to be addressed may differ, depending on whether retail outlets are licensed and regulated.

As discussed in chapter 4, retail outlets should not necessarily be legally subject to licensing and regulation. But if a country decides otherwise, it is advisable for assessors to consider the following questions:

- What criteria are used to license the retail outlets?
- Must they meet a fit and proper test?
- Are retail outlets subject to any oversight from a supervisory authority?
- How effective is the supervision of the retail outlet's compliance with AML/CFT obligations?

The AP is normally held accountable for AML/CFT compliance in regard to the m-money program (see chapter 4). As a consequence, the AP is responsible for ensuring that its retail outlets comply with any obligations that they may have to ensure the integrity of the system. As explained earlier, the AP is the party who procures the retail outlets, trains them, monitors them, and drafts the terms and conditions of the contract with them. As a consequence, it is advisable for assessors to determine whether and how the AML/CFT supervisor considers the following matters:

- Does the AP perform due diligence procedures on retail outlets prior to recruitment?
- Does the AP take sufficient steps to ensure that retail outlets do not compromise any simplified AML/CFT control measures applicable to low-value and low-risk accounts? For example:
  - Are retail outlets subject to the AP's ongoing monitoring and scrutiny?
  - Does the AP perform any on-site visits?
  - How does the AP determine the sites to visit?
  - How often are those sites visited?
  - Does the AP use mystery shoppers?[10]

As part of their assessments of the AML/CFT framework of m-money, evaluators should also consider matters such as the following:[11]

- Do retail outlets have AML/CFT obligations?
- Are these obligations clearly stated in a regulation, or are they set out in a contractual arrangement?
- What is the exact scope of retail outlets' AML/CFT duties?

Reporting Obligations

FATF's Recommendation 13 requires financial institutions to report to the financial intelligence unit (FIU) if they suspect or have reasonable grounds to suspect that funds are the proceeds of a criminal activity or are related to terrorist financing. The reporting requirement must be embodied in law. As already observed, m-money usually involves multiple entities, such as the AP, telecoms, and retail outlets. It may be challenging to regulate the reporting of suspicious transactions in new delivery channels where account opening and monitoring may be split among several entities.[12] There may be uncertainty about who holds the ultimate responsibility for filing a suspicious transaction report (STR) with the FIU.[13] Moreover, because accepting customers, processing transactions, and monitoring accounts may be performed by different parties, there is a need for clarity in the allocation of STR responsibilities, consistent with FATF standards. These important issues should receive attention during an AML/CFT assessment. In particular, assessors should consider whether the legal and regulatory framework ensures that reporting lines are clear[14] and that suspicious transactions are identified and reported effectively.

Before rating compliance with Recommendation 13, assessors may wish to consider the following questions:

- Who is responsible for the identification and reporting of suspicious m-money transactions?
  - Are retail outlets required to report suspicions to the AP?
  - Is the AP legally responsible for reporting to the FIU all suspicious transactions identified by it and by its retail outlets?
  - Where is the reporting obligation for each responsible party detailed? Are the obligations enforceable?
- Do the APs, telecoms, retail outlets, and their staff enjoy legal protection against criminal and civil liability for breach of any restriction on disclosure of information if they report suspicious transactions in accordance with their obligations?
- How does the system ensure that information is disclosed in accordance with the applicable legal rules, including privacy laws?[15]
- How is it ensured that all relevant parties are aware of the reporting obligations and have the ability to identify and report suspicious transactions?[16]
- Is the AP required to provide initial and ongoing training to retail outlets to assist them in identifying and reporting suspicious behaviors?

- Do statistics or other facts indicate that m-money transactions are identified and reported when required? (See the discussion of statistics below.)

Statistics

FATF Recommendation 32 also impacts m-money. This recommendation requires countries to maintain comprehensive statistics on matters relevant to the effectiveness and efficiency of systems for combating ML/TF, including statistics on STRs received and disseminated. According to the common methodology (essential criteria 32.2[a]), authorities should keep annual statistics on STRs received by the FIU, including a breakdown by types of financial institutions, designated nonfinancial businesses and professions, and other businesses or persons filing the STRs. One can infer that in countries where m-money services are used, assessors should determine whether the FIU is keeping statistics on STRs received by those parties that are responsible for filing such reports in relation to m-money (that is, APs, telecoms, and even retail outlets).

Supervision and Enforcement

FATF Recommendation 29 requires supervisors to have adequate powers to monitor and ensure compliance by financial institutions with requirements to combat ML/TF, including the authority to conduct inspections. M-money is a new category of financial activity involving role players who are not necessarily overseen by financial supervisory agencies. In some cases, it is unclear which agency or department is the primary supervisor for mobile network operators that offer m-money services. Conflict between agencies that hold supervisory responsibilities (for example, the central bank, the communications commission, and the FIU) is also possible when there is no clear delineation of responsibilities. These questions may become more complex in the case of supervision for cross-border transactions and cross-border mobile remittances. In this regard, assessors may wish to consider the following questions:

- Who is the primary supervisor for m-money services?
- Does the supervisory regime adhere to the FATF's functional definition of "financial institution"[17] or do some nonbank providers (such as telecoms) fall under different supervision for their financial services?
- If m-money providers are subject to different oversight regimes, is the delineation of duties between supervisory authorities clearly set in law and understood by all parties?

The assessment of compliance with FATF Recommendation 30 is also particularly relevant for m-money in countries where supervision of AML/CFT has been entrusted to the telecommunications regulator, rather than to a financial regulator. Under these circumstances, it is particularly important to assess the extent to which that regulator or supervisor conducts AML/CFT responsibilities. In this regard, assessors should be alert to any gaps in the legal framework or any uncertainty in the delineation of AML/CFT supervision or compliance-monitoring obligations. Telecommunications regulators who license, regulate, and supervise telephone companies are not necessarily familiar with international AML/CFT requirements and with the mutual evaluation process. Assessors must ascertain, however, whether that regulator has adequate financial, human, and technical capacity to supervise and monitor AML/CFT compliance.

Assessors should also pay attention to the licensing mechanism for m-money providers. For example, it is relevant to ascertain whether licensing procedures include effective and appropriate screening of potential mobile banking licensees, including (1) identifying beneficial owners and (2) conducting criminal background checks on potential licensees before granting licenses.

Last, because m-money services are growing fast in many jurisdictions, assessors should also check whether competent authorities have established guidelines and provided feedback to assist m-money providers in complying with their AML/CFT obligations, as recommended by FATF Recommendation 25. In particular, assessors may wish to verify if these guidelines have been circulated not only to financial institutions, but also to nonfinancial m-money providers such as telecoms, when appropriate.

In addition, assessors should evaluate the effectiveness of the m-money AML/CFT supervisory regime. Consideration should be given to the following questions:

- With respect to m-money services, what are the responsibilities of the supervisor?
- Is the supervisor able to supervise compliance by all parties to the m-money program?
  - Are supervisors allowed to conduct on-site visits to all parties (APs, telecoms, retail outlets, and other service providers)? How often do they monitor AML/CFT compliance by these parties?
  - Do supervisory powers extend to all AML/CFT aspects—for example, KYC, recordkeeping compliance, and compliance with STR obligations?

o How does the supervisor ascertain whether the necessary AML/CFT training is provided and whether suspicious transactions are identified and reported correctly?
- When conducting oversight, do supervisors also have access to personally identifiable information that includes the CDD particulars and documents of customers, m-money account balances, correspondence, and other materials?
- Is every party to the m-money business model subject to sanction or other enforcement measures if they are in breach of an AML/CFT obligation?

Notes

1. FATF methodology (2009) is a tool to assist assessors in determining whether countries are compliant with the FATF recommendations.
2. Other electronic means that favor access to finance (such as prepaid cards and automated teller machines) are not addressed in this section.
3. For an example of this complementarity, see FATF/ESAAMLG (2009) and its discussion of Mzansi accounts: "The advent of this product has brought millions of new customers into the formal banking system and has, in effect, expanded the reach of South Africa's AML/CFT regime" (p. 100).
4. Studies such as the International Monetary Fund's Financial Access Survey (http://fas.imf.org/) and the Consultative Group to Assist the Poor's *Financial Access 2010* (CGAP 2010) may be helpful in this regard.
5. Few countries assessed by the FATF have already made provisions with regard to Recommendation 5 to accommodate a flexible approach by not requiring proof of address. In the case of South Africa, for example, Exemption 17 permits the application of reduced CDD to special accounts (such as the Mzansi accounts). To make these accounts available to more customers and to develop further financial inclusion, accountable institutions are required only to establish and verify the customer's identity. They are not required to verify addresses. Furthermore, authorities have established that the ML/TF risks associated with this product are low because of the limits placed on account activity and because customers using these accounts are unlikely to commit these acts. Assessors considered this approach acceptable. For further details, particularly on the risk assessment of Mzansi accounts by the authorities, see FATF/ESAAMLG (2009) and de Koker (2009).
6. In addition to questions on whether simplification or exemption is applicable, consideration of the following would be desirable: (1) whether all (new) customer groups in a country are captured under an appropriate AML/CFT regime and (2) whether the application of KYC/CDD requirements to the new categories of customers is effective.

7. There may not be enough time to gather factual evidence of the abuse of these channels.

8. In a tiered program, a customer who can provide only minimal verification is restricted to basic services and can access higher levels of services after more comprehensive verification.

9. Generally, the customer would be unable to exceed a cap because it has been preset by the system. However, it is important to understand how often and why customers may test the cap.

10. As defined earlier, mystery shoppers are staff who visit retail outlet locations and pretend to be regular customers to test the outlet's integrity and competence in carrying out its role.

11. Many of these questions may be answered through interviews with APs and through document analysis (that is, by analyzing the agency agreement).

12. Retail outlets deal directly with the clients and may be able to identify suspicious behavior.

13. As already stated, the AP retains the ultimate responsibility for filing STRs.

14. Assessors may consider two separate questions in this regard: (1) Are the reporting obligations and lines of reporting clearly stated in regulations? and (2) Does practice reflect the position stated in the regulations?

15. As explained in chapter 4, m-money channels also hold communications data. These data may be relevant to ML/TF investigations, but they normally will be protected by privacy and telecommunications laws. The regulator must strike an appropriate balance that facilitates the inclusion of key information in the STR, investigators' access to relevant information, and protection of customers' privacy.

16. In the Philippines, for example, the central bank has set up a specific department—the Core Information Technology Supervision Group—to help ensure that the information technology systems used by the m-money providers are safe and sound to help prevent any technology breaches or loopholes when the AP files a transaction report with the FIU.

17. Telecoms providing m-money services should be considered financial institutions, as defined by the FATF: among other things, "financial institution" means any person or entity who provides customers with transfer of money or values services or issues and manages means of payment, including e-money.

References

CGAP (Consultative Group to Assist the Poor). 2010. *Financial Access 2010: The State of Financial Inclusion Through the Crisis.* Washington, DC: CGAP. http://www.cgap.org/gm/document-1.9.46570/FA_2010_Financial_Access_2010_Rev.pdf.

de Koker, Louis. 2009. "The Money Laundering Risk Posed by Low-Risk Financial Products in South Africa: Findings and Guidelines." *Journal of Money Laundering Control* 12 (4): 323–39.

FATF (Financial Action Task Force). 2009. "Methodology for Assessing Compliance with the FATF 40 Recommendations and the FATF 9 Special Recommendations." FATF, Paris. http://www.fatf-gafi.org/dataoecd/16/54/40339628.pdf.

FATF/ESAAMLG (Financial Action Task Force/Eastern and Southern Africa Anti-Money Laundering Group). 2009. "Mutual Evaluation Report—South Africa." http://www.fatf-gafi.org/dataoecd/60/15/42432085.pdf.

Mobile Money: Growth Potential, Current Landscape, and Factors for Success

The purpose of this appendix is to give the reader additional details on the current global mobile-money (m-money) ecosystem. It reflects the latest trends and provides some statistics.

The appendix is divided into four topics for discussion. It first gives some statistics on the potential growth of m-money programs and their profitability to providers. It then offers a stocktaking of the current m-money landscape, including the various types of providers and their increasing interest in deploying cross-border mobile remittance initiatives. The appendix goes on to offer a snapshot of potential conditions that could either foster or constrain the success of m-money programs, and then concludes by addressing the current global regulatory scenario.

Potential for Growth

M-money services hold great potential for expanding financial access among the poor. More than 80 percent of the world's population is now within mobile coverage. In 2009, the Groupe Speciale Mobile Association (GSMA) reported that there were more than 4 billion mobile subscriptions globally, with 80 percent of new connections in emerging markets and mostly for lower-income consumers.[1] The growth of global mobile coverage continues exponentially as new mobile network infrastructure and competition in the mobile markets flourish worldwide.

At the same time, there are enormous discrepancies between mobile coverage and access to formal financial services. An early-2009 study by the Consultative Group to Assist the Poor, the GSMA, and the McKinsey Group (CGAP 2009) shows that almost 4 billion people worldwide remain without access to formal financial services. Of this number, 1 billion do not have a bank account, but do possess a mobile phone—a number expected to grow to 1.7 billion by 2012. Therefore, mobile phones can be leveraged to provide formal financial services to nearly half of the world's unbanked population. In addition, approximately 120 m-money programs were deployed in developing countries in 2009; and in 2012, these programs will cover up to 364 million low-income, unbanked people. The total revenues generated for the m-money industry are estimated to be nearly $7.8 billion in 2012.

Despite the great potential of m-money in expanding financial access, its financial incentives to providers and ultimately financial inclusion objectives should be put in context. The expected revenue of $7.8 billion would constitute only 4.6 percent of the m-money industry's expected total income in 2012. In addition, although there are nearly 120 m-money programs operating at the moment, it is likely that only a few will succeed and remain sustainable over the long run (CGAP 2009). Nevertheless, the potential impact of m-money in postconflict and fragile states, such as Liberia,[2] may be significant. The financial sector and the landline infrastructure in these countries tend to be limited, but cell phone companies are among the first major enterprises to expand their businesses into these areas. Thus, if an environment conducive to m-money growth were to exist in either the developed or developing world, national jurisdictions could promote m-money as a key mechanism for financial inclusion. M-money would provide additional service offerings and convenience to consumers. It could also help further reduce remittance transfer costs and improve a country's payment infrastructure, access points, and distribution networks.[3]

The Current M-Money Landscape

The m-money provider[4] and the specific services of m-money may vary greatly from country to country. For example, only mobile-based payment services are offered in some countries, and only domestic (and sometimes international) person-to-person transfers are available in others. A few countries have providers who offer every type of m-money service, from mobile-based payments to domestic person-to-person transfers and even cross-border remittance transfers.

The extent of involvement among the different entities (banks, MNOs [mobile network providers], and third-party providers[5]) in any m-money transaction may vary greatly from one jurisdiction to another because banks may play a larger role in an m-money transaction in one jurisdiction, and the MNO or third-party provider may have a comparatively larger role in another jurisdiction. Chapter 1 has given greater clarity in this regard, discussing the mechanics of the many m-money business models around the world.

Sampling of National Jurisdictions

At the moment, some type of m-money program (typically, mobile phone–based payment services) has been deployed in most jurisdictions around the world. However, domestic or international person-to-person transfer service offered through m-money remained limited to a few jurisdictions, as of February 2010 (map B.1). The authors have used this map because national regulations and supervisors defining an appropriate

Map B.1   Jurisdictions Where Domestic or International Person-to-Person Transfer via M-Money Is Available, February 2010

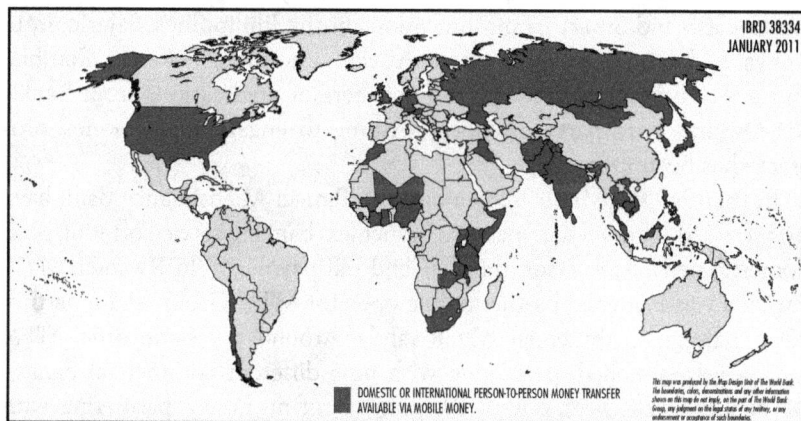

DOMESTIC OR INTERNATIONAL PERSON-TO-PERSON MONEY TRANSFER AVAILABLE VIA MOBILE MONEY.

IBRD 38334
JANUARY 2011

Source: GSMA's Wireless Intelligence unit.
Note: According to the source, this list may not be comprehensive because data are still being collected from additional countries. This map was produced by the Map Design Unit of the World Bank, January 2011. The boundaries, colors, denominations and any other information shown on this map do not imply, on the part of the The World Bank Group, any judgment on the legal status of any territory, or any endorsement or acceptance of such boundaries.

regulatory framework for m-money should focus on the person-to-person transfer risks associated with m-money in those areas. M-money goes beyond person-to-person transfer to include bill payments, but bill payments are not reflected in the map because they do not pose equally serious integrity risks.

As one can see on the map, m-money programs have caught more attention in developing countries than in developed ones, perhaps because they may have a greater marginal impact in expanding financial access in low-income jurisdictions. In the developing world, such as in a few African countries in Africa,[6] m-money may be one of the only means to expand such access. However, in more-developed and in some developing countries, there is already a relatively well-evolved financial sector with a very expansive distribution network and larger percentages of people with access to formal financial services. In India, for example, World Bank research and fieldwork has shown that even sending and receiving money may be done with relative ease and efficiency through the extensive distribution network of the postal service (which can act as a traditional bank's retail outlet). Hence, the deployment of m-money programs in countries like India may be considered more of an additional service for its citizens than a key tool to promoting financial inclusion.

Sampling of M-Money Providers

Some of the more "aged" operators of m-money in the developing world are G-Cash and Smart Communications in the Philippines, Safaricom in Kenya, and Wizzit in South Africa. At the same time, in Kenya, Zambia, and a few other jurisdictions, the numbers of applications from banks, MNOs, and third-party providers wishing to engage in m-money programs has been increasing.

In Pakistan, the MNO Telenor and the Tameer Microfinance Bank have partnered to produce "easypaisa," a branchless banking service offering both domestic person-to-person transfers and bill payment.[7] In Rwanda, MTN Rwanda was launched by the mobile operator MTN Group and a partner bank, Banque Commerciale du Rwanda. Around the same time, MTN Ghana was launched, partnering with nine different commercial banks.[8] MTN Group has been one of the pioneers of m-money, partnering with Standard Bank and launching in South Africa in 2005, and then commercially launching similar services in Uganda in 2009. Other new electronic-money (e-money) issuers engaging in similar services are WebMoney and Yandex in Russia. In Brazil, most banks offer some type of mobile banking service, including transaction-enabling services such as m-money.

M-money is also present in more-developed countries. In Germany, for example, some banks have offered m-money services, including the ability to transfer funds among individuals. However, recent trends indicate that, despite the increase in the number of mobile network users in Germany, fewer banks are operating m-money services now than in previous years. One study on the topic asserts that this probably results from a lack of consumer interest and little overall profitability of deploying these services, partly because of comparatively high service fees. Hence, the introduction of "flat rates"[9] for using such services is posited as one possible initiative to change consumer patterns in Germany and cause an increase in demand for such services (Scornavacca and Hoehle 2006).

Cross-Border Mobile Remittance Programs

An increasing number of m-money operators are offering users the opportunity to send and receive money across international borders. Thus, cross-border mobile remittance corridors appear to be targeted as a growth area by e-money issuers. By "cross-border," we mean at least one mobile account serves to remit or receive funds.

A cross-border mobile remittance model exists between the United Kingdom and Safaricom accounts in Kenya (which opened in June 2009). Senders go to brick-and-mortar, remittance-transfer retail outlets in the United Kingdom, and the money is remitted directly into the recipients' Safaricom accounts. For more than a year, another corridor has existed between the telecommunications company (telecom) Maxis in Malaysia and the telecom G-Cash in the Philippines. There is a third cross-border mobile remittance corridor between the telecom SmarTone in Hong Kong SAR, China, and G-Cash in the Philippines. The latter two corridors possess the only pure telecom-to-telecom cross-border mobile remittance models currently known.[10] Telecom-to-telecom service means that a customer may send funds directly from his or her mobile wallet to the recipient's mobile wallet. This is unlike most cross-border operations that require either the remittance sender or the remittance recipient to go to a brick-and-mortar retail outlet to send funds from his or her mobile account or to receive funds in his or her mobile account.

M-money operators G-Cash and Smart Communications are also studying the feasibility of cross-border mobile remittance corridors between the Philippines and countries of the Gulf Cooperation Council, where many Filipino migrants reside. At the same time, mobile payment solutions companies (such as Germalto) are currently in discussions with MNOs working extensively in the Middle East and North Africa (including the United Arab Emirates) to enable South Asian migrant workers (such as Bangladeshi, Indian, and Pakistani workers) to send remittances home via mobile-based technologies.

Profitability of M-Money Providers and the Factors for Success

The profitability of m-money operators may vary significantly both among countries and over time. Recent fieldwork in the Philippines suggests that m-money is merely a complement to existing communications services and does not present a profitable endeavor by itself. Both G-Cash and Smart have claimed that the only reason m-money is profitable is because of their increases in airtime sales. The service acts as a marketing tool and as a way of increasing customer "stickiness." Thus, neither company has engaged in aggressive marketing or promotion efforts for m-money.

The experience of Safaricom, Kenya's largest mobile operator, may provide a different perspective, however. Safaricom is considered the only truly profitable m-money operation in the world today, and it has become the most widely adopted m-money program. Launched in 2007, the company had nearly 7 million users in 2009—in a country of 38 million people, 18.3 million of whom have mobile phones. As a result, the proportion of Kenyans considered to be part of the formal financial sector has doubled to 41 percent in the last three years (*The Economist* 2009). The success of Safaricom has compelled other m-money operators (such as Zap from the MNO Zain and Yu from the telecom Essar) to enter the Kenyan competitive landscape.

Kenya's unique local conditions have helped drive Safaricom's profitability. The company has been considered successful because having fewer remittance market players has produced more limited competition, leading to an unusually high cost for sending money through traditional transfer mechanisms such as money transfer operators or wire transfers via banks. In addition, during the postelection violence in 2008, Kenyan citizens tended to lose faith in banks, which were entangled in ethnic disputes; thus, people preferred to store their money in an m-money account and send funds to their families through that mechanism. Furthermore, the dominant market share (80 percent) and the aggressive marketing efforts of (and resultant customer loyalty to) Safaricom made Kenyan consumers more likely to test new products and services. Finally, the regulatory and supervisory authorities permitted Safaricom to proceed in its operation without any formal regulatory approval or any formal e-money, anti-money laundering/combating the financing of terrorism (AML/CFT), or other relevant legislation, as mentioned earlier.

In the future, it will be interesting to see whether emerging providers will find that m-money by itself serves as a profitable business proposition in the jurisdictions where they operate, or whether m-money can be profitable only as part of a larger bundle of service offerings provided by all entities (banks, MNOs, and third parties) involved in the m-money transaction. In this regard, the case of third-party providers will be especially interesting because these providers (unlike banks or telecoms) are exclusively in the business of m-money and thus do not have an incentive to deploy m-money programs as simply a mechanism to reduce customer turnover. It is not yet clear if third-party providers generally will find m-money to be a profitable endeavor by itself. It is likely this would diverge greatly on the basis of jurisdiction-specific conditions.

The Current Global Regulatory Scenario

The extent of involvement among the different entities in an m-money transaction often depends on existing regulations in the jurisdiction. In India, as well as most other surveyed jurisdictions where m-money has been deployed, banks are required to play a larger role than the MNO or third-party providers in the various stages of an m-money transaction. This means that banks frequently offer their own customers some type of mobile banking service (such as one that lets a customer view his or her bank account information on a mobile device) and perhaps a transaction-enabling service (such as m-money). However, there are signs that this soon may change in India and other jurisdictions where MNOs are being allowed to play a larger role in an m-money transaction. This wider empowerment often has been the result of national authorities becoming more aware of the intricacies of an m-money transaction and learning how other jurisdictions may be regulating and supervising m-money entities outside of banks to mitigate the integrity, prudential, and other risks associated with the use of such channels.

In certain jurisdictions, not all the relevant regulations that could govern m-money are formally enacted—for example, relevant AML/CFT laws or e-money or payment system laws.[11] In Zambia, for example, there is a national payment system law and an AML/CFT law, but no law governing e-money. In Kenya, an AML law was passed in January 2010, but other relevant regulations have not been formally enacted. Nonetheless, m-money programs are active in these jurisdictions; and some national authorities claim that they have formulated mechanisms to regulate and supervise these services, despite the absence of one or more formal laws. The authors do not agree with these practices and believe it is important to have a legal and regulatory framework in place to govern m-money providers. Although Safaricom was able to proceed in its operation without formal regulatory approval and the enactment of formal (and relevant) legislation in 2007, interviews with Safaricom indicate that they very much desire formal regulatory approval and a clear legal and regulatory framework to provide greater clarity and enhance consumer confidence in their operations.[12]

Notes

1. The source of those data (Wireless Intelligence, GSMA's marketing information unit) is available at https://www.wirelessintelligence.com/.

2. In Liberia, landline service was destroyed in the war and it has not been rebuilt. To call anyone there, one must use a cell phone.

3. In the example of Safaricom, m-money developed more as an alternative to traditional remittance transfer mechanisms, which were more limited and far more expensive at that time. But in more-developed countries like (where greater and more competitive financial infrastructure is in place), m-money services may be profitable and be considered a supplemental or complementary financial service offering.

4. As outlined in chapter 3, any m-money program always includes a variety of providers—a mobile network operator (MNO), a bank, and possibly one or more third-party providers. The term "mobile-money provider" is used to describe the lead entity or account provider (AP).

5. A third-party provider is defined as a nonbank or a nontelecom. Perhaps the most famous third-party provider is Celpay, which classifies itself as a "payment service." Others call themselves "technology platforms" or "mobile payment solutions companies."

6. These countries include Ghana, Kenya, South Africa, Tanzania, Uganda, and Zambia.

7. This service was launched on October 14, 2009.

8. MTN Rwanda and MTN Ghana were launched in February 2010.

9. A "flat rate" means that the funds' transfer cost is the same, irrespective of the amount of funds transferred.

10. What is also unique about the Maxis–G-Cash model is that a customer in the Philippines can use his or her mobile phone to send remittances directly to a recipient's mobile phone in Malaysia. This service is rarely used, however,

because most remittances are sent in the other direction—from Malaysia to the Philippines.

11. A stocktaking of sample regulations governing m-money was provided in chapter 3.

12. The Kenyan AML law passed in January 2010 may have a positive impact in this regard.

References

CGAP (Consultative Group to Assist the Poor). 2009. "Window on the Unbanked: Mobile Money in the Philippines." *CGAP Brief.* December.

———. 2010. *Financial Access 2010: The State of Financial Inclusion Through the Crisis.* Washington, DC: CGAP. http://www.cgap.org/gm/document-1.9.46570/FA_2010_Financial_Access_2010_Rev.pdf.

The Economist. 2009. "Beyond Voice: New Uses for Mobile Phones Could Launch Another Wave of Development." September 26.

Scornavacca, Eusebio, and Hartmut Hoehle. 2006. "Mobile Banking in Germany." Proceedings of the Helsinki Mobility Roundtable. *Sprouts: Working Papers on Information Systems.* 6 (28). http://sprouts.aisnet.org/6-28.

APPENDIX C

Customer Due Diligence Obligations and Mobile-Money Services: Key Questions and Solutions

This appendix introduces the challenges that mobile-money (m-money) providers are currently facing in complying with customer due diligence (CDD) obligations. It also lifts some misunderstanding or misperceptions of what is expected from service providers, clarifies some concepts that are not always correctly understood either by authorities or by the industry, and analyzes the precise obligations under Financial Action Task Force (FATF) Recommendation 5. It also offers some guidance on how best to use the flexibility permitted by the standards and to explore possible alternative options.

Know-Your-Customer and the Risk-Based Approach: Principles and Limits

Identifying the applicant and verifying his or her identity is the first step of the CDD process under FATF Recommendation 5. This applies to all financial institutions, including m-money providers.[1] In the particular context of m-money in developing countries, it is clear that these requirements are difficult to meet, especially in jurisdictions where people do not carry formal identification papers or are unable to provide proof of address. To address this challenge, the FATF recommendations contain provisions that permit flexibility in the way know-your-customer (KYC) and CDD obligations can be fulfilled. Recommendation 5 states that financial institutions (and, implicitly, nonbank financial providers like mobile network operators [MNOs]) should apply each of the CDD measures that is listed, "but may determine the extent of such measures on a risk sensitive basis depending on the type of customer, business relationship or transaction." Furthermore, according to paragraph 9 of the FATF interpretative note for Recommendation 5, "there are circumstances where the risk of money laundering or terrorist financing is lower, . . . or where adequate checks and controls exist elsewhere in national systems. In such circumstances it could be reasonable for a country to allow its financial institutions to apply simplified or reduced CDD measures when identifying and verifying the identity of the customer and the beneficial owner."

Simplified or reduced CDD measures, therefore, should be read and considered in combination with the so-called risk-based approach (RBA).[2] The RBA allows countries to shape some elements of the anti-money laundering/combating the financing of terrorism (AML/CFT) system around risk. It permits countries to exempt a person, entity, or financial activity from some or all of the AML/CFT obligations. However, such an exemption must be on a strictly limited and justified basis—for example, when risk of money laundering or terrorist financing has proved low or when a financial activity is carried out by a person or entity on an occasional or very limited basis (having regard to quantitative and absolute criteria) such that there is little risk that ML/TF activity will occur.

The FATF principles on reduced CDD measures appear straightforward. Their interpretation and implementation in an m-money context in low-capacity countries have proved quite challenging, however. Regulators, m-money providers, and policy makers actually have been struggling to determine a "relaxed" KYC regime that meets FATF requirements and the "particular circumstances" that may justify adjustments of the CDD principles. Despite the FATF guidance on the RBA, several issues around balancing financial integrity with the financial inclusion goals of branchless banking remain unclear to many stakeholders.

One question is whether low-value financial inclusion products can qualify as low-risk products.[3] The interpretative note for Recommendation 5 provides some examples of customers to whom simplified or reduced CDD measures could apply. It also gives examples of simplified CDD measures that may be acceptable for various types of products. However, none of the examples offered either in the interpretative note or in other FATF documents are relevant to m-money services[4] because m-money did not really exist in the developed world when the FATF standards were revised.

The subsequent RBA guidance notes do not bring additional clarity. They acknowledge that low-value transactions may pose a low ML risk, but that there is some risk. Whereas the guidance notes recognize the complexity of the matter, they shed little light on how countries and institutions should treat low-value products.[5]

In conclusion, the FATF principles and guidelines do not provide all the answers; for many developing countries, many questions remain regarding whether low-value transactions and low-turnover accounts associated with m-money meet the definition of a low-risk product that qualifies for simplified due diligence. The authors believe that m-money services observed in numerous jurisdictions carry a low risk, as explained below.

Why M-Money Services Carry Low Risks

The 2007 RBA note states that when there is little risk of ML/TF activity, a country may decide that the application of AML measures is not necessary, either fully or partially. In strictly limited and justified circumstances, and based on a proven low risk of ML/TF, a country may decide not to apply some or all of the recommendations to some of the financial activities.

The FATF does not clarify what is meant by "proven low risk," but there are a number of arguments that could be advanced in support of a partial exemption for m-money services. For instance, the profiles and risks of the services currently in use can be presented:

1. Fieldwork shows that mobile services can be both prepaid and post-paid, depending on the consumer and the services offered. However, the vast majority of services are prepaid, and accounts that are prepaid usually have a ceiling on the amount of credit that can be stored on them at one time. As stated in chapter 1 of this volume, prepaid accounts do not pose a particular risk to a telecommunication company's (telecom's) business.

2. In terms of payment values, mobile transactions are generally very low, averaging about $20–$30. Many of the financial transactions carried

out through mobile phones are micropayments. The typical user makes a total of only $500 worth of transactions annually. Regarding frequency of use, research in Kenya suggests that more than 65 percent of customers use the service at least once a month, and only 1 percent do so more frequently than once a week.

3. Initial users tend to be banked customers who are sending money to their unbanked relatives,[6] so the sender has normally been identified already. Average m-money users typically work in a city and remit funds to family members for regular support. Last, although funds generally flow from urban to rural areas, most services currently function only within one country.[7] Given such common patterns in m-money, anything remotely different could be flagged as suspicious, depending on the context.

4. Information technology companies have developed mature software solutions that provide a robust control environment and a flexible and scalable operating environment for m-money providers. Banks also may deploy sophisticated transaction-monitoring systems (as evidenced by fieldwork), and they are able to implement robust compliance processes that meet FATF recommendation standards (see chapter 4). Also, industry practices that set frequency and strict amount limits for transactions may discourage ML and even TF.

5. The availability of telecommunications data on users of m-money limits the risks posed by this payment system.

6. The MNO often occupies the position of intermediary in the payment process, functioning between a bank—or several banks—and the customer or recipient. As a result, the MNO is able to provide additional transaction information to law enforcement investigators to complement identity data provided by other financial institutions. These data may be equally or more valuable in the chain of evidence than is a repetition of the verification process (see JMLSG [2007]).

7. The statistics are also telling. So far, there is no evidence that m-money services are being used for ML/TF purposes. Empirically, there has been no specific case of money laundering through m-money services in countries where these services have been implemented. And there

have been no reports of TF (Chatain et al. 2008; Zerzan 2009). Although any payment system is bound to be abused at some point, World Bank research and reports from the mobile operator industry (Solin and Zerzan 2010) indicate that m-money has been of little interest to criminals or terrorists.

8. TF also usually involves an international element. In most of the m-money systems currently in operation, international transfers are prohibited. The few systems that do permit such transfers have CDD standards equivalent to any other method of transferring money abroad—for example, wire transfers and the like.

9. There is a common understanding or conception that TF necessarily involves low-value transactions. Evidence from law enforcement authorities shows that transaction sums from the 9/11 terrorist attacks are well above the typical limits in m-money services.

10. Caps on m-money transactions force criminals and terrorists to engage in a large number of transactions, and that increases the likelihood of being exposed to detection.

11. In jurisdictions where cash is easily prevalent, using m-money services for criminal purposes appears too burdensome, greatly reducing the likelihood of using these electronic channels.

All things considered, the authors believe that there are low risks of ML/TF associated with mobile phone financial services when accompanied with limits and monitoring systems. This low risk can justify simplified CDD, as discussed below; but, in some cases, the risk assessment and evidence may convince a regulator that the conditions for a partial exemption from CDD obligations are met.

Relaxed CDD for M-Money: Three Possible Scenarios

According to the FATF, there are two scenarios to consider when it comes to relaxed CDD. At the business level, a country can decide to apply reduced AML/CFT obligations to a given activity or to exempt it—fully or partially—from AML/CFT obligations on the basis of a proven low risk and in strictly limited and justified circumstances. If a country decides to subject a financial activity to AML/CFT obligations, it may allow the businesses that carry out such an activity to apply reduced CDD to their customers where there are low risks. In this latter case, however, full exemption is absolutely not allowed. As matters currently stand, three possible alternatives may be explored to permit more flexibility while ensuring the integrity of the financial system.

The first approach is based on the fact that the *identification* part of the CDD process is perceived to be crucial. The *verification* of names may be given greater flexibility under the "reduced or simplified" CDD procedures. In other words, in particular and clearly defined situations, identification should be required but reduced verification may be allowed.[8]

Reduced verification measures are easy to envisage. As discussed in chapter 2, many developing countries have been imaginative in promoting innovative means to verify the identity of a customer: a letter from a local leader confirming the bearer's identity, a call to a reliable local source to confirm the customer's appearance or voice, or the use of a witness known to and trusted by the retail outlet. Such alternative verification solutions are likely to be tolerated if they are restricted to channels with limited risk. In South Africa, for example, verification of address for holders of Mzansi accounts is skipped because the accounts have very limited functionalities and thus are classified as low risk.[9]

Another argument that can support such an approach is that up-front KYC by itself does not seem to be the most effective risk mitigator.

Because identification information may include a variety of data about a person (name, address, phone number, date of birth, and so on), no single item stands out as always essential. For instance, there are several countries where a person's name is not documented. Why should name be the key piece of information to universally identify a person? Perhaps the person's schoolmates and village elders designate him or her differently. Furthermore, in some small communities, all males or females have the same name (son/daughter of ___). Perhaps the only consistent identifier is his or her phone number—something that would rarely change because it is the way people reach the person or, in some cases, it is where his or her money is kept. Numbers are easier to use because they are less likely to be recorded incorrectly and because illiterate people are able to understand them.

As witnessed in many countries, financial criminals are likely to layer transactions through any number of clean front men who act as account holders or who hold power of attorney over the accounts of the beneficial owner. However, it is most important and quite surprising to learn through discussions with law enforcement experts that many criminals use their real names when they establish relationships with financial institutions. That was sometimes the case during the preparation of the 9/11 terrorist attacks in the United States. The U.S. investigation of financial transactions that supported the plot has shown that one of the main financiers provided an exchange center[10] with his real work identification data, his cell phone number, and his work address. As for the hijackers, they opened accounts in their own names, using passports and other authentic identification documents.[11] The same investigation has revealed that, contrary to numerous published reports, there is no evidence the hijackers ever used false social security numbers to open any bank account in the United States (Roth, Greenburg, and Wille 2004, p. 140). KYC has been of little use in these particular situations.

The second approach relies on the exemption of very small transactions from CDD obligations. The third European ML directive (EU Directive 2005/60/EC) provides an interesting example: it exempts electronic money (e-money) accounts from up-front CDD if the total transacted on the account does not exceed €2,500 in any one calendar year and if not more than €1,000 is redeemed for cash by the bearer in the same calendar year.[12]

It is noteworthy that most of the mobile business models observed during fieldwork have set limits (daily, monthly, or yearly) on the amount of money that can be stored in the mobile phone account. One may infer that m-money services currently available in developing countries match the situations described above and could fall under the exemptions permitted in Europe, for example.[13] However, full exemption of KYC is not permitted under FATF Recommendation 5 when a country decides to subject an activity to AML/CFT obligations—as is actually the case in many visited jurisdictions. As a result, it is not certain that e-money accounts addressed in the third European directive include m-money accounts.

A third option is to apply a graded or progressive CDD approach, whereby a customer who can provide only minimal identification is restricted to basic services and may access higher levels of service only after more comprehensive verification. This progressive CDD approach relies on the quality of information and verification that is provided by the applying customer. In practice, m-money providers (including non-banks like MNOs), have developed technical platforms that automatically manage tiered KYC obligations. In one case, all customers are placed in rule bands that govern the amounts the customers are allowed to transact. The system allows customers with low-risk profiles to move more money. Thus, customers who are able to provide additional identification and verification information (such as a proven address, a photocopy of an identification card, or an introduction from an employer) can be placed in rule bands that permit higher transaction limits.

Notes

1. For natural persons, the Basel Committee on Banking Supervision (2001) advises that the following information should be obtained: (1) legal name and any other names used (such as maiden name); (2) correct permanent address; (3) telephone number, fax number, and e-mail address; (4) date and place of birth; (5) nationality; (6) occupation, public position held, and name of employer; (7) an official personal identification number or other unique identifier contained in an unexpired official document (such as a passport, identification card, residence permit, social security records, or driver's license) that bears a photograph of the customer; (8) type of account and nature of the banking relationship; and (9) customer signature. In addition, the following might be required: taxpayer registration number, employer identification card, and one or two references.

   According to the Basel Committee on Banking Supervision (2001), the identifying particulars that an institution obtains should be verified by at least one of the following methods: (1) confirming the date of birth with an official document (for example, birth certificate, passport, identity card, or social security records); (2) confirming the permanent address with a utility bill, tax assessment, bank statement, or a letter from a public authority; (3) contacting the customer by telephone, letter, or e-mail to confirm the information supplied after an account has been opened; and (4) confirming the validity of the official documentation provided through certification by an authorized person (such as an embassy official or notary public).

2. This approach was introduced by the FATF's 2003 revised 40 recommendations and was explained in subsequent RBA guidance notes. [see FATF (2007)].

3. de Koker (2009) identifies various questions that arise regarding the level of risk of low-value products, and he suggests ways in which the FATF may address the uncertainties.

4. Examples of customers, transactions, or products for which the risk may be lower might include (1) financial institutions, (2) public companies that are subject to regulatory disclosure requirements, (3) government administrations or enterprises, and (4) life insurance policies for which an annual premium is no more than \$/€1,000 or a single premium is no more than \$/€2,500.

5. Of course, there are limits to the clarity that the FATF can provide. Its standards have universal application. Given the complexity of the questions and the fact that risks and risk appetites may differ from country to country, the FATF can and should give only broad, principled guidance.

6. According to recent surveys of customers using branchless channels in Brazil, India, Kenya, the Philippines, and South Africa, today's customers are primarily not the unserved majority—although the unbanked and the poor are starting to use branchless channels. See Pickens, Porteous, and Rotman (2009).

7. However, there is great demand for cross-border payments because of the need to cheaply remit money to relatives back home. See Solin and Zerzan (2010).

8. In South Africa, for example, Exemption 17 eliminates the need to obtain and verify the residential address details on low-value, low-risk accounts.

9. The features of a Mzansi account reflect the following risk parameters: *type of customer:* the product is only available to natural persons; *nationality of the customer:* the customer must be a South African citizen or resident; *limited to domestic transactions:* cross-border transfers are not permissible, except for point-of-sale payments or cash withdrawals in the Rand Common Monetary Area; *monetary limits:* there is a daily limit on withdrawals, transfers, and payments. A capped monthly limit also applies. In addition, there is a limit on the balance that may be maintained in this account. The customer is restricted from maintaining more than one such account at an institution (see FATF/ESAAMLG [2009], p. 100). It is important to note that the FATF/ESAAMLG evaluators had no negative comments on this exemption.

10. The center was the Wall Street Exchange Center of Dubai, from which the financier wired $5,000 to the United States.

11. The hijackers also used multiple aliases.

12. As set forth in the directive, member-states may allow the institutions and persons covered by the directive not to apply CDD in some particular circumstances (Article 11, para. 2). As for e-money issuers, this exemption is permitted (1) if the maximum amount stored on a device that cannot be recharged does not exceed €150 or (2) if a limit of €2,500 is imposed on the total amount transacted in a calendar year on a device that can be recharged (Article 2, para. 5(d). CDD may also be skipped for any other product or transaction representing a low risk of ML/TF (Article 2, para. 5). The full text of the directive may be viewed at http://eur-lex.europa.eu/LexUriServ/LexUriServ.do?uri=OJ:L:2005:309:0015:0036:EN:PDF.

13. The European directive seems to be a good example of a bill that gives policy makers some flexibility when it comes to applying or eliminating CDD obligations.

References

Basel Committee on Banking Supervision. 2001. "Customer Due Diligence for Banks." Basel, Belgium. http://www.bis.org/publ/bcbs85.pdf.

Chatain, Pierre-Laurent, Raúl Hernández-Coss, Kamil Borowik, and Andrew Zerzan. 2008. "Integrity in Mobile Phone Financial Services: Measures for Mitigating Risks from Money Laundering and Terrorist Financing." Working Paper 146, World Bank, Washington, DC.

de Koker, Louis. 2009. "Identifying and Managing Low Money Laundering Risk: Perspectives on FATF's Risk-Based Guidance." *Journal of Financial Crime* 16 (4): 334–52.

FATF (Financial Action Task Force). 2007. "Guidance on the Risk-Based Approach to Combating Money Laundering and Terrorist Financing." Paris, France. http://www.fatf-gafi.org/dataoecd/43/46/38960576.pdf.

FATF/ESAAMLG (Financial Action Task Force/Eastern and Southern Africa Anti-Money Laundering Group). 2009. "Mutual Evaluation Report—South Africa." http://www.fatf-gafi.org/dataoecd/60/15/42432085.pdf.

JMLSG (Joint Money Laundering Steering Group). 2007. "Guidance on E-Money." http://www.jmlsg.org/news.

Pickens, Mark, David Porteous, and Sarah Rotman. 2009. "Scenarios for Branchless Banking in 2020." Focus Note 57, Consultative Group to Assist the Poor, Washington DC.

Roth, John, Daniel Greenburg, and Serena Wille. 2004. "Monograph on Terrorist Financing." Staff Report to the National Commission on Terrorist Attacks Upon the United States. Washington, DC. http://govinfo.library.unt.edu/911/staff_statements/index.htm.

Solin, Marina, and Andrew Zerzan. 2010. "Mobile Money: Methodology for Assessing Money Laundering and Terrorist Financing Risks." GSMA Discussion Paper. London. http://www.mobilemoneyexchange.org/Files/b0a2fa88.

Zerzan, Andrew. 2009. "New Technologies, New Risks? Innovation and Countering the Financing of Terrorism." Working Paper 174, World Bank, Washington, DC.

Reporting Obligations in the Particular Context of Mobile Money

Suspicious transaction reports (STRs) are vital to the anti-money laundering/counter-terrorist financing (AML/CFT) system. The STRs filed by regulated entities provide important perspectives and often trigger further money-laundering/financing of terrorism (ML/FT) investigations. This appendix outlines the challenges posed by implementing reporting obligations relative to mobile money (m-money). In particular, it discusses the different role players, the division of functions, the incidental rights and duties, and the information that should be provided in an STR.

The Financial Action Task Force's (FATF's) Recommendation 13 requires regulated financial institutions to promptly report to the financial intelligence unit (FIU) every time they suspect or have reasonable grounds to suspect that funds are the proceeds of a criminal activity or are related to terrorist financing. Additionally, some countries require that reports be filed on transactions involving cash in excess of a specified amount, regardless of suspicion. The latter appear of less importance in the context of m-money, given the modest transaction sizes and transaction limits involved.

Key issues that arise regarding STRs are the allocation of responsibilities for the filing of these reports and the information that should be set out in them.

Allocation of Responsibilities

In theory, depending on the business model (see chapter 1), there are four distinctive m-money functions that are involved in the m-money mechanism, and as many as four parties may be active in a transaction. Each of the parties has a particular role to play and so may be subjected to reporting obligations. The four parties are:

- the *retail outlet*, which deals directly with the customer and can identify possible suspicious behavior;
- the *account provider* (AP), who keeps the customer and transaction records, processes transactions, and may be able to identify suspicious transaction patterns and suspicious customers and their agents;
- the *telecommunications company* (telecom), which provides the telecommunications service and may have additional customer information, including customer particulars, contact details, and other identifying data; and
- the *settling bank*, which holds the accounts of the retail outlets, receives their deposits, supports their cash withdrawals from the m-money system's pooled account (if the system uses one), and may be able to identify suspicious transaction patterns relating to retail outlets.

Depending on national regulations, a specific institution may act in more than one of these capacities—for instance, a telecom may act as both the telecommunications service provider and the AP. If the AP is not a bank, the m-money program will need to involve a settling bank to hold the pooled account and the bank accounts of the retail outlets.

In an ideal situation, an effective STR system will draw on the strengths of all parties involved, and all parties will share relevant information with each other. In practice, however, ineffective communication channels and legal impediments, such as commercial secrecy and privacy protections, may complicate information sharing. Every regulator and m-money business model will need to consider the best ways to address barriers to information sharing within the context of the relevant laws. Increased information sharing will support higher-quality STRs. It is also important to have clear rules regarding the allocation of reporting obligations. In this regard, the following delineation of functions is suggested:

1. When a telecom provides m-money services on its own and is responsible for the AP function, it acts as a financial service provider and should be licensed as such. In its capacity as a provider of financial services, it should be responsible for reporting STRs to the FIU.

2. If a telecom partners with a bank, questions arise regarding an appropriate allocation of STR responsibilities in relation to m-money transactions. Regulators should be guided by the division of functions within that partnership. The bank will be subject to general STR duties regarding all transactions that it processes. The key question is whether it should share responsibilities with the telecom. If so, how should the relationship be structured? Jurisdictions may consider applying the so-called rule of the account provider (discussed in chapter 1), according to which the provider of the account record services is responsible for AML/CFT obligations (including the filing of STRs). Three examples of the application of this rule will suffice:
   o If the bank acts as the AP, there may be little reason to burden the mobile network operator (MNO) with parallel duties to file STRs with the FIU. The STR obligation should fall under the bank's responsibility.
   o If the MNO acts as the AP, it should be responsible for filing STRs.[1]
   o If an intermediary provider type is neither a bank nor an MNO, the intermediary provider is the AP and should carry the STR responsibility.
3. If the program involves a settling bank, the bank is able to identify suspicious transaction patterns relating to retail outlets, and it will be subject to general AML/CFT duties requiring it to report any suspicious transactions directly to the FIU.
4. Retail outlets should be required to inform the AP of any suspicious conduct by a customer. This duty should be created and detailed by the agency agreement between the AP and the retail outlet. The AP will consider the customer's profile, transaction patterns, and other relevant information, and will file an STR with the FIU if it finds that there are reasonable grounds to do so. A contractual reporting obligation for retail outlets will suffice in many cases. It reflects their lack of access to client records and other relevant information needed to support a high-quality STR.

Although the rule of the account provider may assist a regulator in determining responsibility for filing STRs, it is clear that more than one party may be responsible for filing STRs in some cases. The regulator will need to decide whether such parallel reporting obligations support the country's AML/CFT framework. In some business models, the services may be delivered in such a fractured manner that none of the parties have sufficient information to file a comprehensive STR. When that is true, it is advisable to designate a lead party to coordinate the filing of individual reports or to ensure that a comprehensive report is filed. The lead party and the other parties may need effective information-sharing mechanisms that meet legal requirements, including privacy protections.

Related Rights, Obligations, and Processes

The allocation of reporting duties suggested above will be effective only if the parties also assume the related obligations. For example, the AP must ensure that its employees and retail outlets receive proper training to enable them to identify and report suspicious transactions. Reporting processes (especially reporting lines) and internal responsibilities (such as those of the money-laundering reporting officer) must be clear. Appropriate records should be kept, and all parties should be aware of the need to keep information confidential and should not inappropriately disclose information regarding potential or actual STRs.

The reporting obligation must be linked to the duty to monitor transactions, customers, and retail outlets; and should be supported by sufficient capacity to investigate potential suspicious behavior, including identity fraud. M-money providers must be able to ensure effective and ongoing monitoring of accounts and customers. Accounts and customers that were subjects of an STR must be monitored closely for a reasonable period, and an STR should be filed for each additional suspicious transaction that may be concluded.

The AP also requires processes and capacity that enable it (1) to monitor retail outlets' compliance with their obligations (including the obligation to inform the AP of any suspicious operations) and (2) to take corrective action when required (including terminating an agency agreement, when necessary).

When an international company is one of the service providers—especially when it is the AP—general STR filing duties may be split among group, regional, and local officers. In practice, banks and other financial institutions entrust their designated compliance officers with the task of completing and submitting STRs to the relevant authority prescribed by the national AML law. In the case of financial groups, STR obligations are determined on the basis of internal arrangements and geographic locations. For example, AML tasks can be split among the group AML officer, the regional AML officer, and the country AML officer. The last of those parties actually develops and maintains procedures and systems to ensure that STRs are reported to local authorities in accordance with local law and to the group AML officer (if not explicitly forbidden by local law).

When such a splitting of functions is relevant, it is important to clarify the obligations and to ensure that they support the effective reporting of m-money STRs to the local FIU.

Policy makers must also ensure that relevant authorities are able to access available information and data if they follow up on an STR. The FIU, for instance, must be authorized to seek information from the retail outlet, the AP, the MNO, and the settling bank, irrespective of whether any of the parties filed or contributed to the filing of the STR.

Although the reporting obligation is a vital element of the AML/CFT system, fieldwork has shown that very few STRs have been submitted in the countries that were visited. In the Philippines, the FIU has seen an increase in STRs from the two m-money operators (G-Cash and Smart Communications) since it began recording these submissions in 2007. Only two cases—both relating to petty consumer fraud involving m-money rather than to money laundering—were sent on to law enforcement authorities.

One case involved alleged recruiters of overseas workers who demanded G-Cash payment as a recruitment fee. In this case, the large number of transactions involving similar amounts flowing from various clients to one account triggered the suspicion.

The second case involved a fraud scheme known as "dugo-dugo" (blood-blood) in which a relative is called with news that a loved one has been in an accident and is urgently requesting money. This scam was more difficult to identify because the amounts that were sent differed. Despite the difficulty, however, the m-money providers found sufficient information to trigger suspicion and to file an STR that led to appropriate law enforcement action.

Contents within an STR

Questions arise regarding the nature of the nontransactional information and the extent to which it must be reported to the FIU.

Banks generally can draw only on information about customers and their transactions for purposes of internal control and reporting of suspicious transactions. The m-money channel holds additional communications data (such as general call logs and text messages) that may or may not have a bearing on any particular transaction. Where suspicion is related to a specific m-money service user, it is unclear whether a provider (particularly an MNO) must report to the FIU not only the transaction—or series of transactions—that is suspicious (date, amount, name of the sender, cell phone number, and name of the recipient), but also all communications data that might be related to these operations (for example, details and contents of phone calls and text messages that come before or after the mobile transaction). In certain cases, such data may be of great value to the FIU and to law enforcement authorities because they will usefully supplement transactional information. However, disclosure of those data by means of an STR raises privacy and other legal questions.

FATF Recommendation 13 on reporting obligation refers only to "funds" and does not specify the exact type of information subject entities must disclose. Similarly, Recommendation 10 on recordkeeping does not shed light, simply stating that "transaction records should be sufficient to permit reconstruction of individual transactions." In practice, FIUs usually require reporting entities to send "full details" on the customer, including transaction details and even recipient account details. In the particular context of m-money, it is not known whether an FIU would get full access to communications data.

The questions relating to the disclosure of such data are too complex to address by means of general international principles. Much depends on the particular context of the report and the national legal framework protecting communications and citizens' privacy. Therefore, it is important that every regulator consider this matter and issue clear guidance to the entities being regulated. When considering the matter, the regulator should be attentive to the national legal framework and to the scope of data reportable to the FIU. The regulator may limit the information to be disclosed in the STR to specific data and evidence of specific communications that provide grounds for the suspicion. Such information might include the fact that a short-message transmission preceded or followed a funds transfer and the mobile numbers and particulars of the parties who sent and received that message. If the text of the short message is directly relevant to the suspicion, the regulator should consider whether the national law will allow disclosure of the text in the STR or whether its relevance should merely be recorded in the STR, leaving it to the authorized investigators to follow due process to gain access to the text.

Countries should consider the possibility of authorizing the FIU to seek information from other institutions subject to AML reporting obligations—such as MNOs—that may have been involved in the customer's related transactions or business, even if they have not provided reports.

Note

1. Other players in the system, including the settling bank, would have very little knowledge or awareness of customer activity because they would not hold the account records. Retail outlets' interactions with the pooled account is the one exception to this. Retail outlets generally are required to hold an account in the same bank as the pooled account so that they can make deposits and withdrawals from the system. (Customers use retail outlets as their own deposit and withdrawal points so they need not interact with the bank.) Banks may detect suspicious activity in the retail outlet's own bank account and find it linked to the retail outlet's deposits and withdrawals in the pooled account. This activity most certainly should be reported to the FIU.

Index

Boxes, figures, maps, notes, and tables are indicated by *b*, *f*, *m*, *n*, and *t*, respectively.

A

Abu Sayyaf, 60*n*29
access to formal financial services. *See* financial inclusion
account providers (APs)
  clarification of role of, 130
  defined, xxv–xxvi
  in mobile money transaction flow, 14, 15, 16, 17, 23, 27, 28–29
  proper identification of, 115
  recordkeeping by, 15, 27, 88
  responsibility and accountability of, xxxi
  retail outlets and, xxxii, 92–97, 115–18
  rule of the account provider, 28–29
  simplified know your customer (KYC) requirements, enhanced monitoring due to, xxxiii
  suspicious transaction report (STR) responsibilities, 89–90, 132, 178, 179, 180, 181
accounts
  balance information and transaction history, 14
  types of, xxv
Airtel Africa (formerly Zain), 26, 98*b*, 162
al Qaeda, 130

alternative providers in mobile money transaction flow, 21*f*, 23–24, 23*f*
AML/CFT. *See* anti-money laundering/ combating the financing of terrorism (AML/CFT) regulations
AMLC (Anti-Money Laundering Council), the Philippines, 44, 45, 47*b*
anonymity, as ML/TF risk, 33–34, 37*t*
anti-money laundering/combating the financing of terrorism (AML/CFT) regulations, xii, xv, xxix–xxxiv, 6–7, 63–103
  enforcement regime, 120–25
  financial inclusion, advantages of, 4, 5*f*
  financial inclusion and. *See* financial inclusion
  guidelines, publishing, 52, 112–14
  identification and verification processes, 75–82, 79–81*b*, 82–83*b*, 84–85*t*
  licensing. *See* licensing of providers
  methodology and organization of study, 6–7
  mobile money transaction flow, market integrity procedures in course of, 25–28

anti-money laundering/combating the
    financing of terrorism (AML/CFT)
    regulations (*continued*)
  objectives, scope and audience for study
    of, 4–6
  policy recommendations regarding. *See*
    policy recommendations
  recordkeeping, 81–88, 89*b*, 90*b*
  registration. *See* registration
    requirements
  retail outlets, 92–97, 94*b*, 96*b*, 98–99*t*,
    98*b*, 118
  risk-based approach to, xxxii–xxxiiii
  STRs, 88–92, 91*b*
  supervision of providers, 71–75, 73*f*,
    74*b*, 75*b*
Anti-Money Laundering Council (AMLC),
    the Philippines, 44, 45, 47*b*
APs. *See* account providers
Australia, 86

B

Bangko Sentral ng Pilipinas or BSP
    (Central Bank of the Philippines),
    69*b*, 85*t*, 93, 101*n*14
Bangladesh, 162
Bank Negara Malaysia, 141*n*22
Bank of Japan, 41–42, 43*f*
banks
  AML/CFT procedures carried out by,
    28, 36–37
  bank licenses for m-money businesses,
    59*n*13, 140*n*4
  m-money business models, involvement
    in, xxxi, 11
  ML/TF risks, 38–39
  mobile money transaction flow, role in,
    11, 12, 16, 21*f*, 22–23, 28, 29*n*2
  policy recommendations for m-money
    providers. *See under* policy
    recommendations
  in provider-based licensing
    regimes, 66, 67
  recordkeeping by, 22
  STR responsibilities, 178, 179, 181
  supervisory role of, 73*b*, 74*b*
Banque Commerciale du Rwanda, 160
Basel Committee on Banking Supervision,
    xii, 77, 100*n*5, 174*n*1
Basel Core Principles, 65, 71, 112, 121
branchless banking

AML/CFT regulations and, 74, 99*n*1
customers of, 175*n*6
easypaisa, 160
financial inclusion goals of, 168
MNO leveraging power in, 12*n*59
policy recommendations, 119, 122, 124,
    138, 140*n*15
Brazil, 8*n*10, 58*n*6, 66, 94*b*, 98–99*t*,
    160, 175*n*6
Britain. *See* United Kingdom
BSP or Bangko Sentral ng Pilipinas
    (Central Bank of the Philippines),
    69*b*, 85*t*, 93, 101*n*14

C

Cambodia, 100*n*3
cash versus m-money transactions, ML/TF
    risks of, 40–42, 41*b*, 42*t*, 43*f*
CDD. *See* customer due diligence
CellC, 56*b*
Celpay, 23–24, 24*f*, 29*n*13, 164*n*5
Central Bank of the Philippines (Bangko
    Sentral ng Pilipinas or BSP), 69*b*,
    85*t*, 93, 101*n*14
CFT (combating the financing of
    terrorism). *See* anti-money
    laundering/combating the financing
    of terrorism (AML/CFT)
    regulations
Chatain, Pierre-Laurent, xxi–xxii, xxx
Christen, Bob, xii
closed versus open m-money systems,
    15–16, 16*b*, 17, 18, 19, 20*b*,
    20*t*, 28
collaboration
  between all stakeholders, 119
  between financial regulators and
    m-money industry, 112,
    113–14, 120
  with FIU, 119, 120
  between m-money providers, 131
  between regulatory agencies, 119
  STRs, information-sharing
    regarding, 133
  with supervisors, 119–20
Colombia, 94*b*
combating the financing of terrorism
    (CFT). *See* anti-money
    laundering/combating the financing
    of terrorism (AML/CFT)
    regulations

compliance officers of m-money
    providers, 128
Congo, Democratic Republic of, 9,
    23, 24f
Consultative Group to Assist the
    Poor, 2, 158
consumer fraud versus ML/TF risk, 40,
    44–45, 46–48b, 181
cooperation and coordination. *See*
    collaboration
Core Information Technology Supervision
    Group, the Philippines, 155n16
Côte d'Ivoire, 49
cross-border transactions
    demand for, 175n7
    financial inclusion and fiscal integrity,
        balancing, 110, 141n22
    from Gulf Cooperation Council
        countries, 161–62
    internal procedures for, 127
    market distortion, preventing, 136
    progressive KYC/CDD approach
        for, 77
    supervision of providers and,
        74–75, 123
    terrorist financing concerns
        related to, 53
customer anonymity, as ML/TF risk,
    33–34, 37t
customer due diligence (CDD), 7,
    167–76. *See also* know your
    customer
    broadening AML/CFT regulations
        beyond, 107–8
    defined, xxvi
    FATF on, 7, 167–71, 173
    financial inclusion and, 144,
        147–49, 154
    importance of, xxx, xxxii
    low risk from m-money generally,
        169–71
    low-risk transactions, need for guidance
        on, 138
    progressive KYC/CDD approach, 77,
        78f, 100n5, 173–74
    records obtained through, 83, 86
    relaxed or simplified processes. *See*
        relaxed or simplified CDD/KYC
        processes
    retail outlets, xxxii, 92, 115, 116
    risk-based approach to, 110–11, 138,
        167–69

customer identification and verification.
    See identification and verification
    processes
customer interface, 13, 26
customer profiling, 51

D

Dannaoui, Najah, xxiii
data-enabled phones, impact of, 59n12
de Koker, Louis, xxiii–xxiv, 40
Democratic Republic of Congo, 9, 23, 24f
Devan, Janamitra, xv
DOCOMO, 101n12
due diligence
    customer. *See* customer due diligence
    retail outlets, 97
dugo-dugo scams, 181

E

e-money. *See* mobile money
e-money issuer licenses, 69–70
easypaisa, 160
elusiveness, as ML/TF risk, 34–35, 37t
enforcement of AML/CFT regulations,
    120–25, 152–54
England. *See* United Kingdom
Essar, 162
European Union (EU)
    AML/CFT regulations in, 68b, 69,
        70b, 77, 79b, 101n13
    progressive KYC/CDD approach, 173,
        175n13
    retail outlets, 116

F

FATF. *See* Financial Action Task Force
    (FATF) and FATF standards
FICA (Financial Intelligence Centre Act),
    South Africa, 56b, 83–86
Financial Action Task Force (FATF) and
    FATF standards, xii, xv, xxxi,
    xxxiii, 2
    CDD, 7, 167–71, 173
    on collaborative efforts, 119
    enforcement regime, 124
    financial inclusion and, 7, 138–39,
        143–47, 149, 151–53
    on guidelines for providers, 112
    on identification and verification
        processes, 75, 77

Financial Action Task Force (FATF) and
    FATF standards (*continued*)
  for low-income clients, 5
  ML/TF risks, 40, 50, 51*b*, 52
  policy recommendations, 7, 107, 136–39
  providers, registration and licensing of,
    52–53, 65
  recordkeeping, 81–83, 86, 87
  retail outlets, 93, 94, 95, 96, 101*n*17,
    116, 117
  risk-based approach suggested by, 50,
    51*b*, 110
  on risk management practices and
    transaction monitoring, 128
  sequenced implementation of, 111–12
  on STRs, 88–89, 90, 177, 182
  on supervision of providers, 71, 72
  World Bank working with, 8*n*8
financial inclusion, 7, 143–56
  AML/CTF framework, as part of,
    145–46
  AML/CTF regime as driver of, xv
  AML/CTF regime strengthened by, xxix,
    4, 5*f*
  defined, 144
  FATF and, 7, 138–39, 143–47,
    149, 151–53
  identification and verification processes
    affecting, 76
  importance of, xi–xii, xiii
  KYC/CDD and, 144, 147–49, 154
  mitigation of risks, balancing with,
    54–58, 55*f*, 56–57*b*, 110–11
  mobile coverage and access versus, 2–3,
    158
  policy recommendations, 110–11,
    146–47
  recordkeeping and, 54–55, 55*f*, 149
  relaxed or simplified CDD/KYC
    processes and, 144, 168–69
  retail outlets and, 149–50
  STRs and, 151–52
  supervision and enforcement issues,
    152–54
Financial Intelligence Centre Act (FICA),
    South Africa, 56*b*, 83–86
financial intelligence units (FIUs)
  additional information, access to, 133–34
  collaborative efforts, 119, 120
  enforcement regime, 125
  financial inclusion and, 151–52
  key threat indicators for, 35, 46*b*

  on ML/TF versus consumer fraud risk,
    35, 44, 46*b*, 47*b*, 48*b*
  provider obligation to report to, 131,
    132, 133, 134
  retail outlets reporting to, 117
  statistics, keeping, 152
  STRs filed with. *See* suspicious
    transaction reports
  supervisory role of, 73–74, 121, 140*n*16
  watch-lists, responsibility for circulating,
    141*n*25
Financial Services for the Poor initiative, xii
financing terrorism. *See* anti-money
    laundering/combating the financing
    of terrorism (AML/CFT)
    regulations; money laundering and
    terrorist financing (ML/TF) risks
FIUs. *See* financial intelligence units
formal financial services, access to. *See*
    financial inclusion
France, 6

G

G-20, xii, xiii, xiv
G-Cash, 45, 46–48*b*, 93, 160–62,
    164–65*n*10, 181
GAFISUD, 144
Germalto, 161
Germany, 79*b*, 161
Ghana, 8*n*6, 84*t*, 160, 164*n*6, 164*n*8
Global Communications, 45
global financial crisis, xiv
Global Leadership Seminar on Regulating
    Branchless Banking, 139*n*2
Globe, 14, 15*f*, 98*b*
Great Britain. *See* United Kingdom
Groupe Speciale Mobile Association
    (GSMA), xiv, 2, 40, 157, 158
  guidelines on AML/CFT and m-money, 52,
    112–14, 136–38
Gulf Cooperation Council, 161

H

Hong Kong SAR, China, 8*n*10, 161
hotlines for retail outlets, 118

I

identification and verification processes,
    33–34. *See also* customer due
    diligence; know your customer

acceptable documentation, 82–83*b*,
    84–85*t*, 174*n*1
AML/CFT regulations, 75–82, 79–81*b*,
    82–83*b*, 84–85*t*
anonymity, as risk category, 33–34
Basel Committee recommendations,
    174*n*1
differentiation of, 77
financial inclusion affected by, 76
innovative mechanisms for, 50
relaxed or simplified approaches,
    172–73
risk-based approach to, 77, 78, 79–81*b*
SIM cards, 55, 56*b*
in South Africa, 55–57, 56–57*b*
IMEI (International Mobile Equipment
    Identity), 45, 47*b*
India
    branchless banking in, 175*n*6
    cross-border transactions for migrant
        workers from, 162
    fieldwork conducted in, 6
    mobile money transaction flow, 9, 23
    postal service, sending and receiving
        money through, 160
    provider-based licensing regime in, 66
    regulatory scenario in, 163
Integrity in Mobile Phone Financial Services
    (World Bank study, 2008), 2
internal procedures
    for cross-border transactions, 127
    mitigation technique, internal
        monitoring as, 51–52
    for providers of m-money, 126–28, 134
    simplified KYC/CDD process combined
        with, xxxiii, 49, 55, 57
International Mobile Equipment Identity
    (IMEI), 45, 47*b*
iPhones, fraudulent sale of, 45
Italy, 47*b*

J

Janjalani, Abdulrajak, 60*n*29
Japan, 41–42, 43*f*, 100*n*4, 101*n*12

K

Kenya
    AML/CFT regulations in, 74*b*, 75*b*, 89*b*,
        90*b*, 91*b*, 96*b*, 98*b*
    branchless banking in, 175*n*6
    established m-money providers in, 160

fieldwork conducted in, 6
financial inclusion, importance of
    m-money to, 164*n*6
frequency of transactions in, 170
internal policies of m-money providers
    in, 126–27
ML/TF risks, perceived versus
    actual, 38, 44
mobile money transaction flow in, 9, 13,
    18–19, 22, 26
Orange (MNO), 19
profitability and success factors in,
    162–63
regulatory scenario in, 163–64, 165*n*12
Safaricom. *See* Safaricom
Khalifa, Mohammed Jamal, 60*n*29
know your customer (KYC). *See also*
    customer due diligence
dangers of overly restrictive processes, 4
defined, xxvi, 59*n*22
financial inclusion and, 144, 147–49
importance of, xxx
progressive KYC/CDD approach, 77,
    78*f*, 100*n*5, 173–74
relaxed or simplified processes. *See*
    relaxed or simplified CDD/KYC
    processes
retail outlets, xxxii, 116, 117, 119
risk-based approach to, 167–69
tailored to m-money framework, 49–50
Korea, 8*n*10, 21, 50–51, 52*b*, 100*n*4
KYC. *See* know your customer

L

layering, 35, 45, 172
Lesotho, 84*t*
Liberia, 3, 8*n*4, 158, 164*n*2
licensing of providers, 65–71
    banking licenses for m-money
        businesses, 59*n*13, 140*n*4
    as mitigation technique, 52–53
    non-bank providers of m-money, 109
    payment system or e-money issuer
        licenses, 69–70
    provider-based licensing regimes, 65–67,
        66*b*
    retail outlets, 92–93
    service-based licensing regimes, 67–70,
        68–69*b*
    technology-neutral, 70*b*
    universal licensing regimes, 30*n*15

licensing of providers (*continued*)
    unstructured supplementary service data
        (USSD) licenses usually held by
        MNOs, 29*n*12
limits on transaction amounts, 50–51, 51*b*,
    52*b*, 173, 175*n*12

M

m-money. *See* mobile money
Macao SAR, China, 8*n*10
Malawi, 82*b*
Malaysia
    AML/CFT regulations in, 68*b*, 69, 84*t*,
        90*b*, 101*n*13
    cross-border remittance services with
        the Philippines, 141*n*22, 161,
        165–66*n*10
    fieldwork conducted in, 6, 8*n*10
    settlement process, 14, 15*f*
Maldives, 66
Máxima (Princess of the Netherlands), xi
Maxis, 14, 15*f*, 161, 164–65*n*10
MBank, SK Telecom, 21
McKinsey Group, xiv, 2, 158
Mexico
    AML/CFT regulations in, 66*b*, 79*b*, 83*b*,
        89*b*, 91*b*, 94*b*
    fieldwork conducted in, 6
    retail outlets, oversight of, 123
microstructuring, 35, 58*n*7
migrant workers, cross-border transactions
    for. *See* cross-border transactions
mitigation of risks, 49–58
    customer profiling, 51
    FATF risk-based approach, 50, 51*b*
    financial inclusion objectives, balancing
        with, 54–58, 55*f*, 56–57*b*, 110–11
    government-issued guidelines, 52
    innovative identification and verification
        mechanisms, 50
    internal monitoring, 51–52
    KYC tailored to m-money, 49–50
    limits on transaction amounts, 50–51,
        51*b*, 52*b*, 173, 175*n*12
    m-money as tool for mitigating overall
        ML/TF risk, 137
    motivation for, 59*n*14, 60*n*24
    providers, supervision, licensing, and
        registration of, 52–53
    terrorism, mitigation techniques specific
        to, 53–54

ML. *See* money laundering and terrorist
    financing (ML/TF) risks
MMS (multimedia messaging service)
    messages, 88, 100*n*10, 101*n*13
MNOs. *See* mobile network operators
mobile banking, defined, xxvii. *See also*
    mobile money
mobile money, xxix–xxxiv, 1–8, 157–65
    alternatives to, 4
    AML/CFT regulations, xii, xv,
        xxix–xxxiv, 6–7, 63–103. *See also*
        anti-money laundering/combating
        the financing of terrorism
        regulations
    availability of, 2, 3*m*, 159*m*, 159–60
    CDD, 7, 167–76. *See also* customer due
        diligence; know your customer
    current services and systems, 158–62
    defined, xii, xxvii
    financial inclusion and AML/CFT, 7,
        143–56. *See also* financial inclusion
    growing importance of, xiii–xiv, xxix,
        2–3, 157–58
    methodology and organization
        of study, 6–7
    ML/TF risks, xxix, xxx–xxxi, 6, 31–62.
        See also money laundering and
        terrorist financing (ML/TF) risks
    objectives, scope, and audience
        for study, 4–6
    policy recommendations regarding, 7,
        105–42. *See also* policy
        recommendations
    profitability and success factors, 162–63
    regulatory requirements of, xiv–xv,
        xxix–xxx, 163–64
    STRs, 7, 177–83. *See* suspicious
        transaction reports
    transaction flow, 6, 9–30. *See also* mobile
        money transaction flow
mobile money transaction flow, 6, 9–30
    account balance information and
        transaction history, 14
    alternative providers, 21*f*, 23–24, 23*f*
    APs, 14, 15, 16, 17, 23, 27, 28–29
    banks, role of, 11, 12, 16, 21*f*, 22–23,
        28, 29*n*2
    customer interface, 13, 26
    market integrity procedures in course of,
        25–28
    MNOs, roles of, 11, 12, 13, 16, 19–22,
        21*f*, 23

mobile phone service, provision of,
    12–13, 25–26
multiple participants in, roles of, 11–12,
    19–24, 21*f*, 28
open versus closed m-money systems,
    15–16, 16*b*, 17, 18, 19, 20*b*, 20*t*, 28
retail outlets, role of, 14–19, 18*f*, 20*b*, 20*t*
rule of the account provider, 28–29
settlement process, 14, 15*f*, 28, 178
stages of, 12–14, 12*f*
transaction processor, 13, 26–27
mobile network operators (MNOs)
    AML/CFT procedures carried out by,
        25–28, 37
    financial inclusion balanced with risk
        mitigation, 54
    increasing array of services provided by,
        30*n*15
    licensing and registration, 65–67
    m-money business models, involvement
        in, xxxi, 11
    ML/TF risks, 38–39
    mobile money transaction flow, role in,
        11, 12, 13, 16, 19–22, 21*f*, 23
    policy recommendations for m-money
        providers. *See under* policy
        recommendations
    recordkeeping by, 25, 27
    with separate financial entities, 74, 75*b*
    STR responsibilities, 88, 92, 178, 179,
        181, 182
    supervision of, 72–73, 74
    as target audience for study, 6
    USSD licenses usually held by, 29*n*12
Mobile Transactions Zambia Limited
    (MTZL), 17, 18*f*, 19, 23, 24, 29*n*7
money laundering and terrorist financing
    (ML/TF) risks, xxix, xxx–xxxi, 6,
    31–62. *See also* anti-money
    laundering/combating the financing
    of terrorism (AML/CFT)
    regulations
    actual risk, 40–49, 169–71
    anonymity, 33–34, 37*t*
    assessment of vulnerability, threat, and
        risk, 42–43
    cash versus m-money transactions,
        40–42, 41*b*, 42*t*, 43*f*
    categorization of, 33–37, 36*b*, 37*t*
    consumer fraud risk versus, 40, 44–45,
        46–48*b*, 181
    demand for information about, 1–2

elusiveness, 34–35, 37*t*
fieldwork evidence of, 44–49, 45*t*,
    46–48*b*
key risk indicators, 35, 36*b*
layering, 35, 45
mitigation of. *See* mitigation of risks
perception of risk, 37–40
poor oversight, 35–37, 37*t*
potential vulnerabilities by risk
    category, 37*t*
rapidity of transactions, 35, 37*t*
smurfing, 35, 37*t*, 45
MTN Banking, 8*n*6, 50, 56*b*, 66*b*,
    160, 164*n*8
MTZL (Mobile Transactions Zambia
    Limited), 17, 18*f*, 19, 23, 24, 29*n*7
multimedia messaging service (MMS)
    messages, 88, 100*n*10, 101*n*13
mystery shoppers, 26, 30*n*17, 98*b*, 118,
    150, 155*n*10
Mzansi accounts, South Africa, 85*t*, 154*n*3,
    154*n*5, 172, 175*n*9

N

NFC-enabled mobile phones, 42, 59*n*18
Nigeria, 49, 74*b*, 141*n*24
9/11 terrorists, 54, 173
Nokia, 29*n*3
Noor, Wameek, xxii–xxiii

O

Obopay (India), 23
open versus closed m-money systems,
    15–16, 16*b*, 17, 18, 19, 20*b*,
    20*t*, 28
Orange (Kenyan MNO), 19
oversight problems, as ML/TF risk,
    35–37, 37*t*

P

Pakistan, 160, 162
payment system licenses, 69–70
Peru, 94*b*, 98*b*
Philippines, the
    AML/CFT regulations in
        identification and verification
            processes, 79*b*, 82*b*, 85*t*
        licensing and registration, 69*b*, 70
        recordkeeping, 90*b*, 101*n*13
        retail outlets, 93, 94*b*, 98*b*

Philippines, the (*continued*)
  separate financial entities, MNOs
    with, 75*b*
  STRs, 91*b*
branchless banking in, 175*n*6
BSP, 69*b*, 85*t*, 93, 101*n*14
Core Information Technology
    Supervision Group in, 155*n*16
cross-border remittance services,
    141*n*22, 161, 165–66*n*10
established m-money providers in, 160
fieldwork conducted in, 6, 8*n*10
ML/FT versus consumer fraud risk, 44,
    45*t*, 46–48*b*, 53, 60*n*29
mobile money transaction flow, 9,
    14, 15*f*
profitability and success factors in, 162
STRs, 91*b*, 181
policy recommendations, 7, 105–42
  application of regulations to non-banks
    offering m-money, 108–9
  assessment of m-money system, 108
  branchless banking, 119, 122, 124,
    138, 140*n*15
  CDD, broadening AML/CFT regulations
    beyond, 125–35
  collaboration. *See* collaboration
  for FATF, 7, 107, 136–39
  financial inclusion, 110–11, 146–47
  for national policy makers, 107–25
    collaborative efforts, 112, 113–14,
      119–20
    guidelines for providers, issuing,
      112–14
    regulatory framework, design of,
      107–12
    retail outlets, regulating, 114–19
    supervision and enforcement, 120–25
  for providers of m-money, 125–35
    internal policies, 126–28, 134
    risk management practices and
      transaction monitoring, 128–31
    STRs, 131–32
    training for staff and retail outlets,
      134–35
  retail outlets
    regulation of, 114–19
    training for, 134–35
  risk-based approach, 109–10
  sequenced implementation of
    AML/CFT obligations, 111–12
  technology-neutrality, 109

watch-list screening, 130–31
pooled bank accounts
  defined, xxv
  in mobile money transaction flow, 15*f*,
    17, 18*f*, 19, 20*b*, 20*t*, 22, 28
  STRs, 132, 178, 183*n*1
pooled funds, 39
pooling of mobile phones, 34
poor oversight, as ML/TF risk, 35–37, 37*t*
profiling customers, 51
progressive KYC/CDD approach, 77, 78*f*,
    100*n*5, 173–74
provider-based licensing regimes, 65–67,
    66*b*

R

rapidity of transactions, as ML/TF
    risk, 35, 37*t*
RBA. *See* risk-based approach
recordkeeping
  AML/CFT regulations, 81–88,
    89*b*, 90*b*
  by APs, 15, 27, 88
  by banks, 22
  financial inclusion balanced with risk
    mitigation, 54–55, 55*f*, 149
  by MNOs, 25, 27
  by retail outlets, 15, 88
  STRs and, 182
registration requirements
  m-money providers, 52–53, 65–71
  SIM cards, 25, 49, 57, 60*n*32, 81
Regulation of Interception of
    Communications and Provision of
    Communication-Related
    Information Act (RICA), 2002
    (South Africa), 56–57*b*
relaxed or simplified CDD/KYC processes
  AML/CFT regulations and, 77–82,
    79–81*b*, 100*n*5
  financial inclusion products and, 144,
    168–69
  internal monitoring, combined with,
    xxxiii, 49, 55, 57
  mitigation of risks and, 49, 55, 57
  possible approaches to, 171–74
reporting obligations. *See* suspicious
    transaction reports
Republic of Korea, 8*n*10, 21, 50–51,
    52*b*, 100*n*4
retail outlets

AML/CFT procedures carried out by, 26, 95–96
AML/CFT regulations and, 92–97, 94b, 96b, 98–99t, 98b, 118
APs and, xxxii, 92–97, 115–18
Brazil, regulation in, 98–99t
CDD, xxxii, 92, 115, 116
defined, xxviii
due diligence regarding, 97
ensuring compliance of, xxxiii
FATF on, 93, 94, 95, 96, 101n17, 116, 117
financial inclusion and, 149–50
identification and verification processes, innovation in, 50
integration into regulatory framework, xxxi–xxxii
KYC, xxxii, 116, 117, 119
liability for, 93, 94b, 96b, 101–2n17
licensing, 92–93
ML/TF risks, 39–40, 59n14
mobile money transaction flow, role in, 14–19, 18f, 20b, 20t
policy recommendations regarding regulation of, 114–19
training for, 134–35
recordkeeping by, 15, 88
risk management of, 97, 98b
STR responsibilities, 117, 132–33, 178, 179, 183n1
supervision of, 93–95, 117
telephone hotlines for, 118
RICA (Regulation of Interception of Communications and Provision of Communication-Related Information Act), 2002 (South Africa), 56–57b
risk-based approach
to AML/CFT regulation, xxxii–xxxiiii
to CDD/KYC, 110–11, 138, 167–69
FATF on, 50, 51b
guidance on, need for, 137–39
to identification and verification processes, 77, 78, 79–81b
in internal policies, 127
to mitigation of risks, 50, 51b
policy recommendations regarding, 109–10
risk management
for providers, 128–31
of retail outlets, 97, 98b

risk of consumer fraud versus ML/TF risk, 40, 44–45, 46–48b
risk of ML/TF. See money laundering and terrorist financing (ML/TF) risks
rule of the account provider, 28–29
Russian Federation, 6, 71, 98b, 100n3, 140n15, 160
Rwanda, 160, 164n8

S

Safaricom
cross-border transactions, 161
established business of, 160, 164n3
internal policies, 126–27
ML/TF versus consumer fraud risk, 44
mobile money transaction flow, 13, 22, 26, 29n8
profitability and success factors for, 162–63
regulatory scenario in Kenya and, 164
retail outlets, 96b, 97, 98b
Saudi Arabia, 53
September 11, 2001, 54, 173
sequenced implementation of AML/CFT obligations, 111–12
service-based licensing regimes, 67–70, 68–69b
settlement process, 14, 15f, 28, 178
short message service (SMS)
defined, xxviii
recordkeeping requirements, 87–88, 100n10–11, 101n13
staff training, use in, 135
STRs, 92
supervision of providers and access to, 74, 123
USSD compared, xxviii
SIM card. See subscriber identity module (SIM) card
SIM Toolkit (STK), xxviii, 13
simplified CDD/KYC processes. See relaxed or simplified CDD/KYC processes
SK Telecom, 21
Smart Communications, 160, 161, 162, 181
SmarTone, 161
SMS. See short message service
smurfing, 35, 37t, 45
South Africa
AML/CFT regulations, 66b, 76, 80–81b, 81, 83, 85t

South Africa (*continued*)
  branchless banking in, 175*n*6
  established m-money providers in, 160
  FICA, 56*b*, 83–86
  fieldwork conducted in, 8*n*10
  financial inclusion in, 154*n*5, 164*n*6,
    175*n*8
  mobile money transaction flow in,
    29*n*10, 30*n*16
  Mzansi accounts, 85*t*, 154*n*3, 154*n*5,
    172, 175*n*9
  RICA, 56–57*b*
  risk mitigation techniques, 49, 50, 55,
    56–57*b*, 57, 60–61*n*33
Spain, 72
speed of transactions, as ML/TF
    risk, 35, 37*t*
Standard Bank, 160
statistics on STRs, 152
STK (SIM Toolkit), xxviii, 13
STRs. *See* suspicious transaction reports
subscriber identity module (SIM) card
  consumer fraud regarding, 45, 47
  defined, xxviii
  identification and verification process,
    55, 56*b*
  in mobile money transaction flow, 13,
    25, 29*n*13
  registration requirements, 25, 49, 57,
    60*n*32, 81
supervision of providers
  AML/CFT regulations, 71–75, 73*f*,
    74*b*, 75*b*
  collaboration with regulators, 119–20
  financial inclusion and, 152–54
  FIU, supervisory role of, 73–74, 121,
    140*n*16
  as mitigation technique, 52–53
  policy recommendations regarding,
    120–25
  retail outlets, 93–95, 117
  rulemaking authority of supervisors, 124
  training for, 125
suspicious transaction reports (STRs), 7,
    177–83
  accessibility, 141*n*19
  allocation of responsibility for, 178–80
  AML/CFT regulations on, 88–92, 91*b*
  AP responsibilities, 132, 178, 179,
    180, 181
  bank responsibilities, 178, 179, 181
  contents of, 181–82

defined, xxviii
  FATF on, 88–89, 90, 177, 182
  financial inclusion and, 151–52
  FIU, filed with. *See* financial intelligence
    units
  guidance and feedback, FIU
    provision of, 112
  by international companies, 180–1812
  MNO responsibilities, 88, 92, 178, 179,
    181, 182
  policy recommendations, 112, 117,
    131–32
  provider obligations, 131, 132,
    133, 134
  recordkeeping and, 182
  regulations regarding, 88–92, 91*b*
  retail outlet responsibilities, 117,
    132–33, 178, 179, 183*n*1
  rights, related obligations, and processes,
    180–81
  rulemaking for, 134
  statistics on, 152
  telephone hotlines for retail outlets, 118

T

Taliban, 130
Tameer Microfinance Bank, 160
Tanzania, 60*n*32, 83*b*, 164*n*6
technology neutrality
  in AML/CFT regulations, 109
  in licensing of providers, 70*b*
telecommunications companies. *See* mobile
    network operators
Telenor, 160
telephone hotlines for retail outlets, 118
terrorism, financing. *See* anti-money
    laundering/combating the financing
    of terrorism (AML/CFT)
    regulations; money laundering and
    terrorist financing (ML/TF) risks
third party providers in mobile money
    transaction flow, 21*f*, 23–24, 23*f*
training
  m-money provider staff and retail
    outlets, 134–35
  for supervision of providers, 125
transaction amount limits, 50–51, 51*b*, 52*b*,
    173, 175*n*12
transaction flow. *See* mobile money
    transaction flow
transaction processor, 13, 26–27

U

Uganda, 60*n*32, 85*t*, 160, 164*n*6
United Arab Emirates, 162
United Kingdom
  AML/CFT regulations in, 78*f*, 100*n*4,
    101*n*13
  cross-border transactions with
    Kenya, 161
  fieldwork conducted in, 6
  Global Leadership Seminar on
    Regulating Branchless Banking,
    139*n*2
  mitigation of risk in, 47*b*
  mobile money transaction flow in, 9*b*
United Nations Security Council
  Committee, 130
United States, 47*b*, 83*b*, 86, 101*n*13, 173
universal licensing regimes, 30*n*15
unstructured supplementary service data
  (USSD)
  defined, xxviii
  in mobile money transaction flow, 13,
    29*n*12

V

verification. *See* identification and
    verification processes
Vlaanderen, Paul, xv
Vodacom, 56*b*

W

watch-list screening, 130–31
WebMoney, 160
Wireless Intelligence, 2, 7*n*3
Wizzit, 50, 66, 160
World Bank, xiii, xiv, 2, 8*n*8, 31, 32
World Bank Financial Market Integrity
    Unit, 8*n*7
World Savings Bank Institute (WSBI), 76

Y

Yandex, 160
Yu, 162

Z

Zain (now Airtel Africa), 26, 98*b*, 162
Zambia
  AML/CFT regulations in, 68*b*, 69, 70,
    74*b*, 75*b*, 90*b*, 98*b*
  established m-money providers in, 160
  fieldwork conducted in, 6
  financial inclusion in, 160, 163, 164*n*6
  mobile money transaction flow in,
    9, 17, 18*f*, 19, 21, 23,
    24*f*, 29*n*11
  MTZL, 17, 18*f*, 19, 23, 24, 29*n*7
  regulatory scenario in, 163
Zap, 162
Zerzan, Andrew, xxii

www.ingramcontent.com/pod-product-compliance
Lightning Source LLC
Chambersburg PA
CBHW070410270326
41926CB00014B/2769